Wars are Never Enough:
The Story of João Matwawana

WARS ARE NEVER ENOUGH

the João Matwawana story

BY JOHN F. KEITH
foreword by David Kilgour

BayRidge
BOOKS

Wars are Never Enough: The João Matwawana Story
Copyright ©2005 Canadian Baptist Ministries
Canadian Baptist Ministries
7185 Millcreek Drive,
Mississauga, Ontario, L5N 5R4

Author - John F. Keith
All rights reserved
International Standard Book Number: 1-897213-04-2

Published by:
BayRidge Books
Willard & Associates Consulting Group
1-1295 Wharf Street, Pickering, Ontario, L1W 1A2
Tel: (416) 573-3249   Fax (416) 226-6746
E-mail: info@bayridgebooks.com
www.bayridgebooks.com

Copy editing by Beryl Henne
Cover Design by Essence Publishing
Printed at Essence Publishing, Belleville, Ontario

This book or parts thereof may not be reproduced in any form without prior written permission of the publishers.

Scriptures marked NIV are from *The Holy Bible, New International Version*. Copyright © 1973, 1978, 1984 International Bible Society. Used by permission of Zondervan Publishing House. All rights reserved.

Library and Archives Canada Cataloguing in Publication

Keith, John F. (John Frederick), 1932-
    Wars are never enough : the Joao Matwawana story / John F. Keith.

Includes bibliographical references and index.
ISBN 1-897213-04-2

    1. Matwawana, Joao. 2. Clergy--Angola--Biography. 3. Clergy--Canada--
Biography. I. Title. II. Title: Joao Matwawana story.

DT1424.M37K44 2005   967.304'092   C2005-904716-X

Table of Contents

Foreword 7
Prologue 9

Part One: The Early Years in Angola

1. João's Childhood, Youth and Early Studies 15
2. Nora 33
3. Teaching and Marriage 43
4. Studies at Calambata Bible Training Institute 65
5. War in Northern Angola, 1961 .71

Part Two: The Democratic Republic of the Congo

6. Studies at Kimpese, Kinkonzi, Then Birmingham 85
7. Chaplaincy at IME Kimpese 93
8. Additional Responsibilities Accumulate 103
9. Brief Return to Angola 117

PART THREE: CANADA

10. Arrival in Canada, Studies at Acadia Divinity College 139
11. Pastorate at Lockeport and Ragged Island 157
12. Prison Chaplaincy at the Halifax Correctional Centre 183

PART FOUR: THE GREAT LAKES REGION OF CENTRAL AFRICA

13. Kenya 207
14. Kivu Province, Democratic Republic of the Congo 211
15. Nora's Work with the Women .261
16. Reconciliation Work in Rwanda 269
17. Back to Kenya 283

PART FIVE: MINISTRIES FOLLOWING RETIREMENT
REAPING THE ADVANTAGES OF AGE AND EXPERIENCE

18. Burundi 289
19. Transition to Angola, Visiting Refugees in Zambia 309
20. First Peace Mission—to Angola (Aug-Sept 2002) 319
21. Second Peace Mission—to Geneva, Didcot (UK),
    and Angola (Feb-Mar 2003) 331
22. Third Peace Mission—to Zambia
    and Angola (July-Oct 2003) 343
23. Fourth Peace Mission—to Angola (Dec 2003-Feb 2004) . .353
24. Fifth Peace Mission—to Angola
    and Congo (May-Aug 2004) 363
25. Sixth Peace Mission—to Angola
    and Congo (Jan-Feb 2005) 373

Conclusion 377
Appendix A: Key to Abbreviations 381
Appendix B: Chronology of the Matwawana Family 385
*Appendix C: National Fellowship for
    the Reconciliation of Angola* 397
Bibliography 401

Foreword

João Matwawana, who has done and seen so much in both Africa and Canada, brings the deep wisdom of an African elder to bear on a wide range of issues. He was called, at various periods of his career, to function as a hospital chaplain in the Congo, a pastor in a Nova Scotia fishing village, a prison chaplain in Halifax, an agent of reconciliation in Hutu-Tutsi tensions that continued following the Rwanda genocide of 1994, and contributed to the reconstruction of civil society in his native Angola as it emerged out of forty years of brutal conflict.

Matwawana illustrates how immigrants to Canada contribute much of importance to the quality of Canadian society by bringing experience, different perspectives, and fresh approaches to the problems Canadians face in a country that is increasingly multicultural in its nature. As a Canadian, he has contributed significantly to the pursuit of world peace.

The book, *Wars Are Never Enough*, is full of international dimensions, highly relevant to an era where the flow of populations from continent to continent results in a constant interaction between and among cultures. Among other things, it is a study in cross-cultural adaptation.

For the Matwawana family, the process has continued fully across seven decades through a kaleidoscope of very different environments.

War and violence set the stage, but the theme of this book is essentially about how forgiveness and reconciliation are the basic building blocks of a peace that has the capacity to endure. It brings us interesting case studies, the painful struggles of individuals who have progressed through pain and hatred to an ability to pronounce pardon and peace. It carries us through a range of emotions from tears to laughter.

The story of this couple carries with it an analysis of the root causes behind so many of the ethnocultural conflicts that plague not only Africa, but the Balkans and many other troubled areas, as well. Hatred and the desire for vengeance are exposed in their true light, experienced first hand, and dealt with effectively. Dimensions of personal religious faith and experience are related in personal and practical terms, showing how they can be highly relevant.

The careful detail and painstaking research with which this book is written, make it a book of merit. It is fortified by the demonstrable effectiveness of Matwawana's work in the field. João Matwawana's experiences and struggles are related extensively in the first person. We move with him through experiences that most of us would never want to face.

The author, with his wife, Virginia, have worked on five continents, and have known João and Nora Matwawana for 45 years—remarkably in relation to each of the contexts that make up the five parts of the book: Angola, the Congo, Canada, Rwanda, Burundi, and Kenya.

It is, indeed, an honour to write a foreword for a book such as this.

David Kilgour
Ottawa

Prologue

Welcome to the life story of Dr. João Matwawana and his wife Nora. The impact that this remarkable couple have made upon Angola, the Democratic Republic of Congo, Canada, Burundi and Rwanda would be difficult to quantify. They themselves would insist that they were only serving God by serving others. They passed through many situations of great peril and considerable hardship, demonstrating that even in such circumstances they could carry themselves with dignity and poise. In retrospect, one sees that because they were often in the right place at the right time, they were able to make a difference. Their influence on individuals, on institutions, and even on nations continues to be unique, even as they themselves are unique.

As author of this biography I am more than its narrator. At several junctures I am an integral part of the story, beginning with our first meeting at the Bible Institute in Calambata in 1959. The Matwawana and Keith families interacted daily over the following two years. We experienced together a scary evacuation from Calambata in the face of war. After the onward evacuation from Mbanza-Kongo, of my wife, Virginia Keith, pregnant with son John, and accompanied by daughters

Carol and Shirley, I was a daily part of life in Mbanza-Kongo under siege, part of the preparations for the flight of the Matwawana family and others through forest and grassland to their safety in the Democratic Republic of the Congo.

When a country changes its name and then later reverses that name change, it can easily lead to confusion. Under the presidency of Joseph Kasavubu, this vast country at the heart of Africa was the Democratic Republic of the Congo. But for several decades under the presidency of (Joseph Désiré) Mobutu Sese Seko Kuku Ngwendu Wa Za Banga, it became the Republic of Zaïre, its river and its currency being given the same name. The Matwawanas and others who lived there as refugees in the late 1960s and 1970s came to know it as Zaïre. At the time of writing it is once again the Democratic Republic of Congo (DRC)—usually referred to just as "the Congo," although Congo (DRC) is occasionally used to distinguish it from the French-colonized Congo, across the river, with its capital city Brazzaville.

The events of Part Two of this book affected the lives of both Matwawana and Keith families for four years, but not on the same campus. The Keiths were at Sona Bata, while the Matwawanas were at Kinkonzi or at Kimpese, a scant hour distant by road.

Our paths then diverged for some years, but when João Matwawana's safety and security in the Congo came into question, my own position at the time in Toronto as General Secretary of Canadian Baptist Ministries permitted me to be part of his extraction from peril, helping to secure arrangements for the Matwawana family's shift to Nova Scotia, Canada, where Part Three of this narrative takes place.

The themes of forgiveness and reconciliation were well rooted in João Matwawana's life long before the assignment of João and Nora to work in Congo's turbulent Kivu Province. It was here that João emerged as the reconciler, working with ethnic diversity, then engulfed by the wave of refugees from Rwanda's genocide, and swimming against the flow with his message of reconciliation. Part Four of his story covers these momentous events.

When João moved into active retirement in 2000, as described in Part Five, we came full circle to the kind of close fellowship we had shared in Part One, but with our roles reversed. João, the *Peace and*

PROLOGUE

Reconciliation Consultant, became the teacher, and John, the *Diplomatic Liaison* person, also in retirement, became the student. Africa took central stage for Dr. João Matwawana, the reconciler, while I did what I could to support his efforts through Ottawa.

Eventually, CBM asked me to tell João's story for the rest of the world, which required a number of interviews and personal conversations, many of which you will find recounted in João and Nora's own words in the course of this story.

With these words of explanation, I will now step back and tell the intriguing story of the way God has been working through the lives of João and Nora Matwawana.

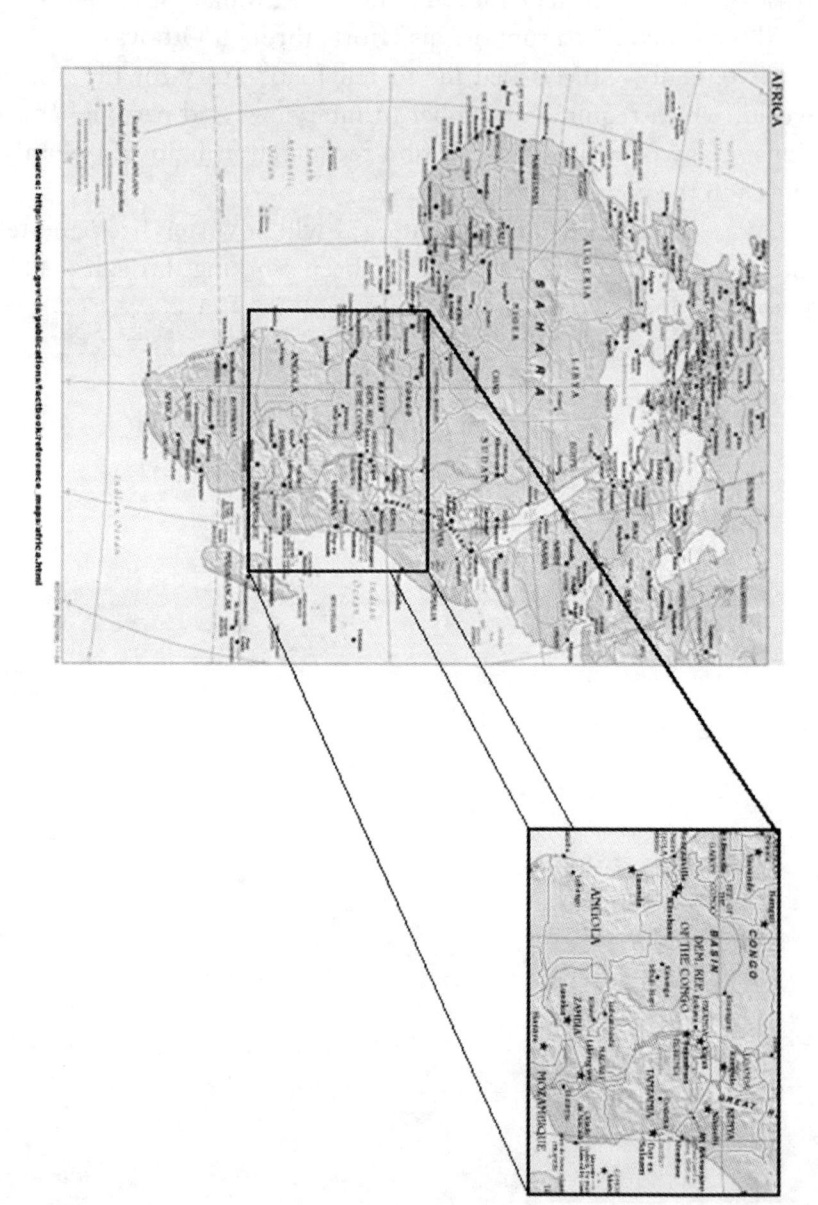

Central Africa

PART ONE

The Early Years in Angola

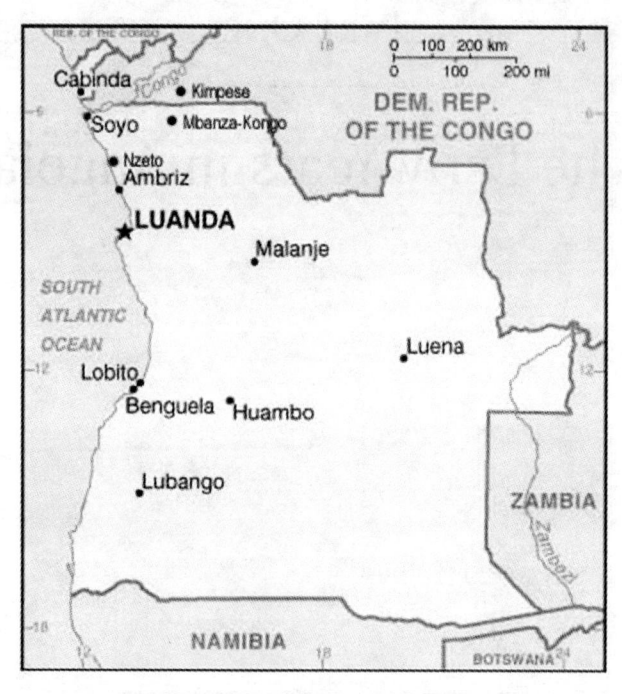

Angola

1

João's childhood, youth, and early studies

Family roots in Angola

João Matwawana spent the carefree days of his childhood at Luanika, in northern Angola, in the household of his father, Pastor Zakuadia. His father was close to the people, and the people lived close to the land.

The area was rich in game both small and large. Herds of elephant roamed the forests, marsh, and grasslands, along with wild pigs and several types of antelope. The wily bush buffalo, wary of humans but dangerous and aggressive when wounded, found cover in the gallery forests along rivers and streams.

Luanika was a comfortable day's walk from Mbanza-Kongo, capital of the ancient Kingdom of the Kongo, which had its roots deep in the time before written records were kept in that part of Africa. The famed kingdom at its peak had stretched well northward across the mouth of the great Congo river and reached inland as far as today's Kinshasa. It extended across segments of territory that would eventually be colonized by three European powers—France, Belgium, and Portugal. This was a prestigious and historic land.

THE ANCIENT KINGDOM OF THE KONGO.

The Kingdom of the Kongo had already passed its peak, weakened by internal struggles, when Portuguese explorers edged their way southward past the hump of Africa and farther along the coast, which was previously unknown to Europeans. João, and also Nora, who would eventually become his wife, were both descended from the royal families that had held the title of king.

It was at the Conference of Berlin in 1885 that the international borders delineating French Congo, Belgian Congo and Portuguese Congo (Angola) were established. What had once been a united and autonomous kingdom became part of three distinct colonies.

PORTUGAL'S COLONY OF ANGOLA

João grew up in Angola in an era when Portugal's colonial rule had not yet been seriously challenged, although his people had made one move in that direction about twenty years before he was born. Colonial rule had a profound impact on their life, both directly and indirectly, deliberately and unintentionally.

The customs and relationships of the Kongo peoples were based on matrilineal patterns of kinship. Each person belonged to the *luvila* of his or her mother, grandmother, great-grandmother, great-great-grandmother, etcetera. The anthropologist would insist that the *luvila* is technically a "matri-sib," but we will use the term "clan" for simplicity. The rule of marriage, by local custom, was that each marriage partner should be from a different clan. Lineage was traced through the women, yet it was not a matriarchal society. A male member of the clan, normally a mother's brother, traditionally held the last word of authority over children, relating especially to matters such as discipline, financial obligations, choice of marriage partner, and choice of vocation.

The Early Years in Angola

Zakuadia, Father of Matwawana

João's maternal uncle, his clan figure of authority, lived in this same village, Luanika, but his most valued relationship was with his father, Zakuadia, something of a departure in terms of local custom. Zakuadia was a Christian pastor serving the village of Luanika. The family spent most of their time at Luanika, on the road to Buela, rather than at Zakuadia's own village, Ngandu. Wanting the children to appreciate his extended family, he would take them to Ngandu at least once yearly.

Both Catholic and Protestant missions worked from bases in São Salvador, the name given by the Portuguese to Mbanza-Kongo. Zakuadia's affiliation was with the Baptist Missionary Society (BMS) of London, which has historic roots in the work of William Carey and others in Asia, and in that of Holman Bentley and others there at São Salvador.

Zakuadia was baptized at Mbanza-Kongo on Sunday, June 2, 1907, and was accepted into church membership there. He was first recorded as "Ndualu Zakuadia," Ndualu being the standard Kikongo handling of the Portuguese name Eduardo. Later he came to be known as Alvaro rather than Ndualu. He did his studies at Kimpese in the Belgian Congo, he was faithful and diligent in his work, and he was a trainer of others. Zakuadia's impact on the life of his son was profound. Following Zakuadia's death in 1956, Pastor Pedro Dimiti, trained by him, not only replaced him as pastor of the church at Luanika, but also served as role model to João. Pastor Dimiti was a man of great patience, and this made its impact on the younger man.

My first African teacher in the village was a man who was almost like an angel. His patience was beyond understanding. I myself was a joker, a clown, one who often disturbed the class. Pedro Dimiti would need to discipline me from time to time, but I could see in his eyes, even then, that he loved me, he loved his students. His godly example was imprinted in us without his need to say anything.

(João Matwawana)

Building modern roads had forced the relocation of Luanika and other villages. The colonial administration dictated that all villages must relocate to these new highways, which were, in fact, still dirt roads. These relocations were mandatory and had a profound impact on rural life, as they caused great inconvenience to the population, then forced to walk great distances to their gardens and to where their fruit trees had been planted, as well as to their hunting and fishing territories, defined by inheritance.

The new roads and the decrees that villages must be located on these roads all served the colonial government well in their attempts at population control, and in the manipulation of populations to service the plantations that fed its growing export trade. The Belgian neighbour to the north followed similar practices.

When one begins to look at the patterns of traditional life and behaviour in Kongo society, the areas of conflict with the colonial administration and its policies immediately stand out. The *confiscation of traditional lands* granted to the settlers whose influx increased after the end of World War II; the *forced resettlement* of traditional villages along newly-constructed highways; the violent and brutal *conscription of forced labor* to work the plantations; the *taxation*— levied on males over sixteen, whether employed or not. The annual sum of 120 *escudos* was a great burden to bear. Those who did not pay their taxes were imprisoned, or beaten, or both, or even deported, especially if personnel demands were heavy in offshore plantations. These and other points of tension cast their shadow over the life of every Angolan adult and child.

Luanika was a conglomeration of seven villages brought together as a mega-village in 1934 by forced resettlement. As a result it had seven different chiefs, each of which governed a clan that had lived in a different village. These people, forced to live together, found ways to live together peacefully. The government insisted that it have only one "chief" as its representative to whom they could send directives and who could be called in on occasion to listen, or speak, or account for activities that had taken place. So one man represented them to the government, but he could decide nothing without consulting the seven chiefs. These seven were automatically his counsellors, something the government did not know and showed no concern about. Internally in the village, there was no allegiance to that one chief designated by the government. Each individual was committed to his or her own clan chief.

Each of these seven chiefs was now separated from his *zumbu*, his traditional village. The people returned to these *mazumbu* (plural) on foot with regularity, for there they could make large gardens for beans, or hunt and fish. They might go for as long as three weeks at a time.

Discipline was very strict, based on clan structure and authority. When an act of violence or vandalism was noted and the culprit was caught, the very first question was "Where do you belong?"—the local equivalent of asking "Who are you?"—for identity lay not with the individual but with the clan. Nor was punishment individual. Rather, one's group was involved. This resulted in very careful calculation of all activities, the overall concern being to avoid bringing shame on one's clan.

> *When one hears that people who went to military service turned against their own people, there is an explanation. Nobody wants to send their youth to military service, because in doing so he is not defending his own tribe. So Kongo youth are surrendered to the military only when their elders find them uncontrollable.*
>
> *For example, the administration might call for each mega-village to provide two persons who must then serve as* cipaios, *(military-style messengers).*
> *The chief will call together the seven chiefs: "How do we resolve this? Let's see the records." What they will do together is determine who among the young people have already been before the village court three times:*
> *The first crime is an accident.*
> *The second is a flashback.*
> *The third is real, you did it on purpose.*
> *The third crime is the one which is not forgiven.*
> *People know this. The clan chief cannot defend such a person for the record is already there.*
> *The person who cannot be defended becomes the one given up to the military.*

When they return, they have become the enemy, and their own people will suffer because they are taking revenge against the very people who sent them to the system.

Notorious African military leaders who became a scourge on their country and who abused their own people may have had their beginnings in a similar fashion, when village elders recognized that they could not be controlled by traditional methods. Could it be that Idi Amin of Uganda and Mobutu Sese-Seko of Zaïre, soldiers both, were surrendered to military life by their own elders because they did not fit into traditional patterns of behaviour in their villages or towns?

In João's immediate family, the concerns became very personal. In 1947 and 1948 there was a lot of unrest, and many were arrested. Youth were being sent to the coffee plantations in the areas of Uige, Songo, and Negage. It was perilous for youth to remain in their villages, where they were subject to detention and deportation as forced labour. João's father, Zakuadia, approached the local chief:

"What will happen to my son? Will he be drafted? Does it make a difference that I am pastor of the village?"

Although he delayed, the chief was eventually forced to give the difficult answer. "Your son also must go."

Leaving home

João's earliest instruction had been at Luanika, where his father's pastoral duties had included teaching basic literacy. João wanted to move on to study in the boarding school on the Baptist mission at Mbanza-Kongo, but there was a problem. His older brother was already there, and families could not afford to sponsor everyone in studies.

When he finished the first term, his argument to his father was convincing:

"The government doesn't touch anybody who is in boarding school." Zakuadia agreed, but the agreement of the maternal uncle was also needed. This, too, fell in line, and his future in the boarding school was secure.

The Early Years in Angola

Before João could enter the BMS boarding school, he had to work in the palace of the Kongo King, King Dom Pedro VII, for one week, as part of the forced labour plan involving young people (something distinct from the contract labour scheme already mentioned). This happened in an era when the Kongo king was only a figurehead of the colonial government and no longer exercised any real power. João's assignment was to carry water, and he remembers the queen to have been a very kind person. They referred to the queen as *Ntinu Nkento*. She judged João to be too young, at the age of ten or eleven, to be required to do this kind of manual labour, and spoke in favor of his replacement by a bigger lad. João remembers that, in the end, the king paid him twelve *escudos* for the work he had done, although the way the system was set up this was not required. He remembers this as the first money he earned in his life.

Then João was sent away on conscript labour at the age of twelve. In this he was very fortunate, for his assignment was not a distant one.

When we were on the road for considerable distances, we sang to ease the travel, to ease the strain. Singing is a therapy. The song itself might be a complaint, but it eases the stress. Singing helps us to walk faster, and singing, we were happy. Walking was best in the early hours, before the heat of the day. If someone has a necessity he would speak up, and the whole group pauses to wait for him. Otherwise he could never catch up. A harmonica really speeded things up. Our travelling group to Mbanza-Kongo might have fifteen to twenty people, adults and youth. Children would not be brought into such a group until the age of twelve or thirteen.

I was always anxious to carry the coffee of a certain Nkaka Nemiala, *for he was the most generous payer that I knew. He would give another* escudo *on top of the regular ten percent. The pay for carrying someone's coffee from his plantation was ten percent of the sale value at the market. If coffee sells for sixty* escudos *then six* escudos *goes to the carrier. The man who has a harvest of coffee to sell works out how many carriers he will need, and engages them.*

Organization and discipline in a Kongo mega-village

In Kongo society, the individual, by careful conduct, protected the clan and its good name. The clan, in turn, protected the individual, until the three offenses of the individual established that he/she was not defensible. João was very careful about his conduct, but he was caught once. He threw a stone and the leg wound was more serious than he had intended, although he admits that the stone was thrown deliberately.

> *I knew I had only two chances left in life. My family would tell me that if I didn't stop throwing stones I would be gone. "If you don't change, you know the consequences and where you will end up?"*

> *Note that the village does not betray an offender directly to the government for imprisonment. They will eventually betray you when the government insists that workers or soldiers must be provided by the village. Imprisonment was considered an abnormal and cruel form of punishment. Once the individual's record of behaviour is established, that information will be mentally filed until the government appears looking for "volunteers," in which instance the offender is volunteered by the elders. The government's need for personnel surfaced with regularity, and when they called for personnel, they were insistent. The system worked out at Luanika and elsewhere helped to prevent stealing, adultery, lack of respect, violence, laziness, and drunkenness (a behaviour that was called weird). That was the framework.*

> *Those were among the major offences, though the list is not exclusive. Lack of respect is a serious anti-social crime, assaulting as it does the very fabric of Kongo society and its social order, along with theft and violence. Disrespect was a serious matter and needed to be checked.*

> *Obedience was the first requirement for any boy and girl, whether in a Christian home or other. In my case I was in a*

Christian home. My daily routine was therefore different. At 6:30 a.m. was the bell for morning devotions. Within three minutes came another call from a parent. "Go to church now."

Morning prayer was a daily thing, not prolonged, perhaps a song and a reading with brief exhortation and a prayer, then to breakfast. After breakfast we went to the garden or to hunting with father or to cut some big trees so that the women could dig and plant.

My father knew that by two in the afternoon, as a teacher, he must be back. He rang the bell for the school, with studies until five. By then mother was already home. I might be called on to wash dishes or pound manioc flour while girls got water from the river for cooking and for chores.

Boys were not exempt from duties and responsibilities. Maybe I should get firewood for a fire for the men.... The women of the neighbourhood will bring the food for the men to eat there. Cooking had to be fast enough, for who wants to be last providing the food? The men share.

After that the girls take back the dishes and food containers. Maybe they don't even clean them yet. Then the girls always go to the middle of the village to dance and play unless someone is very sick in the village.

Early in the morning every old lady goes around the village with her greeting which is also an inquiry:
"Nusikamene?"
She asks if all have awakened well. When the whole village is well there is reason to rejoice. While the girls dance, the boys are around the fire, grandfather giving the story of his zumbu *with its land, rivers, lakes, and where one finds borders with other clans.*

Village mothers keep watch on time.
"Anna, it's time to sleep."
Then another mother, and another. The girls disappear. Once one or two call their daughters and the circle is destroyed, the dancing and singing stops. If one girl stays behind that will be showing bad behaviour and she will not be trusted; she will get a bad name.

The boys have a bit more freedom. They are sometimes still wandering around. If the historian finishes early, the boys in turn like to circle the inner circle where the girls are dancing. They develop their preferences as to who performs best. The girl who is always behind talking with boys will be looked down on.

If an engagement has been established, it's OK. Couples could then prolong their talk.

Religious conversion

The relationship with his paternal grandfather was held in equally high esteem as that with his father, but the two were radically different, with opposing messages, and João was trapped in the dichotomy. It was from grandfather he learned to hate his enemies. Grandfather warned him against foes out there whom he must intentionally hate, living in fear of their attacks and on guard against their wiles.

Under the spiritual influence of my father, Zakuadia, I knew I should make a decision to follow Jesus as my Lord very early in life. I did that, at age thirteen, but my spiritual progress was very slow because of the traditional village environment in which I lived. My grandfather, Mfutila, was not a Christian, and he had a lot of influence on me when I was small. So many times I used to go sit by the fire in the evening with him. This was my father's father. He was acknowledged to be a

The Early Years in Angola

teacher, a wise man, a historian. He would tell us all about our country, our lands, our lakes, our forest, the borders between us and other families.

Grandfather Mfutila would also tell us who our enemies were and where they lived. He considered that information vital to our upbringing. He would tell us that from a certain hill to a certain other hill these people were our enemies. We formerly had wars with them, so we are not allowed to marry girls from that hill, for that would be breaking tradition. It's too dangerous. Katusompananga ko "We do not intermarry with them." Then also there was a point at which, in marriage prohibitions, they calculated prohibitive distance by the number of intervening rivers. Once you cross three rivers it's considered a foreign land and you can't marry a girl from there. So I was lucky that when I married Nora, my grandfather was already dead. Otherwise it could have been a problem, because I crossed five rivers to marry Nora. Five rivers would be too much for my grandfather to accept. Those are the things which complicated my understanding of the gospel, because although my father's preaching was excellent, I still had to double-check with my grandfather for his evaluation.

Sometimes his grandfather would ask João what his father was preaching about that day.

"He was preaching about loving our enemies. What do you think about that, Grandpa?"

"Bad thinking, and that's dangerous talk. You know, if war should come to us, your father is number one in stupidity in this area because he is not encouraging our people for readiness. He is encouraging people to be lazy and to be attacked without any preparation. We are living here among other tribes and you have to know that loving your enemies means that they will attack you first, so I don't agree."

"But grandfather, he's a pastor, he is preaching, he has to preach these things. They come from the Bible."

"Before your father went to boarding school, he was a smart boy. It was only after being in Mbanza-Kongo and coming back home that he lost all his knowledge. That boarding school experience was a disaster for him."

João looks back on that conflict of input and values between his father and his grandfather, which went on for most of his childhood. He says he always had some doubts, caught between the two of them, with both respect and love for each.

I was always worried whether this conflict would ever end. But then my father decided I had to go to boarding school anyway. By then my grandfather had died, and I went to boarding school. The same school where my father learned to be "stupid."

Educational patterns

Within the educational framework of the schools set up by the colonial government, there were firmly established practices and rules. Only Portuguese was to be spoken at school. In village schools, led by *catechists*, students remained in zero grade until they were able to speak Portuguese, and only then could they begin grade one. They only entered rural schools, such as those eventually directed by João, when ready for grade one, taught in Portuguese. Students who completed the fourth year, *quarta classe*, were thereby qualified to teach the lower classes. Protestant missions that opened schools were required to have, in residence, a qualified Portuguese national educator. This was one way of ensuring that grammar, pronunciation, and usage of the Portuguese language were correct and current.

No effort was either undertaken, or permitted, which would make formal education relevant to children living in rural Angola. On the contrary, the education system's goal was to introduce an awareness and familiarity with things and places of Portugal. Those advancing as far as *quarta classe*, fourth grade, were expected to be making progress toward true assimilation into Portuguese life and culture. Those who were successful in gaining that status by a clearly determined set of rules and conditions moved into the official status of *assimilados*, a process which was considerably easier for Catholics than for Protestants.

Obstacles

The colonial regime in Angola placed many obstacles in the way of Protestant individuals and institutions. Males in Catholic schools were exempt from paying taxes, those in Protestant schools were not. Officials responsible for registering births would go so far as to record the children of registered Protestant weddings as being *illegitimate*. A certain administrative officer called João into his office, closed the door and spoke to him benevolently: "I can change your life today. If you will become a Catholic, your life will be different."

Another administrator, Manuel Martins, informed a group of eight young men that their baptism was not recognized, so they would not be able to secure an effective *padrinho*, or godfather, to plead their cause, to sponsor their expenses, and to facilitate important documentation. This would make it difficult for them to ever obtain the coveted status of *assimilado*. It was a clear indication that as long as they remained Protestants it would be difficult for them to be fully assimilated into the privileges of Portuguese society. In theory the *assimilado* status was open to all who were able to fulfill the requirements. In practice it would prove especially difficult for Protestants to attain.

To reach the status of *assimilado*, there was a rigidly established process. The applicant had to meet certain academic, technical, and cultural requirements. To begin with, the successful completion of *quarta classe*, fourth grade. The second requirement involved a working mastery of the Portuguese language, and the practice of speaking it habitually, to the exclusion of a mother tongue such as Kikongo. Beyond that, it was necessary, in the North of Angola, to have under cultivation a minimum of twenty-five hectares of coffee. To be assimilated required changing one's eating habits, giving up native foods such as manioc, and abandoning native styles of dress. It meant living on a diet of rice, potatoes, beans, sardines, and codfish. It meant living under a tin roof rather than under thatch, even though the result would be greater discomfort under the powerful African sun. Although not formally stipulated, someone applying for *assimilado* status really needed the goodwill of the local administrator, as well. Without that, the browbeating and scoffing of an official could easily dishearten and turn aside even those who came to the project with determination.

As João prepared for his *quarta classe* examinations, he was required to know in great detail the features of life in distant Portugal. For instance, students must recite the stations, in order, on the railway line from Lisbon to Cascais, students who had never seen a train in their life and didn't necessarily know the meaning of *caminho de ferro* (railroad). They had to be able to name Portugal's lakes, rivers, mountains, cities, castles, and monasteries. They learned Portugal's history and the battles fought with the Spanish.

Decades later, in Halifax, a Portuguese, Rui, came to learn details of a project directed by João's son, Edward. As Rui inquired about João's earlier experiences in Angola and his education there, he was fascinated by the amount of detail João knew about a Portugal that he had never seen, citing mountains and rivers that Rui himself no longer remembered.

Attending the BMS boarding school at Mbanza-Kongo

At boarding school I had trouble relating to kids from other clans. I was still remembering what my grandfather used to tell me. Grandfather had a lot of influence on me. A child's wisdom was supposed to come from his grandfather, not from his father. Everywhere I was afraid of other tribes. In school, in the classroom, on the soccer field, always afraid of others. That fear went on until one day I think the Lord met me in this special way.

An incident happened which allowed me to open myself. We had a soccer game. Our team usually won, but this time we were defeated. I was very mad that afternoon and the other kids knew that I get mad when we lose. So I tried to avoid contact with anybody, in order not to say something nasty. I went away from everybody, walking around the yard by myself. Then I crossed over near the church in Mbanza-Kongo. I looked at the tombstones of the first missionaries. I looked at those tombs and I was reading names, English names: Phillips and other names like that. I couldn't understand why one of the tombs had this text:

> *Greater love has no one than this,*
> *that he lay down his life for his friends.*
> *(John 15:13)*

I couldn't understand why this triggered a reaction in me. I went to see the missionary, Clifford Parsons, and asked him why this man had to die for a friend.
"Where did you find that?"
"On one of the tombstones."
"You were at the tombs! Why?"
"Just walking around. But I don't understand those words, their meaning. Who was the friend, and who died?"
"Sit down. You have never understood this?"
"No."
Clifford explained how Jesus died and He wanted to make a point to His disciples in His teaching that He was dying for His friends. He was considering His disciples friends and He was dying for all of us.
"Jesus, yes. But what about this man, Phillips?"
"This man was probably dying and said to his cook, or his houseboy, 'When I die, write this verse on my tombstone.'"
"Oh. So, who was the friend that Phillips died for?"
"His friend was you, and all Angolans. Rev. Ross Phillips came to die, like Jesus, to try to help you, to bring you the gospel. Then he was taken by malaria. So he was just following the example of the Lord Jesus."
"Oh, so this guy was not a Muxicongo, *not an African! I can't*

believe that someone who is not a member of our tribe can die for us or because of us."
"That's the point."
"I would not die for someone who was not a member of my tribe."
"But João, you made a decision that Jesus is your Lord. Do you mean you have some doubts about your faith?"
"I have."
"Do you have problems relating with other tribes?"
"That's my big problem. That's why I keep changing rooms all the time, because I am always afraid of the others."
"So what do you feel now?"
"Now I understand it better. As a Christian, I should love the other kids, even if they come from a different clan."

Clifford called this a breakthrough. He thought we should pray. Clifford prayed a very short prayer. "Lord, help this boy. Take away all the hatred, replace it with Your unconditional love, so that he can be an ambassador of love to his tribe and other tribes. Amen."
"It's late. Go to sleep."

Clifford didn't know that I had skipped supper because I was angry about the soccer game. That's the way the Lord used to bring me closer to Himself and to make a genuine decision for my salvation. So I went to sleep and I slept like a baby. It was the first night I had slept without fear of this guy or that guy. I was delivered completely. I would have been 14 or 15 years old then.

I had made a profession of faith earlier at Luanika with my father, but this crisis at school was the real one that changed my life. While I was near my grandfather in the village, it was a struggle. I couldn't grow. I had a lot of doubts. I had been doubting even my father's faith and my father's preaching because of what my grandfather was telling me. I was not baptized in the village. That happened after I went to boarding

The Early Years in Angola

school at Mbanza-Kongo, but even the baptism had not changed my attitude. This experience that I have just talked about took place after my baptism."

At breakfast the next day, the other kids expected to see my anger from losing the soccer match, but they didn't see it. Surprise. Then at break they tried to provoke me. No result. So someone asked if I were sick.
"You're in a different mood. You're not responding."
"I'm responding in my way."
This was a sign of the turning point in my life. I had that peace inside me already and that went on to cover other things in life."

João affirms that through the soccer incident, his time of reflection in the cemetery, and his interaction with missionary Clifford Parsons, he was brought to a life-changing transition in his life, and he has never turned back from that. He was spiritually liberated and emotionally prepared for a later decision to undertake a teaching assignment in an area considered hostile, where his other classmates were not prepared to go.

The school director at Mbanza-Kongo, under whom João studied *quarta classe*, was Guilherme Ribeiro Neves. He was pursuing a plan to open a network of rural schools that would feed students into the third and fourth year classes of the boarding school at Mbanza-Kongo. João Matwawana was probably his most advanced and most promising student, and one of those on whom Senhor Neves depended to open these new schools.

Of course, after that, we faced this problem of going out to strange villages to start new schools. Guilherme Neves was having trouble convincing anyone to agree. Nobody wanted to go out too far away from home. They were scared. They heard traditional stories that if you went from this area to that area they will curse you, or they will poison you. You will not be accepted by other clans. It hasn't been done before. We were six in quarta classe *that year: Alvaro, João, Andre, Sozinho, Cano, and Pita. We were the first group in history to graduate from* quarta classe *through the BMS school system in northern Angola. I have a picture from Neves, and we were six altogether. They said, "We can't go out in these areas to start schools. It's too dangerous." Before the coming of Neves as a resident Portuguese educator, the government restricted the BMS to the level of third class.*

Neves made the proposal that I should go to Buela, which was 71 kilometres away. For us at that time such a distance was like going to another world. "Those people are different from here, do you accept to go?" I accepted.

João was sent to Buela, and he remembers that the other classmates were laughing at him and taunting him that he would never return alive. However much these fears and suspicions may seem like fantasies now, the fears were very real at the time, and people believed such tales.

In one year I came back alive with a good report. It was not that bad.

Because of that breakthrough, two other teachers then accepted assignments outside Mbanza-Kongo and school director Neves' plan for opening new schools was able to proceed with another new school the second year.

2

NORA

CHILDHOOD

Nora's mother was Mpasu Celina, her father Alvaro Artur, and they lived at Mbanza-Kongo. Of their eight children, Nora was born fourth. The impact of the Christian gospel through the Baptist Missionary Society was strong in her family and in her own personal life. The roots of that influence lay in the experiences of her maternal grandmother, Dilembwa, counted among the first generation of students who attended the BMS boarding school at Mbanza-Kongo. There she met her husband, Garcia Deves Tola, who was older than she. Dilembwa was a dedicated Christian lady who learned to read and write. Nora's mother, Mpasu, followed in the same tradition of commitment to her Lord. She worked closely with BMS missionaries, helping them to learn the Kikongo language. Mpasu was also a teacher at the BMS mission school in Mbanza-Kongo. A great singer, she continued singing in the church choir until late in her life. Her paternal grandparents were Isabel Mona and Manuel Mwanda, who did not live their lives as Christians, although her grandmother accepted Jesus as her Lord and Saviour late in life.

Growing up in a family of eight, it was Nora who emerged early as the one who was especially trustworthy, even though she was not the oldest. That trustworthiness included matters of family finances. She was the one who knew where money was stored, for there were no banks or safety deposit boxes. Her integrity did not always appear as an advantage to her, for it meant she would be the one chosen to run errands that involved money, since she was trusted to handle it properly and to bring the full value home. Grandmother Dilembwa, for instance, would send Nora to sell her manioc at the market, assured she would get the full proceeds. For this Nora would be given a coin.

Responsibility and maturity were recognized in other ways as well. When Nora was seventeen, her parents were away for a period of time at Kinshasa. Nora noted that grandmother Dilembwa was not well, and brought grandmother to live with her temporarily to care for her, even though there were uncles at hand who might have been expected to take that responsibility.

Nora and her childhood playmates were not expected to be seen a lot with boys. There was much to be learned around the house. The matchmakers of village and family began watching young girls at an early age to see that they were not lazy, that they kept themselves tidy, that they were good at cleaning and keeping the home tidy. They were expected to learn cooking at a young age. Girls had duties such as carrying water and wood, and they were expected to be cheerful in disposition, helpful by nature. These were some of the criteria by which young women were judged as potential wives and mothers. By the time Nora was twelve, one of the older ladies had already approached her grandmother, making preliminary proposals that they consider trying to match their grandchildren in marriage.

In preparing a child for responsible life in Kongo society, there were norms of propriety to be learned. Grandmother Dilembwa provided an important part of that teaching. One must be prepared to accept a rebuke, however unpleasant, without answering back. It was considered disrespectful for a speaker to call an older person by name. Someone the age of one's mother would be addressed as Mama.

The Early Years in Angola

Someone the age of one's grandmother would be addressed as *Nkaka*, grandparent. Even an older brother would not be addressed by his name, but would be *Mano*, a familiar form of the word *brother* in Portuguese. When an item was passed from one person to another, it was not to be handled with only one hand, and most certainly never with the left hand! Full respect required the use of both hands when passing and receiving objects. One would not pass directly in front of an older person, but should always pass behind. It was definitely not courteous to jump over another person's legs, nor to step on another, for these were symbolic acts implying a master-to-slave relationship. These few examples are only a suggestion of the rich store of attitude and behaviour to be learned as second nature if one was to be considered cultured in Kongo society.

Nora's maturing and her education were destined to set her apart. From her early years, Nora was an exceptional child, and she was to emerge as the first young Protestant woman in the entire province to graduate from the prestigious *quarta classe*. Angolans, in general, were not encouraged to proceed as far as *quarta classe*, and certainly it was not expected of girls.

School fees represented one of the acute needs for young people. Nora did a lot of gardening with her mother, Mpasu, but she also did her own gardening for the income that would pay school fees. In this she and other girls worked together, working in rotation on the gardens of each. In the end it was only Nora who completed *quarta classe*.

Maternal Influences

A girl growing up in the Kongo society of that era looked to her mother and her grandmother as her sources of wisdom, the models around which her life would be built. Nora's mother, Mpasu, and grandmother, Dilembwa, were unusual women. The impact made on both of their lives by missionaries of the BMS was profound. For one thing, they were both literate.

Decision-making for both boys and girls was not a private matter, not something to be handled by the individual. Decision-making was a process of constant interaction with one's elders, family, and community. Opinions would be exchanged and discussed. One must not give the impression of knowing everything. The big decisions, in particular, belonged to parents and other elders. That was certainly true for choosing a life partner, for deciding what profession or work was to be undertaken, and where to live.

Her Christian heritage, and we must remember that Nora was already the third generation, showed up in several ways, beginning in early childhood. She could not accept an idea if she was not sure. Church leaders encouraged young people to attend classes in preparation for adult baptism. To these she replied, "I can only accept when I believe."

Her relationship with grandmother Dilembwa was very important in that regard. Mpasu, her mother, had a very heavy schedule, while grandmother had more time. Nora recollects that family income generated by her father, Alvaro, tended to be seasonal, so her mother carried more daily responsibility that was very demanding. Nora remembers sitting down repeatedly with her grandmother on Sunday afternoons, together with her cousin, Carlotta. Dilembwa would read to both. Grandmother exercised an important influence, but it was Nora who made her own key decision of faith. At the age of sixteen, she trusted Jesus to be her Saviour and she pledged her life to Him as her Lord.

COFFEE

Nora describes how coffee was prepared as a drink in their home. They lived in a coffee-producing area, where the beans were readily available. One started with the red beans that were ripe; otherwise, if prepared from green beans, coffee would taste too strong. The ripe beans were spread in the sun to dry until they rattled when shaken together in the hand. These dry beans were pounded in the mortar, then winnowed to sift out the dried flaky skin of the beans. They were roasted until black and then pounded again. After a sifting, the powder was ready for making coffee.

In Nora's home, none of the children was allowed to drink coffee, only the parents. Children were given only tea. The parents would prepare coffee in the morning, drink some, and put the rest away to be reheated when they returned from their day's work:

The Early Years in Angola

My parents thought the caffeine was bad for us, unaware that tea also contains caffeine. The coffee they drank smelled so good, that I figured out a way of cheating. I would remove a cup of coffee after they had left the house, replacing it with a cup of water.

Father commented that the coffee seemed weak. I told him that this is what happens when coffee has been left all day. I did this for a year or more, and my parents never caught on. Their explanation for denying children coffee was that caffeine takes away the intelligence. I always had the highest marks in my class, and I noticed that my marks did not go down as I drank coffee, so I kept on.

Graduation day came, and with my top marks my parents prepared a party. Father announced that I now had permission to drink coffee. That is when I confessed that I had been drinking it all along. I was forgiven, but the rule of "no coffee" didn't change for the younger ones.

The fact that Nora was somewhat quiet and pensive by nature was not always looked on favourably. It was not at all useful in helping her to be readily accepted as a candidate for baptism. She had no problems with the instructions or the questions to be answered. However, several times in relating her story to me, she mentioned that others classified her as *fidalga*, proud or perhaps even haughty. That accusation was raised by someone at the time when Nora's letter to the church, requesting baptism, was considered publicly. However, a missionary who had been one of her teachers had left a note when she returned to England, commenting on her qualities, and that note tipped the scales in her favour.

Because of those studies, and the years in school, Nora's friends included boys as well as girls. In fact, Nora's older sister, Ana, moved away to Kinshasa to live with their mother's sister. Their younger sister, Juliana, was ten years younger. So Nora grew up among boys. Anything they did, she matched. She followed them to make traps for birds and rats. She became especially adept at climbing, but also admits to fighting:

> *I had a cousin, my uncle's first daughter, who was a very best friend. She was always in trouble but she was not strong at all. I would go to her rescue and fight on her behalf.*

Climbing trees became Nora's thing. By the time she got home at the end of the day a piece of her snagged dress had often stayed up in a tree somewhere. Her father became so upset about her climbing that he finally announced she should no longer wear dresses of fine material—her dresses would be made of heavy khaki cotton. Even these often snagged in a tree:

> *At one point when the authorities were arresting young boys to work in the coffee plantations, we went as a family to our* zumbu *(abandoned village) to hide my brothers there. Dad ended up taking the boys on to safety in the Congo. At our* zumbu *we found many people hiding, both boys and girls. For cooking, we made sauce from oil palm nuts, the ones we call* ngazi. *But in the abandoned and overgrown forest, these* ngazi *palms were hard to find. One day a group of us girls went looking for firewood. We noticed a palm with ripe and ready* ngazi, *but they were up there very high We didn't bother calling the men. I would go up and harvest them.*

Those who have watched the harvest of *ngazi* know that there are standard safety practices, which include clearing all the fallen branches from around the base of the tree, for the edges of the branch near the trunk have strong and dangerous prongs on both sides of the frond. Nora and her companions failed to clear away this perilous rubble—their first mistake.

The climber goes up with a machete, bare feet against the trunk, using a strong loop made from split fronds which encircles trunk and climber. This loop is flipped upward each time the climber advances. The girls improvised a loop from vines and Nora headed skyward with her machete. Nora's second mistake happened when, in the process of cutting out the *ngazi*, her machete mistakenly cut her climber's loop. She took a straight and immediate fall. Her shoulders landed directly on the spiny rubble below, causing multiple wounds. There was one serious thorn which penetrated the back of her hand. She remembers:

How will I face mother?
When we arrived mother noticed something out of order.
"What's up?"
"Aunt, Nora fell down."
"She was climbing again, right?"

My whole back was bleeding. My hand was already swollen badly from the thorn. Mother boiled water, sterilized a pin, and took it out. But what about some medication to prevent infection? Remember, we were in the bush with no first-aid supplies. Mother used small red peppers. She made a paste and put it all over my back and my hand. The pain was overwhelming and I cried so much. I went to bed without eating and was able to sleep through until the next day. Pepper is so strong. By three days all the wounds were healed.

I thought this would be the end of my climbing, but it went on. Even when I was pregnant with my first son I was climbing a mango tree. I came back with mangoes. João was angry when he noticed I had been climbing—pregnant!

Later, at IPE Kimpese, we found lots of mango trees. I climbed again when I was pregnant with Ambrose. That time I was out after firewood when my labour pains began. I knew that my pains often went on intermittently for up to two days before delivery. I would stay on the ground during the pains then climb between them, to get firewood. That happened during both Julie's and Ambrose's pregnancies. Before going to maternity, I always wanted to make sure I was leaving enough firewood.

Grandmother watched Nora interacting with boys and wondered whether such unusual patterns for a girl would bring complications when it came time to marry. However, the fact that she readily held her own in competition against boys was building Nora's confidence and self-esteem. She was highly competitive, and did not lag behind.

The educational years were difficult ones for Nora's mother, who was herself educated, but had those heavy burdens of gardening, cooking, the processing of manioc through its several stages of peeling, soaking, drying, pounding, and sifting, carrying water and caring for the house, mostly without her daughter. A visit to Mpasu by her brother, who was quite upset, brought sharp criticism: "You allowed her to go to school. Now you suffer. And where will she find employment?"

Her father, Alvaro, on the other hand, was supportive: "She has to get that diploma that boys get. If necessary I'll sell my trousers to help her with fees."

Nora's father, Alvaro, was less educated than Mpasu, but he was a thoughtful man, and kept careful written records of all that was happening, including politically-related events, hiding these carefully in the ground. Nora regrets that their eventual flight as refugees was so sudden, and the eventual bulldozing of the indigenous sector of Mbanza-Kongo was so complete after its burning, that it was later impossible to determine just where the house would have been located. And so the records written and buried by her father are forever lost.

There were teenage conflicts, and there were specific difficulties related to Nora's studies. Grandmother worried that with studies delaying her marriage, they were not getting the number of births necessary to keep the family up to strength. The real riches of a family were seen as being in its people. Nora's own concern was not with getting a husband early, but rather with getting the right one! She wanted a partner who did not use tobacco or alcohol.

Nora had received affirmations of interest and intent from suitors. A number of these from men who had been living and working in Matadi or Kinshasa. They included some with promising financial prospects. Her friends encouraged her to consider such prestigious opportunities. None interested her. She turned them all down. She said she was not interested in their money, for it could threaten her happiness later on if she were to marry a man who might then turn around and spend it on other women. Furthermore, some of them were drinkers, and of that she did not approve.

Crocheting

Crocheting was a skill that beautified the home, and dignified the one who produced the work, establishing that she was a talented person. It also offered an opportunity to earn extra income.

Nora was not given direct lessons in crocheting. She would slip in to watch her older sister, Ana, who was about six years older. Ana, with her friends, did not usually want little Nora around, but she would sneak back in and watch what they were doing over their shoulders. She began crocheting, preparing a stick as a crochet hook.

Later her brother, Deves, found umbrella ribs and made crochet hooks from them, giving one to Nora. Then she was really ready to produce. She was always trying to build up her own hope chest—cushions, pillowcases, bedsheets, tablecloths.

Since we never had enough time for that work, we were always building up our own supply of fancywork.

3

Teaching and Marriage

Pioneering a new rural school at Buela

In 1955, having graduated from *quarta classe*, João, still single, was assigned to Buela with the responsibility of opening a new rural school there. There was a technical difference between village schools, which were run by *catequistas*, and had no official standing, and rural schools, which were those that slotted into the officially recognized educational system. Village schools could teach literacy using the Kikongo language. Rural schools operated only in Portuguese. When João opened new schools, they were always rural schools.

The total responsibility fell on him in every way, but with the backing given by his School Director at Mbanza-Kongo, Guilherme Ribeiro Neves. Indeed, João *was* the school. As he set out, it was vitally important for him to register the students officially with the *Chefe de Posto* at Buela. The *Chefe* resisted, for he could see that this would cut down on his access to young people who could be rounded up as forced labour, one of the realities of life in the Portuguese colony. João knew that if his students were registered with the *Chefe* in Buela, that registration would also be recorded in far off Luanda, the capital. The *Chefe* pretended not to have the appropriate registration forms.

The opening of this school was a significant event. Area BMS School Director Neves was on hand for the registration process, along with missionary Clifford Parsons. These two men stayed up all night typing out the appropriate forms that were required. Neves and Parsons were considered "big people" as they visited the area. When they had gone, the *Chefe* called together the "little people," locals, including the new teacher, João Matwawana. "You have embarrassed me by bringing these big people here without warning me. That includes this bandit, Neves, who has changed his religion."

As a matter of fact, Guilherme was a Portuguese Baptist who had been engaged by the BMS to help in the development of their school system. The *Chefe* could not acknowledge that anyone could be a true Portuguese and, at the same time, a Baptist. To demonstrate his displeasure with the entire process, the *Chefe* ordered, as a punishment, for the people to cut away all the elephant grass to a distance of 2 kilometres, so he could more readily see who was approaching his *Posto*.

In reality, João was much more than a teacher to these children. He was breaking new ground as he opened this first new rural school. In it he was functioning as mother, father, and grandparent as well as teacher, nurse, sports coach, and more. He was helping rural village children take their first steps toward interacting with the modern world. The model on which he was building his experience had come from his own experiences at the boarding school he had attended in Mbanza-Kongo, where missionaries from the U.K. had carried these same multiple functions.

At Buela I had to teach the kids how to play soccer. When they got hurt I would treat them. I had medications.

I was very young when I was doing this kind of work, yet it went well. I give thanks for the years I spent in the boarding school. While I was a student in boarding school I may have felt I was being abused and forced to do things, but when I later came to have responsibilities of my own I thanked God for the boarding school experience. Otherwise, how would I have been able to bring discipline to these kids if I hadn't learned to obey?

The wisdom for this task came from my Grandpa. He told me that as a chief he didn't do much of the work himself. He delegated most of the responsibilities to others. He told me all that. He often confided in me. He would say something like this. 'You see, I could go to that party, but instead I will send Pedro, because he will be happy to represent me there'. These recollections came to me when I was overwhelmed with responsibilities in a primary school. I realized that if every dormitory has a chief, that person will take pride in being a chief, even at ten years old, and he will perform well to keep his position. The teacher could be overwhelmed if required to track all the details of every day's operation. As it was, those details fell on the dormitory chiefs. With so much wisdom, I'm so sorry that my Grandpa didn't know the Bible at all.

A teacher's status at Buela

At the time when João taught at Buela, only four people living there were generally considered to be "civilized" according to standards established by the Portuguese. They included João, the teacher; the diploma nurse, an Angolan, from another area, who used only the Portuguese language; the *Chefe de Posto*, the government's representative on site, functioning under the Administrator in Mbanza-Kongo; and Francisco Neves the storekeeper, a Portuguese, and also a long-standing friend of João. Francisco and João had been classmates in school. The language spoken was an important consideration if one was to be classified as "civilized."

When the four of us talked together, we would talk about the indigenas, natives.

I didn't believe in the rightness of those things, but we had to keep that level of conversation, you see. One day I suggested to the Chefe *that these natives don't have toilets. "What do you think?"*
"No toilets?"
"No toilets. That's why there is a lot of sickness"
The next day the Chefe's cipaio *(indigenous police) was circulating with an announcement that everybody had to dig a toilet behind his house. That was my idea but it came out as if it were from the* Chefe. *But it really started because of my boarding school knowledge.*

So the Chefe *relied on us for his work because we are the civilized, as the teachers. The storekeeper had kept quiet to avoid losing face before the* Chefe, *but when our gathering broke up he was furious.*
"João do you know what you have done?"
"No, what?"
"I don't have a toilet myself."
"Where do you go?"
"I go to the bush."
"Come on, Senhor Francisco, I always thought that any white person has to have a toilet."
"The previous storekeeper didn't have any, so why should I?"
So he had to hire workers to dig. Those Portuguese, they really identified with the people.

As for the others of the village, they dug their latrines, afraid as always that they might go to prison. Government decrees were dangerous things to disobey, from whatever level they were issued. The hierarchy from the top down included the Colonial Governor, the District Governor, the Secretary, and the Chefe de Posto. *Below that were chiefs and sub-chiefs, these last being Angolans.*

That digging of latrines helped a little bit to diminish the sickness among the children.

Being a teacher is something. You are respected. You can also intervene for the people because you speak the language of the ruler and you speak it well, so when problems come you can intervene and the Chefe *will listen to you. You are not only a teacher, you are also intervening for the population.*

CALLING TO CHRISTIAN MINISTRY

João's calling to Christian ministry was first sensed at Buela:

People were commenting on all the extra time I was spending beyond the classroom. They thought it was too much. Finally one evening a parent, a father, came to speak with me.
"Why in the world do you love my children? We expect you to teach them, but not to love them."
"Because I am a Christian and my Lord Jesus tells me to love everybody."
"I never learned about this Jesus. Can you teach me?"
"I know very little, but one thing I know, the love I have is the love of Jesus."
"I think one day you should teach us that Jesus."

God used that man's question as the voice to carry His call for me to serve Him in ministry. When I went on vacation, for some reason that voice went with me, "I think one day you should teach us that Jesus."

João crossed the border to Congo and spent a school vacation at Kinshasa, which was called Leopoldville at the time.

For the whole trip I could not get away from the voice of that man. "Teach us that Jesus."

I stayed with my cousin, who was married to a leader in the Baptist church at Kinshasa. Many people came to their home

for a variety of reasons. For some reason, the evangelist Jean Makanzu came for a visit to the house and my cousin introduced us.
"Here is a man who has something in common with you, João. His father is a pastor who trained in Kimpese long ago, where your father studied. Now Jean is training in Kimpese. You are John and he is John. You have the same name. He is a teacher and you are a teacher, but now Jean is becoming a pastor, filling in for pastor Nkomi who is on vacation."

Then the probing went a little further. Makanzu said, "Maybe that's why you've met me, to make your decision clear." Although this comment may have been made as something of a joke, it hit its mark. They didn't know about my struggle, but this came to me at the right time and at the right place. They were confirming me. I told them I was thinking about those things, but that they shouldn't push me. Then we separated.

When I returned from my vacation to Mbanza-Kongo, I went to see Tata Ambrosio Ngonga and told him I wanted to be a pastor. He said he would talk with Clifford Parsons, and that maybe they could present my name to the church assembly. They did that. The response was not what I hoped for.
"Forget it. João is still a bachelor. He is too young."
The dossier was put away somewhere. But I didn't forget. I knew I was working toward following that calling.

At the end of João's first year of teaching in Buela, his director, Guilherme Neves was due to take a furlough in Portugal. Since João had been helping him correct exams, Neves asked João to accompany him to Luanda, as a reward. He enjoyed seeing the sights of the big city for the first time, and saw Neves off on the ship.

I went back to Buela but I was already determined to make that change. God was leading me from teaching to preaching.

But it was a tense situation for João in terms of informing his family. After all, with a teacher in the family, it will be financially secure. He didn't tell his uncle until a whole year later.

Friendship with Nora

While João attended the BMS boarding school, he developed a close friendship with António Cano, whose home in Mbanza-Kongo was the second house away from where João's aunt lived. When he visited his aunt, they were always together. António's cousin, Nora, lived in the same house. She was a younger girl who was always around, and was treated as a sister, someone to be protected and cared for. It was in a sister-brother sort of relationship that João and Nora became acquainted. At one stage when João was supervising classes in Mbanza-Kongo, Nora was actually one of the students in his class.

When João was returning from his special trip to Luanda, he began to wonder... Nora... What about Nora?

At this point João went back to his friend António, Nora's cousin, to sound out the matter, asking for his advice. Was it appropriate? Would it work? António thought so. How then should João present his case to Nora? That was the question.

João asked António to carry João's proposal to Nora, which he did, and the response was just what João had feared. Nora insisted that João, the prankster, was not serious about this affirmation that he loved her. It was some sort of practical joke, she said, and she persisted in that attitude for about a week. António returned at João's urging, and convinced her that this proposal of marriage was for real. She began to take it seriously. It was the first and only proposal of marriage that had ever interested her.

Before dating began, this relationship ran its traditional respectful course in proper sequence:

João spoke with António, who became his advocate.
António spoke with Nora.
Nora spoke with her mother.
Mother spoke with Father.

Father spoke with Uncle, her Mother's brother, who had the final word.

The uncle was Henrique Deves. Uncle gave his approval, and from that point it became proper for João to negotiate a time when he and Nora could have their first serious meeting, face to face. Even as an engaged couple, all meetings required the presence of a third party—a sister, a brother, or a cousin—so that all contact was proper. Even at this stage, kissing was going "a little too far." Everyone in the society lived under intense scrutiny.

Upon completion of her *quarta classe* Nora taught for one year at Mbanza-Kongo prior to marriage.

After graduation the question to be faced was whether I should marry or work for a year. My parents had been supportive, expecting that in return I would help my family and my younger brothers. João had asked if I could go to the home of Pedro and Sonia Neves in the mornings to learn housekeeping, but this would restrict my teaching to half-time and would reduce my income. There was a certain element of unhappiness that continued through the rest of that year because I was now cut off totally from assisting my own mother. I was neither producing full income, nor was I helping with the work of house and garden.

Since João was considering marriage, he was also caught in the conundrum of needing his family's support to provide the traditional marriage dowry. Dowry continued to be important, for it brought dignity, legitimacy, and validity to marriage. João went to his uncle. By this point, he had announced his intentions to go to Bible school:

It was very confusing. I needed help from my family for the dowry, and at the same time I was saying that I would not be providing support for them after that. Well, that was seen as nonsense. My uncle, Antonio Nunes, was mad. He was mad, mad, mad.

With no money for dowry, João would need to forget marriage. He went to his alternative support system, his network of Christian friends:

I was determined that I will marry Nora. I will pay the dowry. I will go to the Bible school, even if my uncle is against me. I have no choice. My decision is made. The marriage was considered by the family to be a disaster, and my going to Calambata was, for them, a big disaster.

Disaster after disaster.

The Kongo family which had someone in that kind of employment which I had as a teacher is a secure and happy family. They are confident of a dependable source of income. To be a teacher was a very advanced position for an Angolan in my Angola of the 1950s. There was really no other higher position that an Angolan was allowed to hold, unless he belonged in some way to a Portuguese family, like being the illegitimate son of an administrative officer. In our thinking at that time, being a teacher could only be compared with being a storekeeper, except that as a teacher one gained greater respect.

In deciding about a career in Christian ministry, and also in the matter of marriage, João turned repeatedly for wisdom from his friends, his family, and the Christian community. His call to ministry was fortified to some degree when Clifford Parsons, at the funeral service for João's father, Zakuadia, said: "When a big tree falls in the forest there are always some small shoots that will grow to replace that huge tree. Who here will be that replacement for pastor Zakuadia?"

Again, facing the issue of whether to continue as a teacher or to train for pastoral service, he went to Brandon Merricks, a BMS missionary, who counselled him with two suggestions. First, he should beware that family did not stand in the way of vocation. Second, he should go to see a certain deacon, Pedro Peterson, who had been a friend of his deceased father, Zakuadia.

With the elder Peterson, in turn, João asked about wisdom in the search for the needed resources to marry.

After my father's death I always felt that I could go to him without fear to discuss any matter at all. We talked about my career, and more. One of the most serious struggles I faced at the time was the issue of how I would ever be able to arrange a dowry to marry, and the related question of who should become my wife. On one of my last visits to Pedro Peterson I took these issues to him. He taught me to trust God, and to believe that whatever was right, and whatever represented a real need in doing what was right, would be provided in due time by God. God would provide for all my needs, including my dowry. With his guidance I dared to approach Nora to be my wife, and we have been together ever since. Deacon Peterson referred me to this Psalm:

> *Fear the Lord ... for those who fear him lack nothing.*
> *The lions may grow weak and hungry,*
> *but those who seek the Lord lack no good thing.*
> *(Psalm 34:9-10)*

As he struggled through issues of his vocation, his marriage to Nora, and the realities of providing for their basic material needs, a passage from the Psalms took on special meaning for João. And it later encouraged both of them during difficult days of their study together at Calambata:

> *Commit your way to the Lord;*
> *trust in him and he will do this:*
> *He will make your righteousness shine like the dawn,*
> *the justice of your cause like the noonday sun.*
> *(Psalm 37:5-6)*

This word from God served to counteract the questions that were being raised by his teacher and his family, and which may have been circulating even in his own mind. There came a conviction that God was in control and that he, as the follower, was on the right path.

The Early Years in Angola

The primary school at Mongo Zulu

When Guilherme Ribeiro Neves, the BMS director of schools, targeted a certain area for the opening of a new school, it was normally far away from the central school, which was at Mbanza-Kongo. He had João work with him in these projects, being his pioneer for new schools. Once João had opened a new school, some other teacher would be appointed to follow him as teacher there after a year or two. His second assignment, after two years in Buela, was to open a new school in Mongo Zulu.

The Roman Catholic sisters, who were in charge of the Catholic rural schools in that area, were not at all pleased when João arrived to open the new primary school in Mongo Zulu. Catholics carried significant weight with the Portuguese colonial authorities and used it to restrain Protestants. As a result, they asked *monitor* Chaves, their best teacher, to open a new school at Mongo Zulu as competition.

> *I was informed that I would have a hard time in this village. I started my school at Mongo Zulu in September 1957. Two months later they started their school, and they already had a Catholic church on site. It was amazing that I never saw a priest. It was always the sisters who came to give instructions to their teacher, how he should combat me. For my part there was no animosity, I just did my work. That continued for almost six months during which time Chaves and I had not met or said hello. I just saw him outside with his students during recreation period. Our schools were not very far apart.*
>
> *I prayed that one day God would open the door. It happened in a unique way. I heard that he was very sick.*
>
> *One of my students, Pedro Santos, had family on the Protestant side, but his parents were Catholic.*
> *"Professor Chaves is sick, and very depressed."*
> *"Please take me there."*
> *"Why?"*

"To visit my sick colleague."

I knocked on the door. He thanked me for coming as a colleague. I asked what he needed, whether help or medication. In our school we kept a few medical supplies to treat our students with first aid. They did not have such provisions. I sent over some cold medicine. He came to me later for a reciprocal visit and to express thanks.
"Now I know I should never have followed those instructions. I heard so many bad things against you that were not true. I know now that you are my brother even if we are in different religions."
"Be careful not to lose your job."
"It will be my secret."
"Have a Bible."
"I have never seen the whole Bible. I will read it. We are not allowed to have the whole Bible, only the four Gospels."
"Did anyone ask the priest why?"
"Only those who studied theology in Rome are allowed to read it all. They tell us we will become maluco, *(crazy,) if we read it all."*
"Read it all, see if you're maluco."
He read the whole Bible. He was accused by the catechist *(Catholic teacher-evangelist).*

THE LOCAL SCHOOL COMMITTEE

Director Neves established a good system for handling local administrative problems that might arise in the rural schools. It was called the *conselho escolar* (school council), which was in effect the local school committee. The council met once monthly or more often, depending on the need. The teacher took whatever problem had arisen to the council. There were maybe ten men and ten women.

All the women in the village were listed and given an assignment month by month. Each family then supplied food and made one meal per day for the teacher. The students were expected to be "on campus" from Sunday afternoon through Friday afternoon of each week. The students returned home each weekend for the new supply of food that would provide their meals for the coming week. Those supplies would certainly include peanuts, manioc, and bananas, with beans or corn in season, if they were lucky. A student would not expect the luxury of eating meat.

We finished the school year very well, it was a fruitful year. But it was also a difficult year as I prepared for my upcoming wedding. It required many trips to Mbanza-Kongo by bicycle, sometimes without even knowing why Neves wanted me. The big coffee plantation called Primavera *was nearby. Neves might send a message to me by their truck saying that I should come to him immediately with the truck when it returns, but the truck would be gone by the time I got there. So I would cycle most of a day on the dirt road, with many hills. I borrowed the bike of the area pastor, Pedro Mbata. There were ten such pastors; the BMS provided a bike to each of them for visiting their churches.*

While I was trying to make arrangements with Nora, and Neves was making other demands on me, there were community demands that piled up as well. My house was the cleanest house in the community. A government official would come, for instance, to do the census, which was the basis for levying taxes. The community would assign him to live in my house for the two or three days. Or it might be the registered nurse from the government clinic, checking on sleeping sickness in the area, or doing tuberculosis vaccinations. "Go to the teacher's house." In effect, because I was living at a higher standard of cleanliness than the village, they used me as the community guest house, without remuneration. They might provide some food, but the lodging had to be with me. But I found that these government people were appreciative, and became my supporters. The Chefe *might ask if I have business in Mbanza-Kongo when he needs to* go there. He would provide a ride. If there is persecution he would protect me from it. So I found it important to give favours and open doors, which made life easier in the end. Co-operation becomes more important to people living in rural areas.

Senhor Fortunato was the registered nurse serving locally, who had come from the Malange area. He told me he was impressed with how well my house ran, considering I was a bachelor. The secret, of course, was the two lads I had trained to keep my house in order, Fernandes and Rosada, who were living with me. The other thing that impressed him was our medical care at this little rural school, done also by those same lads. They could clean wounds and apply bandages. The boys were not trained as nurses but I had taught them to do these things.

"These kids are not just with me to learn to read and write. The activities of my helpers, beyond keeping the house and helping with food include: prayer in the morning, time in school to learn to read and write, caring for those who have wounds or need medical care. After school they do manual work, some form of gardening, as required by all children in school in the country. Participation in sports is also required, that usually meant soccer. In the evening they are part of the choir, learning music. Every Sunday my school presents a song."

The nurse was really impressed. "I have never seen organization like this in the bush. Usually it happens only in the big centres where we have a pastor and a superintendent."

Since João was the very first of the teachers to open new rural schools, he had to be innovative. He was the pioneer who invented and established the working patterns which came to be copied (or modified) by other teachers as they, in turn, opened additional rural schools. In the schools João directed, he set up a pattern under which each of the lads, in turn, would cook for the others from his village, one week at a time. The average minimum of students to a hut would be five, the maximum ten.

The Early Years in Angola

The kids were so happy in their little kingdoms there, alone. I appointed a chief for each house. When a problem arose, they would solve it, unless it was really major, and then it would be brought to me. The hut chief would bring the problem. Problems were minimal, because each student wanted his village to be seen as a good village, so they managed to solve most problems among themselves, in order not to be seen as trouble-makers.

Once a week the schools' "chiefs" would be called together in order to run a check on how well they were eating. If certain students were not bringing an adequate share of food this would be noted, and João would then speak with the parents of those students. Every parent should provide equally so that all could eat well.

When leaving Mongo Zulu, or any school that I have been starting during the past year, I would not know the program for next year, I had to take all my things with me. For sure the next year's work would not be in the same village. That next year it was to be at Lomba, in the Cuimba Post area. When I went on vacation I had this already in mind, but I expected I would probably be married by then.

The Matwawana wedding

While teaching at Mongo Zulu, even without the financial support of his maternal uncle, João amassed the required funds to proceed with his marriage plans. Helped by friends and by BMS missionaries, he came up with all the money needed for the dowry and their wedding. Local tradition by then had established the expectation that one must go to Kinshasa to get everything in order for the purchases to be considered first class. In those days, only Kinshasa offered the desired prestige.

Traditions were followed. The fiancé should also travel to Kinshasa, to insure the measurements were right. Nora went, and stayed with relatives there. Travel costs to Kinshasa were her family's responsibility, while the shopping costs fell on João.

Shopping for the bride called for a wedding gown and at least seven new dresses, for the village people would appear before her on seven successive days and a different new dress was expected each day. The complete outfit required new lingerie. João's cousin, Ida, was there to help with that. Two pairs of shoes and a pair of sandals were needed to complete the bride's outfit. All this had to travel back to Mbanza-Kongo in João's luggage. They would both wear white gloves on their wedding day.

The best tailors were in Kinshasa. João's two suits were tailored there, one black and one white, which allowed long term for mix and match combinations. Of course he needed shirt and tie, socks and shoes to complete his wardrobe.

Kitchen items were totally the responsibility of the wife, along with house decorations, which accounted for the advanced crocheting and embroidering Nora had long been accumulating.

The wedding was multi-cultural. The whole event could not be completed either in Mbanza-Kongo or in Luanika. Those in the village expected the accompanying celebration to stretch out to seven days. How could one satisfy city friends as well as family and friends in the village? The conclusion they reached was to hold the wedding at Mbanza-Kongo, followed by refreshments at Nora's home, then all the invited guests from Mbanza-Kongo would be bussed to Luanika for the big party. The bride's beautiful wedding bouquet was prepared by BMS missionary, Roma Shields. Clifford Parsons officiated, then changed out of his heavy wool suit to the traditional Parsons shorts, for events in Luanika.

It was a full busload—indeed the bus was overcrowded—with close to a hundred people. Missionaries used mission vehicles. The mission was closed for the day. The missionaries waited at Calambata until the party started.

Luanika village had been alerted only to the numbers of people expected, with no details of who would be included. Food was prepared in abundance. João's brother, Lambourne, hunted a wild buffalo for the party, they had *fufu* (manioc paste), beans and more, cold drinks were kept in refrigerators at Calambata—everybody was happy. João had rented the bus for the day. Manuel, the bus owner, stayed through the day, returning his passengers to Mbanza-Kongo in the evening.

There was one unpleasant incident. Cousin Eduardo, who made the arrangements, had not wanted to overwhelm Luanika people, so didn't tell them a big bus was coming, and didn't mention the participation of the missionaries. As the bus pulled up to Luanika and as João was handing down Nora, an uncle appeared, disturbed by such momentous surprises. "Where did all these people come from?" This was not the right moment for a disturbance. Tradition has it that the bride and groom are not supposed to speak.

"Where will we put them? We don't have enough beds."
"Be calm. Go ask Eduardo Nsonga."
"These people come from Mbanza-Kongo and change all our traditions."

It was an embarrassing moment for João because of the tradition that required the bride and groom to keep silence. In fact it was the expectation that they be quiet and sombre for virtually all day. Nora was expected to shed tears, especially at the wedding itself, to display her grief at leaving mother and family. People want to see the bride cry at the church, and they will remark then on what a nice girl this is, missing her mother so. "If there were no crying it could be something of a disaster." Nora admits that she cried a bit, but maybe at the wrong time, for it happened when her friends were getting back on the bus to return to Mbanza-Kongo!

The missionaries and the overloaded bus returned to town, and the village ceremony continued through the week. The first day was the dowry day. Usually that is finished before the wedding. In this case, the families were spread over a considerable distance, Nora's along the Songololo road, João's along the Cuimba road. They had agreed to wait and do it all during the wedding party.

To fully meet all traditional requirements, the marriage should involve two distinct clans. There were exceptions, and this was one of them, as they both belonged to *Ntumba Mvemba* clan, just different family branches. In any event, dowry requires meeting and negotiating, normally incorporating some pretense at aggression or at least confrontation. Being all the same clan, this dowry negotiation was smooth, but the payment of a fine was required because family research should have been more scrupulously followed. The fine was in the form of a goat to the bride's family, termed *nkombo a nsoni*, "the goat of shame." With that fine paid, the record was cleared and the situation considered normalized. Harmony reigned.

Instead of aggressive negotiation, it became a harmonious formality. The people from the Songololo side came to João's side, those from the Cuimba road came to Nora's side to show that there was harmony.

Then we ate and ate and ate. Every day for a week there was a big dinner, a goat killed each day. People then went back to their gardens happy, everyone having participated. All week the bride had to be treated as a princess, doing no cleaning, not carrying wood or water. We stayed in my father's house. Water for bath arrived already boiled. An aunt or cousin of Nora was appointed to do all these services, aided by other young girls from Nora's family to assist.

Photos of the wedding and the feast were kept with the family through their first exile to the Congo, but were lost in the haste when they had to return for a second time as refugees to the Congo in 1975.

From Luanika and the feast, João and Nora went directly to their teaching assignment in Lomba, without returning to Mbanza-Kongo.

Teaching at Lomba

The last teaching assignment that João and Nora carried was at the village of Lomba. This was the first year of that school's operation, so again they were pioneering in a village which had just been granted its first school. They worked in a single large classroom. This school had proper desks and a table for the teachers, made by local carpenters. Most of the students had attended church schools of the BMS, similar to the one in which João himself had learned to read under his father's instruction. They had studied in the Portuguese language, since Portuguese was required to enter grade one. They sorted out the more advanced students and put them in grade two. Nora taught the first grade, João taught the second. Their work was done simultaneously in one classroom, with fifty to sixty students in all. Ballpoint pens did not exist. Students had no textbooks as such, but they had copy books, notebooks, and they were working with fountain pens. However, much of the work was done with chalk on a blackboard. Between them, João and Nora might have owned fifteen to twenty books, most of which would be textbooks from their own upper grade studies.

The school complex at Lomba. Credit: Pamela J. Buckler

First-year schools had only one classroom. After two years, the local population was so eager to advance their school that they would fire bricks and build a bigger school. Thus the schools grew without assistance from the government or the mission.

Wars Are Never Enough

Morning exercises at the Lomba school.

Our "bell" at Lomba school consisted of a suspended truck rim struck by an iron rod. It was the responsibility of the catequist *(the village's teacher-evangelist) to ring the bell each morning at approximately six-thirty. One student from each of the little kitchens stayed behind to get the fire started and prepare breakfast for his group. Prayers lasted from a half hour to forty-five minutes, and consisted of a Scripture reading, one hymn or song, and a brief commentary. That responsibility alternated between the* catequist *and João. Our church at Lomba had mud block walls, a thatched roof, window openings without glass or shutters, and a dirt floor. It also had a table rather than a pulpit, and proper benches.*

Students lined up and were marched to chapel, a distance of half a kilometre from where we lined up. All of them were in bare feet, and they came awake as they marched. The school system began to bring disciplined routine into these young lives of students, whose age at Lomba ranged from about ten to fifteen years of age. That is exactly what their parents wanted and expected to happen. It was part of school life in every school, whether sponsored by the Protestant or the Catholic missions. Nobody else was operating primary schools in rural villages. The students marched.

After prayers we marched back to the school compound for breakfast, students and teacher. After breakfast the bell rang again, calling the students to assemble in front of the flagpole for the required flag raising ceremony at which the children sang Portugal's national anthem:

Herois do Mar, nobre povo, nação valente, immortal,
Levantai hoje, de novo, o esplendor de Portugal.
Entre as brumas da memória, Ó pátria, sente-se a voz:

The Early Years in Angola

Às armas, às armas, sobre a terra, sobre o mar,
Pela pátria lunar.
Centre as canhões, marchar, marchar.
Heroes of the sea,
Noble people.....

Following the national anthem we went directly to classes. We had classroom studies through the morning, then in the afternoon, manual work and sports.

Nora's perspective

Nora makes the following observations on their first married year, teaching at Lomba:

We were married in September, and the first month was all right. By October I was pregnant. I was often sick, but I continued to teach some in the mornings. We had good helpers, Fernandes and Rosada. I had grown up in a busy household. We always had many people in our home.

At Lomba we lived in a compound with many kids around, and at nineteen years of age, I was already a mother to all these kids. They had their own kitchens, but when they were missing something they come running. "Mom, do you have salt?" I have to make sure they have food. Otherwise, for that house I may provide something.

I was teacher of the youngest class, all subjects; João had the second class, with the older children. Sometimes after school in the afternoons we had games, my class against João's class in soccer, which they always won, for they were older. Once my class won and I remember how João was upset.

Fernandes and Rosada were like extended family members. They had been with João at Buela and Mongo Zulu, then went with the newly married couple to Lomba. They were helpers, but they also kept learning. They knew the routines of his household. Although they had not finished *quarta classe* as Nora had, they were advanced enough as members of João's second class that they were able to fill in and carry the load of teaching for Nora when she was not well.

It was the custom that parents would bring a child to João asking that he be raised as if he were a son. Rosada had been a problem child, brought by his parents and committed to João's care. Fernandes, Rosada, and Paulo slept in his house when he was single and simply continued as household members after he married.

At eight months of my pregnancy, lightning struck while I was in our little kitchen out back, separated from the house. João was inside. I was making donuts there in the kitchen with Rosada, and Paulo was also with us. I was almost killed. It was not a heavy thunder storm, only a shower, but it brought a lightning strike. We were thrown in different directions. The kitchen was red. I was unconscious, unable to move. Fortunately there was no fire, but there was that smell like gunpowder (the smell of ozone). The boys ran into the main house to inform João.

From then I was not well at all, and I had a high fever daily. Village people came, wanting to send me to Mbanza-Kongo for treatment. In June I gave up teaching and returned to family in Mbanza-Kongo. One of the symptoms was excessive thirst. My mother noticed it and inquired what was wrong. We concluded that there were continuing problems from the lightning strike, and when Samuel was delivered the problems continued to show up. His birth was difficult, life-threatening, and his whole body had the appearance of being burned. He was swollen and he carried scars.

I didn't return to teaching. With July came the school summer vacation, then in September we were off to studies with John Keith at the Bible Institute in Calambata.

4

STUDIES AT CALAMBATA BIBLE TRAINING INSTITUTE

Calambata was a modest training program, on a very modest compound, being developed north of Mbanza-Kongo on the road to Cuimba. The BMS missionary, Clifford Parsons, had brought this small institution into being. He and and his wife, Lottie, were assisted there by Eileen Motley from England, and Anibal and Luisa Machado from Portugal. Clifford and Lottie were called to an executive position in London, and departed at the beginning of September, 1959. John Keith and his wife, Virginia, came from their Cabinda posting to replace them. With new students and a new director, the program resumed.

The transition from Lomba to Calambata

Nora was expecting Samuel, and was already living with her parents in Mbanza-Kongo as their year of teaching at Lomba drew to a close. During that summer vacation period, João continued to work with school director Neves, enrolling students for the coming term, to attend their new schools that would be opened.

Mfutila, Chief of Sanga, standing on land he granted to Calambata Bible Institute, circa 1960

During the first few months of their first term at Calambata, which began in September, 1959, some new student housing was being built, three units in all. One of the houses was designated for the Matwawana family, but would require many weeks to complete. From September until Christmas of that year, João camped in the little kitchen behind student Manuel Senguele's house, while Nora and Samuel lived in Luanika with João's mother. This meant that Nora had a walk of 2 or 3 kilometres to school, with Samuel on her back.

The Bible Institute at Calambata was still in its fledgling stage and was beginning to serve two groups of churches, those inland affiliated with BMS missionaries who had pioneered there, and those from the coastal area north of Luanda and in the enclave of Cabinda. The latter were identified as the *Igreja Evangélica de Angola* (IEA), only recently associated with Canadian Baptist Ministries (CBM), following the death of their founder, Matthew Zachariah Stober from the U.K. Some of the churches in Cabinda had been started by missionaries of the Christian and Missionary Alliance, but all were now identified as IEA churches.

Students were sent to Calambata from both areas. They would come as families, and with a helper if needed, so that both husband and wife could enter into studies, which were both academic and "applied," or practical in nature.

There was a wide spectrum of academic capacity among the wives at Calambata, ranging from Nora, who was the most advanced, and Ermelinda, who was also able to follow the content of the men's courses, to others who were totally illiterate. A range of studies was set up for the wives, taught by Eileen Motley, Luisa Machado, and Virginia Keith, with programs in health, nutrition, home care, child care, cooking, and handwork such as crocheting. Nora remembers that that from January on, she was more active on campus, both with her own classroom studies and also teaching crocheting to other student wives.

Classroom studies for the men began early, with classes from 6:30, after which they went back to their families to have breakfast before 8:00. A bell signaled the beginnings, the comings and goings.

Outbreak of War

João relates events around Calambata in the days leading to the outbreak of war:

Calambata students were regularly invited to preach on Sundays at the BMS central church in Mbanza-Kongo. My turn came up to preach there on the weekend before the war actually began, in March 1961. Nora was already there, staying with her parents as she awaited Edward's delivery.

Monday I was returning to Calambata to go back to school. My first shock and surprise was that on that walk of 25 kilometres from Mbanza-Kongo to Calambata I met absolutely nobody on the road. One would normally expect to meet people constantly, or if you were walking too slow others would be passing you. I asked myself what was going on. So I pressed on to find out what was happening.

Rumours of war had been building. By the time I got there the word was going around that maybe some action was about to happen, but what? We had no specific word. A lot of people were interpreting the coded messages that were arriving. Sometimes they interpreted them very wrongly. There were even wild reports that maybe foreign armies were coming to fight the Portuguese.

I was not happy with the explanation I got from the students. However, I had no choice but to go to class. The next day we were to go to the pentamedina *camp at Sengue village.*

Angola's public health service set up camps in rotation from region to region, in an attempt to control sleeping sickness, for it was endemic in much of the area, the tsetse fly being particularly prevalent in the valleys and low-lying areas. Pentamidine was given as an intramuscular injection. It was painful to receive and painful to live with for a few days afterward. The camps were simply referred to as the *pentamedina*.

The next evidence of unusual activity was at the *pentamedina*. Everybody who was present got injections, but there were no men there at all, except the men from our Calambata Bible Training Institute. The men of the villages just did not show up. Because there was such a press of women and children, the nurses were kept busy. They seemed not to notice that no men had come. João and others concluded that the men of the region must be preparing for something big.

Nobody could inform me. I was too close to the white people at Calambata. Everyone kept me ignorant of all the developments, and since most of the students were from other parts of

The Early Years in Angola

Angola they would not be in on strategic secrets in any event.

As we were returning I told the other students that I would be stopping in at Luanika to visit my mother. I would come on to Calambata later. My brother-in-law Matias saw me there.
"What are you doing here?"
"I came from pentamedina, *I will return to Calambata tonight"*
"Don't do that. By night you won't be able to go."
"Why?"
"There will be things happening tonight you won't want to be involved in."
"Maybe I'll have supper with Mother first, and then go."
"Not if you want to be alive. The war will start tonight."
So that's why there were no men at pentamedina!*"*
"Nobody wants to go to war with all the swelling and pain in your butt that comes from a pentamedina *injection. A person is too sore to move. Certainly one could not run. By tomorrow many people will not be alive. Tonight there will be roadblocks everywhere. At Calambata you will be safe."*

So finally I knew, and precisely in those hours when the action was starting.

I ran back all the way to the students' camp, without waiting for supper. We heard shots that night, which made us aware that the rebellion had started. There were UPA (União das Populações de Angola) soldiers patrolling. Later they would be known as FNLA (National Front for the Liberation of Angola). They patrolled back trails, and one of those trails passed through Bairro Parsons, *our student camp. Some of them knocked at midnight. We were afraid, and it was raining a little. They told us to open the door.*
"We're cold, can we have tea?" (That didn't sound too threatening, we made them tea.)
"Do you have an antelope skin? (They cut our rug in pieces as a rain shield to keep the powder dry in their muzzle loaders' firing action.)

These young freedom fighters became friendly, and they stopped in various times during those four days of waiting until the Portuguese army patrol arrived to end all our days at Calambata. The last two of those four nights I couldn't sleep. The dialogue concerned what should be done with the white people, thirteen of them:

- *Anibal and Luisa Machado, with Lidia and Maria Lina, a staff family.*
- *Eileen Motley, staff.*
- *John and Virginia Keith, with Carol and Shirley (Virginia being pregnant), a staff family.*
- *Dr. Walter and Mrs. Winnifred Johnson, in Kikongo language study.*
- *Tony Bourne and his wife Jill, in Kikongo language study.*

It was at that point, I came to John Keith, telling him that the bridges were all burned or destroyed between Calambata and Mbanza-Kongo, as well as in the other direction. I had been asked to tell him that everyone was safe on the mission compound itself, as long as nobody left the compound, and as long as nobody from outside was allowed in to increase the numbers. Very fortunately, nobody came to ask asylum, for he would have been in a very difficult spot.

5

WAR IN NORTHERN ANGOLA, 1961

The unresolved tensions that had been building for 500 years between an expanding colonial power and a declining traditional kingdom set the stage for the violent uprising of 1961, which deeply affected the lives of everyone. Angola's war of independence was a conflict that did not spring up overnight. Its roots were five centuries deep, and it is a story of a colonial administration attempting to be effective, efficient, and productive by its own standards, but whose efficiency was in conflict with African culture and traditions that were deeper and more profound than the European presence.[1]

On March 15, 1961, the staff and students at the Bible Training Institute at Calambata awoke to a new day which looked much like those preceding it.

It was an eerie morning of total stillness in a countryside where the bustle of life began with daybreak. That morning held no ringing of bells, no sound of voices, none of the usual barking of dogs at whatever pedestrian, bicycle, or vehicle might be in movement along the dirt roads or private paths. It was the kind of stillness that brings a lighthouse keeper wide awake when the foghorn stops its intermittent blowing. We at Calambata were not in the direct line of action, but the war that was making itself known elsewhere left us caught in a surreal suspension.

The roads were free of traffic, for all bridges had been destroyed, in both directions. The primary school on the hill nearby stood empty. The workmen with whom we interacted daily had all gone to ground, knowing that government reprisals would be swift and without mercy when the initial smoke cleared. The Calambata student families were in a different situation from that of local inhabitants, as all but the families of João Matwawana and Henrique Josias were from other regions of Angola. Without any guarantees, everyone hoped that security for the student body would ride on the presence of expatriates: British, Portuguese, and Canadian. History indicated that government treatment of Angola was always moderated under the eye of foreigners, especially British. A common proverb, *Para Inglês ver...* (For English to see...) bears testimony to that.

For the small expatriate community at Calambata, our only source of information was short wave radio, the BBC's foreign service, as bits of information began to trickle in over the next few days. We were in isolation. There was a pencilled notice, on paper, stuck in a forked stick, indicating that inhabitants of this mission station were safe as long as we did not leave our compound, or allow outsiders to seek refuge in our midst. Fortunately that was never tested, for how could we have refused asylum?

For four long days and tense nights Calambata was in isolation, broken on the afternoon of the fourth day by the roar of army trucks. When the military convoy arrived, their bearded commander displayed no joy at finding this pocket of undisturbed foreigners in a countryside where Portuguese nationals were under attack, many already dead. There was a brief period of intense negotiation. The commander insisted on evacuating Calambata's foreigners, and he needed a local whom he could take back with him "to answer a few questions." This would surely have been a death sentence for any unfortunate person taken for questioning. John Keith refused to leave unless the student families and remaining house help were all evacuated, as well. In the end, expatriates travelled in Mission vehicles, inserted into the military convoy, while student families were loaded on the back of the trucks that carried the heavy planks with which temporary bridging was arranged over the streams which could not be forded.

Grenades and gunfire in the wooded valleys assured the nervous soldiers that they would not be ambushed while building temporary bridges. When all had crossed, the planks were loaded once more on the trucks. It was a tense time with jittery soldiers, nervous adults, crying children, the uncertainty over the future, and the smell of explosives. The destination was the BMS mission compound in Mbanza-Kongo, a distance of some 25 kilometers. They arrived just after nightfall without incident. That night João was reunited with Nora and their four-day-old son, Edward, born in the hospital there at Mbanza-Kongo. Samuel, only eighteen months old, was also with Nora.

The following day there was a wholesale evacuation of those most anxious to leave. That included the Guilherme Neves family from Mbanza-Kongo (João's former school director), and the Anibal Machado family from Calambata. It included missionary wives and children, and others who could be persuaded to go, such as Kikongo language students. They were shuttled by six-passenger aircraft to a larger airfield at Toto and from there to Luanda by flying boxcar, sitting on their luggage. From there they proceeded at different stages to their destinations in Portugal, the U.K., Canada, and the United States. As John Keith's students were still in Mbanza-Kongo, he remained, as did a number of BMS missionaries.

Life for the Calambata student families inside the walled mission compound of Mbanza-Kongo became very tense. That included the Matwawanas, who remained roughly one more month under those conditions.

The Flight out of Mbanza-Kongo

João, Nora, and their colleagues were passing through perilous days. Their faith and their judgement were being tested by the hour, with no assurance on most days that they would live to see another sunrise.

Tensions and suspicion in the town were such that it was not safe for the men to stray outside the walled compound of the BMS mission property. Tension built by the day, with taunts flung in over the wall by passers by:

"We know you're in there..."

"One of these nights..."

It was considered only a matter of time until the men would be seized and taken out forcibly, whether officially or unofficially:

We had devotions every night. Every night each man would say goodbye to his wife, unsure that there would ever be another opportunity.

Nora had gone into labor for the birth of Edward on the night of March 15, and she delivered the next day. That meant that when the April arrangements were being made for the departure in secret to safety in the Congo, João and Nora were fleeing with two children, Edward just five weeks old, and Samuel only nineteen months. Nora comments on that interim period while the pressures were building toward their departure from Mbanza-Kongo:

When I went for Edward's delivery, I stayed with my parents until I had the baby. My father was in terrible danger, for he really knew what all was going on. When mother and dad felt that it was too dangerous for them to stay any longer, they both went to sleep in the forest. But from time to time mother returned to Mbanza-Kongo to see how we were doing, sometimes bringing peanuts. The day my dad was almost caught they decided that João and I must leave, too. Dad told my mother "go and get Nora and the children, then it would be easier for João if he has to run." They knew if we were trapped with small children it would be hopeless.

Mama Nuneza has been telling people that João is being indoctrinated by his in-laws who do not have faith. When my Mom and I were crying, Nuneza came again and said, "Celina, I can't understand, you lost your faith." But Mom knew how dangerous it was, and so we said a farewell as if we were to die, comforting each other that we will meet in heaven. Although my mother and father left then, the rest of us stayed around for one more week before we left.

John Keith called the students together just before they fled on April 24. He gave them their standard living allowance, which the students referred to as "pocket money." Then two distinct communications: First, that this would be the last of the living allowance payments. Second, that he was not instructing students either to flee or to remain at Mbanza-Kongo, but that there was solid evidence pointing to 10 a.m. on Sunday as being the safest time for those wanting to flee to slip out through the city's perimeter defences to the safety of the forest. The army seemed to show a consistent pattern of calling all the guards and watchmen in at that time for a roll call.

Preparations

There were intense meetings held non-stop among the student families. The majority of students felt that to flee would be suicide. They were certain they would be sighted and shot. They did not know the area and its forests, as local people did. They did not have assurance that they would find either friends or relatives along the way. Some had come to study from considerable distances, spoke Kikongo with different accents, and would not be considered local people by those they might encounter in the forests.

These intense consultations among ourselves went on through the night after the rations had been distributed. There was scurrying back and forth to confer with one or another, then we came together for a major collective decision.

The only ones who didn't agree with the majority were Henrique Josias and João Matwawana; both of us were from

Mbanza-Kongo. We knew that we were more vulnerable than the others. If soldiers came to pick us up for questioning, as they were threatening to do constantly, we local students are the ones for whom there would be guaranteed beatings and torture.

"Let us separate a little."

Henrique and João met and decided that since the pressure on them was now intense, they should leave as quickly as possible.

We informed John Keith and the others on that Sunday morning that we had decided to leave. Eileen Motley brought some sandwiches and peanut butter for the road, with sugar and tea.

But then John Keith came and mentioned a complication which had arisen:

"João, we just remembered something. You, with Josias and your wives, are the only residents from this area who have not fled, apart from a few elderly people. There are children in both the girls' and boys' boarding schools. If you two families go, the children are doomed. They don't know where to go. There will be nobody left who can guide them. Their parents are not here. Are you willing to take them with you as you go?"

João and Nora can't remember how many students there were, certainly more than twenty, probably less than fifty. The parents of these children, in many instances, would be in villages they would pass along the way, and, in fact, this happened repeatedly as they travelled through the forest.

João:
Our numbers in the group kept changing. Those who met relatives would step out of our group to travel with their family. Others, for their own reasons, would wish to attach themselves to us to travel with us. Pedro Vieira, the Keith family's cook,

was the other adult who accompanied us—Pedro and his infamous travelling companion, the Keiths' dog.

João and Josias, in consultation perhaps with Pedro, played the role of Moses leading that multitude through the wilderness:

Our worries increased as we realized our contingent was growing, making it more scary trying to slip out of the city under siege, with guards posted all around. But as you said, there was nobody on guard at 10:00 in the morning. We left Mbanza-Kongo without seeing even one soldier.

Nora:
Mama Nuneza followed crying for her grandchildren. We took immediately to the paths in the bush, but she circled around openly on the main road, to where the path would cross it. She carried one single banana, and kept shouting loudly to us, pleading with her family not to leave. And this was supposed to be our departure in secret. We were terrified. We met her where we had to cross the road to the other side. If she were seen or heard we would all have been killed.

It was on Sunday morning that we left. We walked for three days, but it was terrible. It was the rainy season. I was still weak from childbearing. I remember, too, that we had received injections against TB. I had a reaction on my arm. I was carrying Edward, and his umbilical cord was not yet healed. After walking two days, my arm ruptured and I could not carry him any more in my arms, so I transferred the small baby to my back.

It was so slippery that at times we would just fall. We walked for three days. Mom and Dad and my sister were coming from a different direction and we met just like that in the forest.

João:
We didn't have a plan to meet. That was just God's plan.

They did not travel by day on any roads that would take cars. It was all on the forest paths and through grassland as far as the Congo border.

These paths had been there for a long time. These were the traders's paths used by people going to and from the markets for generations past. It was known to be the way from Angola to Songa, which was a big market on the Congo border. Our people would go there to sell beans and to buy good things, cloth, and more. These paths had been there for ages.

On the way, we met people who were already living in these areas, so that food was not a problem. Everywhere we came to people who welcomed us with peanuts and bananas. Without our being aware of it, there was a network already in place for us. Whenever we were tired, we would just lie down and sleep under the trees in rain or whatever. We had no choice.

In our escape, I had taken a big umbrella. When it was raining, I could cover the two boys. Five to six days were needed to get us across the border into Congo, then we were safe.

They met family along the way, Nora's parents first, then a day later João's mother and Nora's sister. Their meeting was not planned—it was God's plan for them.

The number of people travelling together kept increasing. We collected people from different directions coming to the same major paths, which led to the big market at Songa. There were too many paths to be guarded by the Portuguese. And also they didn't yet have enough soldiers at that time. The war was fresh and they were still bringing more soldiers out from Portgual.

The advantage we had in getting safely out of Mbanza-Kongo was that wherever you happened to be in the town, you could find a nearby path that would lead to the forest and connect with other paths going to Congo. For instance, when Marques

The Early Years in Angola

and the other group left, they followed a completely different set of paths from ours, but they, too, were successful.

The survival system for those exiting Mbanza-Kongo lay in the vast network of paths, but also in the co-operation of people. They knew that half of the former population of the town were living in Congo because of the oppression.

That was the reason why large refugee camps were not required for Angolans in Congo. We were always able to find an uncle or somebody from the clan.

When João went to change money, Derrick said, "We missionaries cannot tell you when to go, but I am so glad you are going. If it were me, I'd be there already." That was a nice confirmation. Then he gave us a very thick blanket to cover the baby on the road. That helped a lot.

There was one particularly dangerous spot where we had to cross the Songololo highway the second time. It would be so easy for them to kill us at that point. It was at this second place where Vieira gave our children's food to the Keith's dog to keep it quiet.

An older man was there, an acquaintance of my father, who had taken it on himself to be a guide to help various groups cross the road at this perilous spot. He spotted me. "Oh Mwana Zakuadia..."

We could not travel fast because of fear. We would travel a bit, then stop and listen. We didn't go very far that day. We slept under the trees that night. Amazingly, the babies were quiet all the time. That was like a miracle, as if they knew something was wrong.

As we approached the border, even the students kept bumping into their relatives as they travelled along the path. We might have been about 100 people at the time we crossed the highway. It was very fluid with people joining and leaving.

There were many times when we would hear the surveillance aircraft approaching. We would all scatter to hide in the tall elephant grass. In April it would be about 2 metres high everywhere. There were no serious spottings by the aircraft because of that good cover at that time of year. On arrival at Songa we found a huge gathering of about 10,000 people.

Those who fled had food with them, especially peanuts. It was Nora's responsibility to distribute some food to the students. Before they left, she had gone to Dr. Shields and asked for some medications and especially aspirin. Along the way, whenever anyone had cuts or wounds, it was Nora who cared for them and give aspirin to those who had headaches. They had enough peanuts to share with the boarding school students whose parents did not live nearby. Nora comments:

When we met João's sister at a certain place along the road, she took over and carried Samuel from that point.

Rivers were difficult. I was not used to balancing on a log to cross rivers. I was so scared. That part was hard. There were times at rivers when I thought I would die. João would make trips across to take all the baggage, then take the babies, then lead me by the hand.

Although the border was not clearly marked we knew distinctly when we were there. Once we had crossed, we felt very safe.

When we arrived at Songa, we found João's mother in the hospital there, running a high fever. When we left Mbanza-Kongo, Dr. Shields had said, "Nora must go straight to see a doctor at Songa." My TB reaction had ruptured before we got to Songa. Edward's umbilical cord had not healed and it had an infection.

The Early Years in Angola

I remember arrival at Songa. What would we do now? João had no employment. We slept in some leaves on the verandah of somebody's house. My father went to ask João if they could take me to Kinshasa for treatment. João agreed. The next day we were able to get to Kimpese by truck. We prepared to sleep.

We spent one night at Kimpese, then someone informed me that my brother had been seen at Mbanza Ngungu.

We flagged down a truck and jumped in. It was a meat truck with blood over everything and all over us. As we arrived at the first gas station in Mbanza Ngungu, there was my brother, Deves, buying gas. Imagine that! God gives us such wonderful evidences of his care. My father called to the driver, "You stop here. I want my family out."

The men spent that night at Deves' home in Mbanza-Ngungu, the women and children were lodged in the home of a woman who lived nearby, with instructions for food to be prepared for them all.

This was the first properly prepared meal that they had eaten in more than a week, having snacked along the way as they travelled. Nora remembers that the lady prepared *fufu* from manioc flour and that Deves brought in corned beef, which can quickly give substance to the sauce that accompanies *fufu*. The next morning Deves appeared with a huge basin of bread loaves, with tea, sugar and milk. "What a treat! I will never forget the amount of tea I drank. We didn't eat lunch that day, that was enough," Nora recalls.

Deves faced a dilemma: how to get these people to Kinshasa? His own truck was loaded merchandise. The solution lay in the special train that came from Kinshasa to Mbanza-Ngungu on the weekend, known as the *train soùlard,* the drunkard's train. It was set up for people who chose to spend their weekends away from the city, in a drinking party. That train would meet their needs. Nora would go immediately to Kinshasa on the *train soùlard,* with her parents and the two boys. The others would follow in the evening. Deves would meet the first group at the train station in Kinshasa, for family members there were as yet unaware of these recent arrivals from Angola.

Brother Deves took us to the train station. In the train, we had no identity papers at all. Police came through the train checking for documents. With family in Kinshasa , and having made frequent visits there over the years, ours was a family in which most people spoke some Lingala. Our strategy was to pretend that none of us understood what we were being asked. Each in turn pointed to my father. When the police came to him he chose to pretend insanity. They ask him for documents and his response is a jumble of words accompanied by a blank stare. It's the other passengers who get us off the hook. "These are just people running for their lives, leave them alone." The police moved on.

In Kinshasa, Deves picked us up and delivered us home. He was renting a very large house, close to my Uncle David's house. The two shared the burden of hospitality. Most of the women stayed with Uncle David, the men with Deves.

Now, how would the treatment be managed? Elderly Tiago worked at Amadeus' store back in Mbanza-Kongo. His daughter Maria Matrosa worked at the big hospital in Kintambo. She came, saw the baby, got medication at the hospital and began treating Edouard's umbilical cord. The Medical assistant at the Baptist clinic in Kintambo was Afonso Constantino, João's cousin. Networking solved everything. Edward's treatment and mine was looked after without spending a penny.

Thus began the Matwawana's lives in the Congo. Nora and the children stayed three months in Kinshasa, before joining João at Kimpese.

Endnotes:
[1.] Additional details about this crisis period are recorded in the author's earlier book *The First Few Wars Are The Worst* (Keith 1998:30-46).

Part Two

The Democratic Republic of the Congo (DRC)

Democratic Republic of the Congo

6

STUDIES AT KIMPESE, KINKONZI, THEN BIRMINGHAM

ÉCOLE DE PASTEURS ET D'INSTITUTEURS—EPI KIMPESE

When João arrived at EPI Kimpese in 1961, he went immediately to look for the pastor. He learned that the chief mason at EPI Kimpese was a man of Angolan origins.

> *I asked to meet this Angolan head-mason, and was taken to meet Tata Isaac. When I asked where he was from, he said Mbanza-Mpangu. That village is only a few kilometres from Mbanza-Kongo, and I told him I knew most of the people in Mbanza Mpangu.*
> *"Where are you staying?"*
> *"I'm sleeping on a verandah here at Kimpese."*
> *"Where do you come from in Angola?"*
> *"From Luanika."*
> *"Who is your father?"*
> *"Zakuadia."*

"Oh no! My wife is Zakuadia's niece! This year we have had a baby which we named Zakuadia. Come, I must introduce you to my wife. This is a real discovery! We thought perhaps most of the people were dead. We have found one who is alive—a member of the family."

Tata Isaac took me straight to his house. And when he announced me! Well, this lady couldn't believe it. She jumped, she cried, she sang. This kind of welcome in a new place in a strange country—I couldn't believe it.

"This is your house. Your father is the one who kept the family going."

Zakuadia's "family" lived far away on the Songololo Road and João didn't know them well, but those were the people his father had visited regularly. Now, in Congo, João reaped the benefits from his father's continued contact with his extended family.

This head mason, Tata Isaac, was highly esteemed and considered an important man on the campus at EPI Kimpese. João needed an interview with the governing board of the Pastors' school at EPI, where he hoped to enroll as a student. Nothing would do but that Isaac accompany João, the principal, and the pastor, to that critical interview with the committee.

These were unsettling times. Congo was less than a year past the turbulence which accompanied its own independence. Many were jittery about their safety, with the influx of tattered and scarred people who were coming to them now with regularity out of Angola. João understood the fear of some of those he first contacted at Kimpese, and he was sympathetic to those fears. In his first contacts with EPI's Principal, João found him to be skeptical and even fearful, suggesting that João should return the following day when more people could be drawn together. When he went in the following day it was "like a press conference":

So I went already armed with some backing, to prove that I'm not a rebel. The general reaction was favorable.

"Because Tata Isaac knows this person João, even though he is barefoot, we have to listen."

The committee sat away off at a distance, asking the questions. They were afraid of this man in bare feet with cuts and scratches on his limbs from travelling through the forest, someone who had just come from northern Angola where people had been killed.

"So, you say you were in Calambata?"
"Yes."
"I know that Calambata, because it is a BMS school. Do you know Eileen Motley?"
"Yes, she was one of my teachers."

Then it began to be evident that João was not dangerous, and that he was telling the truth. Reference was made to Clifford Parsons and others who had figured in João's life. By the next day, the committee did not need to be on hand. João simply proceeded with Director Bert Cox to deal with details of regularizing his relationship to EPI as a student candidate. For someone who had been through the perils of fight, flight and forest, God's coincidences were a glorious smoothing of the way, providing a real ray of hope in the midst of such dark circumstances and following his family's exposure to so much peril.

It became clear that he needed to locate a place immediately where he could settle with his family. Beyond that, it would take some time to determine the academic level at which João could be admitted. He had no documentation to show precisely what he had been studying at Calambata. They were interested in seeing the last report card.

"But these things are in Angola."
"Well, that's the problem."
"And if I showed you a report card, might that open the door?"
"Yes."

Back into the fire!

When João came out from his interview, he ran to the shopping centre to confer with Pedro Vieira, his companion on the recent flight from Angola.

"We're going to Calambata."
"That was always in my mind anyway. Let's go."
Then we located Josias, and I told him that if he wants to study, he must have his report card.
"But it's too dangerous to go back."
"What's the difference? If I go I will be dead. If I'm here, I'll be just sitting around as a refugee."

Vieira declared his intention to go, regardless of whoever else went. Josias agreed to accompany them. He proceeded to convince his wife, who insisted that he must return with her sewing machine. João's problem was to convince his mother, Ditina, who was living near the Angolan frontier. He found ways to clear that obstacle as well, with stories that may have fallen short of full disclosure!

Well, we went. Our arrival there took four days through the forest and grasslands. We stood on one of the hills overlooking Calambata for almost a full day, just to monitor whether there was movement. We saw no vehicles passing, and concluded that the area was almost abandoned, though we kept wondering whether someone was hiding. Maybe they have spotted us already. That's the kind of fear we had.

After waiting for hours, we proceeded slowly and carefully to the campus where the new student houses had been built. Josias and I decided that we would not cross that little stream to where the school and the rest of the compound was located. Vieira had to go there, because his house was on the other side. He rushed quickly and got a few things from his house. We were really saddened by the place, seeing the chickens fleeing from fear of people. That was another confirmation that nobody was around.

The essential was to get that last report card, and then I found it! ...I also brought class notes and exercise materials. Going from Kimpese to Calambata was easiest, without anything to carry. Coming back was slow and more difficult, with our additional loads.

Back at Kimpese, I went to Mr Cox with my documents, and showed my report card. He was surprised by the range of what we had studied at Calambata, commenting that I had already covered almost everything on their curriculum at EPI, but that I still needed language.

"Now," he said, "I don't have any doubts. I'm going to write today to Clifford John Parsons in London." And he did. When the reply arrived from Clifford, one of its components was an appeal that the family should be treated as students rather than as refugees, since they were still considered to be under the BMS Calambata program. We benefitted from the reality that BMS missionaries such as Mr. Cox and Mr. Parsons were working under the same organization even if it was in two different countries.

MATWAWANA ASSISTS IN COORDINATING RELIEF TO REFUGEES

The relief organization *Secours Protestant* was swinging into action, and twelve warehouses were put at the disposal of Edna Staple and Jean Comber, missionaries who had also fled from northern Angola. They looked up João and invited him to join them in their distribution of relief supplies during this interval while his status as a potential student at EPI Kimpese was being decided. They made João keeper of the keys for those twelve warehouses. Shipments of food would arrive, normally by rail, in up to four boxcars. It might be as much as fifty tonnes at a time—rice, beans, milk, salt, flour, oil, dried fish, soap, and bulgur wheat. Occasionally there were canned goods.

French language study at Kinkonzi

Deliberations at Kimpese confirmed that the level of studies completed by João at Calambata in Angola justified admission to pastoral studies at EPI Kimpese, apart from the question of language. He would need to acquire French, and a year should be set aside for that purpose.

The speaker that year at EPI's graduation ceremonies was the senior pastor from the Maiombe district of Bas-Congo Province, pastor Albert Mpaku, from the church community founded by the Christian and Missionary Alliance. The missionaries at Kimpese, including Edna Staple, arranged for João to speak with him about enrollment at their Bible Institute in Kinkonzi. The proposal did not focus so much on learning the Bible, but rather on learning French in a context where theological vocabulary would be a natural part of every day, and in the context of a caring Christian family. In order for João to be accepted to participate in the entrance exam for the school of theology at EPI Kimpese the following year, he would need to pass the hurdle of that examination, in French.

> *That is precisely what André da Costa and I did, and we passed. We were admitted together to Kimpese.*
> *During those four years of study, the summers did not include any vacation time, but rather I spent that time visiting refugee settlements located all along the Angolan border. I was visiting with them and preaching. It was this close contact with the refugees which later resulted in my being invited to England.*

While João was in studies at EPI, Nora studied English and home economics. She also gave birth to both Ambrose and Julie during their time at EPI Kimpese.

The Democratic Republic of the Congo

Studies at Westhill College of Education in Birmingham, U.K.

It was not normal procedure for the BMS to send any African pastor to England unless they had worked for a minimum of five years in ministry. Then sometimes workers would be taken to England for a visit of fellowship.

I wrote a letter to Clifford John Parsons concerning the plight of Angolan refugees, especially those situated in villages I had visited along the Angola/Congo frontier. I stated that the older generation of believers remain faithful, and are full of hope. However, I expressed concern for the younger generation, which was not being reached, because they are all influenced by the political movement. Their thrust is nationalistic, they want to fight in the war. I mentioned that for youth, the church holds no attraction at this moment.

Even at Kimpese, João received no instruction on how to reach youth. It was his conviction that unless some way could be found to reach these young people, they would be lost. Clifford took that letter from João as a challenge. He began checking out colleges in England where one might focus on Christian Education and ministries to youth. His research led him to Westhill College of Education in Birmingham, which had such a program. Westhill was part of a cluster known as Selly Oak Colleges. It offered scholarships; Clifford applied and secured one of these, then wrote to João affirming that when he finished his course at Kimpese, he could proceed to England.

He told me it was because of that report I made. Because I showed concern for youth, I was given a chance to go to England to learn how to do those ministries. That touched my heart. They started arranging it, and Jim Grenfell helped out with the documentation.

Arrangements for travel to the U.K. were in place by the time of João's graduation from EPI Kimpese in 1966. Nora and the children stayed at Mbanza Ngungu with Nora's sister and her family during João's year in England. That year was not an idle one for Nora. There was a Bible School at Mbanza Ngungu. In addition to caring for the children, Nora gave literacy instruction to student wives who were illiterate.

During the months of João's study in Birmingham, planning for the future focused on the prospects of returning to do ministry among refugees located in villages along the Angola border, just inside Congo. His concerns were consistently on how he could contribute to the betterment of his people.

João as a student at Birmingham, U.K.

7

Chaplaincy at IME Kimpese

IME Kimpese

North and east of the town of Kimpese, where EPI was located, lay a vast medical complex: the *Institut Médical Evangélique*, commonly referred to as IME Kimpese, sponsored by many of the same Protestant mission agencies that supported EPI. The distance by road separating these two institutions was about 11 kilometres. The administration of each was entirely distinct from the other, but with a good sense of co-operation between the two.

IME was a teaching hospital of about 450 beds. It encompassed a range of specialties including:

- Surgery (with a large pavilion designated as "surgical")
- Pediatrics (with a designated pavilion)
- Orthopaedics (with its own pavilion)
- Physiotherapy
- Outpatient treatment

- Public Health
- Internal medicine
- Gynecology
- Obstetrics
- Tuberculosis
- Leprosy, with a designated leprosarium
- Pathology
- Laboratory
- Dentistry
- Nursing, with a designated School; IME was a government-approved teaching hospital for nurses.
- Laboratory techniques, with a designated School
- Pharmacy, with a designated School of Pharmacy

In addition to serving the staff, students, and patients of the above, the Chaplain's duties covered personnel connected with:

- CEDECO, *Centre de Développement Communautaire*
- Guest House
- Mission Aviation Fellowship (MAF) with its pilots, support staff, and training programs

IME was also an approved hospital where expatriate medical staff destined for posts in the Congo served periods of internship.

It was to this vast and complex medical institution that João Matwawana was appointed as its first African-born chaplain in 1967:

While I was in England, before I finished, I got a letter from Dr. David Wilson who was the General Director of the hospital saying, "João, we are asking you, when you return from your studies, to come as our first African chaplain."
To this I replied "Why me? I am a refugee."
"It's exactly because you are a refugee. Fifty percent of our patients are refugees. Only you can understand Portuguese. And we get more grants for the hospital because of refugees. You are the one. Also, you will minister to some staff who use

English, and you will minister to Congolese in their own language, Kikongo. You would immediately be part of the Executive Committee of IME Kimpese."

This prestigious appointment came as a total surprise to João, especially since he was not a Congolese national.

Programs and responsibilities as IME Chaplain

João had a number of major programs and pastoral responsibilities by virtue of being the Chaplain of IME Kimpese.

1. **Pastor of the IME Church, with pastoral care of staff, students, and patients.**

During the time that João was studying in England, the Religious Activities Committee at IME Kimpese began to act upon their long-standing conviction that their campus should have a formally-constituted church. This would enable those for whom IME was their permanent place of residence, to take full part in church life. The inaugural meeting of the church was held on November 20, 1966, with 97 members. A chapel was constructed and in use before João appeared in the area.

Just one year later, the annual report registers growth and a church membership of 115, commenting that with the arrival of pastor Matwawana the church had become increasingly active in the life of the institution and the surrounding area.
(Andersen: 1967-68: 12)

It was a weighty assignment, beginning with the expectation that ministry would be conducted in French, Portuguese, English, and Kikongo. Services had an average attendance of around 200. João perceived the real challenge to lie in his ministry to the staff of this remarkable institution, one of the most prestigious in the country. Furthermore, he was undertaking this as a refugee, a community that in general was despised.

That challenge helped me to be careful in my preparation and the research of my messages, because I knew that I'm not just addressing village people, so I have really to be sure of what I am preaching.

It was reassuring to have doctors come to me and tell me that they had been helped by my message. It also pushed me beyond my limits, working too hard, because I wanted to be sure I had something of value to offer.

The IME church had a deacons committee with fourteen members and we met once monthly. They were carefully chosen to represent all the participating mission agencies. So together we had Canadian Baptists, American Baptists, British Baptists, Americans from the Christian & Missionary Alliance, Swedish Congregationalists, Methodists from the USA, Disciples of Christ from the USA, together with Congolese and Angolans. ... We found it interesting that people could keep their differences and still do something together, and we managed.

Remember, too, the complexity of the membership in my congregation. The staff, students, and patients, whether from IME hospital, the nursing school, CEDECO, the Leprosarium, the dispensary—all were considered IME church.

João Matwawana was also a gifted evangelist who had learned through life experience that the most valuable gift he could bring to his people was a relationship with Jesus Christ, the Son of God. Through him, many have come to that personal relationship with Jesus which transforms the one who believes.

2. Chaplaincy of the hospital Complex

The most profound joy João experienced during his eight years as chaplain at IME lay in his relationship with the patients in the wards. From his own point of view, there was no preference of nationality. But to refugee patients, he was something very special. They considered him as their own, at a time in their lives when there was so very little they could claim to own. They also recognized him as an ally at a time when most refugees felt that they had nowhere to turn.

> *I remember people coming from Kinshasa for treatment. With accidents, they knew that at IME their people would be treated well. Companies would transfer their patients from the Kinshasa hospitals to IME direct. We had directors of companies coming for treatment. These people said that the thing they appreciate most here is the gospel. We also had a lot of government people as patients.*

> *There was a period, including when I was chaplain, when IME was considered by most as the finest hospital in the country, even though it was not the largest. We worked hard at maintaining high professional standards, we had excellent specialists and good equipment, and there was a genuine desire to show Jesus' compassion through the care given at IME.*

3. The nursing school at IME

The School of Nursing was in transition from being a three-year diploma course to being a four-year course that included the High School diploma. The chaplain was among the many part-time teachers giving instruction, João's subject being religion.

4. The Leprosarium

IME Kimpese had a leprosarium called "*Kivuvu.*" This translates from Kikongo as "The place of hope."

> *This was a large leprosarium, and it attracted specialists. I saw many of the leprosy patients come to Christ, many whose lives were changed.*

João preached first each Sunday morning at Kivuvu, then later at the IME church. It was his custom to prepare announcements in advance and deliver them identically at both services.

So it was that following a disastrous flood in Bangladesh, the chaplain relayed to both congregations a special appeal from the *Église du Christ au Zaïre* (ECZ) office in Kinshasa for contributions to help flood victims. A week passed, and it was with some surprise João noticed that despite the dozens of doctors and nurses working at IME, he had received no response at all to the special appeal. He proceeded as usual to Kivuvu the next Sunday morning for worship there. He noticed with irritation that the chapel was half-filled with peanuts, the product of local fields.

Who put their peanuts in here?
Edna Staples asked whether I had forgotten my announcement from last week. "The patients have responded generously," she said. These bags of peanuts were their gift to others in great need. I couldn't hold back my tears. I said "Lord, what are you trying to teach me?"

So I brought this news immediately to the worship service at IME. From that I saw the money pouring in. Everybody was touched. The leprosy patients had given us a lesson. When you suffer you recognize the suffering of somebody else. We sold the peanuts. We sent the money to Kinshasa with an explanation of whose donation it was.

5. CEDECO

The *Centre de Développement Communautaire*.(Community Development Centre), CEDECO, was begun as a trade school to teach carpentry, tailoring, and mechanics to Angolan refugees.

As other former Angolan missionaries joined CEDECO, they brought new specialties. With Dr. Allen Knight (United Church of Canada) came agriculture, with Ian Pitkethly (BMS) a focus on the raising of chickens, with Eric MacKenzie (CBM) new skills in propagating and grafting citrus trees. Both Congolese and Angolans benefitted as CEDECO students, and the enrollment tended to run at about thirty to forty students.

6. Air Service IME—MAF (Mission Aviation Fellowship)

From 1974, the Mission Aviation Fellowship service became a reality in conjunction with the *Communauté Évangélique au Zaïre (CEZ)*. Because of the Swedish government's interest in the work of Swedish missionaries serving in the Manianga area of Bas-Congo with CEZ, they donated a six-seated Cessna aircraft to IME. At every mission outpost in Manianga, due to the lack of decent roads, a small airstrip was created. This permitted the airlift of patients to IME.

A base for MAF service to the Province of Bas-Congo was located at IME. The pilots and their families were part of the IME church community. They gradually expanded to train both pilots and mechanics, both Congolese and Angolans. So both personnel and students relating to this air service were expanding, and a new element of ministry came into play.

> *So we had the MAF pilots and two of our own IME pilots. They used facilities together.*

> *We even made the national news broadcast. The Governor of the Province was visiting Manianga, and his back was disabled because of the bad roads. They called to have him air-lifted out, and we facilitated that.*

Nora Matwawana's contributions at IME Kimpese

Among the Angolan refugees in Congo, a multitude of women and single girls were not fully literate. One of the ministries undertaken by IME Kimpese was to teach them.

When she arrived at Kimpese as a refugee, Nora began teaching, for she was the most advanced of the women coming out of Angola, having been a teacher there herself. That same year she was appointed president of the women's organization in the Kimpese church. All the women, including refugee women, supported her and helped her. There were many facets of the teaching program which went far beyond mere literacy. In all of this she gives credit to BMS missionary Jean Comber, who was her encourager, helping to equip Nora for this work, and guiding her in it.

Certificates were provided to women and girls finishing the course, to help them get employment. The women's program conducted lessons in cooking, French, hygiene, reading, religion, and sewing, under Jean Comber's guidance.

Nora's presidency of the women's organization lasted three years, after which she resigned, continuing to contribute to the ongoing program as a member.

Nora was chosen by the hospital's public health program to go to Kinshasa to take a course in nutrition, under that department's supervision. This involved being separated from her Kimpese family for about a month. In Kinshasa she stayed with her brother, Deves, who supported her while she was studying there at Ndjili. At the end of the course she returned to Kimpese. She accompanied Dr. Sid Gilchrist to conduct seminars in villages, accompanied by two other women, but soon found to her disappointment that there were no funds to sustain her in women's work. That being the case, Nora moved to a salaried position at IME's maternity ward, to help support the family. There her assignment included weighing-in the babies, while she continued to do women's work as a volunteer in the afternoons.

Ordination

Pastor João Matwawana was ordained to Christian Ministry in the church at Kimpese on June 7, 1970, from which time he was officially Reverend João Matwawana. This significant event was attended by a rich array of delegates from the denominations and the mission agencies which were sponsors of IME, as well as by friends, family, and acquaintances.

An interesting and significant set of events happened the night before João's ordination. Congolese elders came and asked to see the address which he had prepared to deliver the next day. They wanted to make sure that there were no mistakes and that it would be the best. This was a two-hour speech, and they pronounced it okay. Immediately a second delegation appeared, this time of Angolan intellectuals and elders from Kinshasa, with the same set of concerns. "We want to see the speech. We want to make sure that it is correct and that it will not embarrass anyone." The appearance of these two spontaneous delegations from distinct communities demonstrated the chaplain's broad personal base of support. It also highlighted the fine touch that was required to maintain various sets of expectations in balance. Matwawana the diplomat was being shaped both by God and by circumstances.

> *A few patients in wheelchairs rolled down the concrete walk leading from the hospital. Solemn men in black suits and white clerical collars gathered around the entrance leading to the pulpit—senior pastors from the churches in the province. A few yards away stood another group—young men in bright blue shirts with red cuffs and yellow scarves and straw hats. Someone touched a match to a little pile of straw, then held a succession of small drums over the flames to heat the drum head and make it more resonant. A dozen of the men tuned their hand-made flutes and began stepping in time to the music. The band was ready. The big drum at the front of the church boomed out. Inside the building, the organist began to play the prelude. The band moved into the church. More people arrived. Unable to get inside, they stood around in disappointed little clusters. The foresighted ones had brought little wooden stools. Others sat down on the grass.*
>
> (Ross: 1971)

The ordination featured a combined Angolan choir of more than fifty singers representing all of the Angolan Protestant denominations and including even Catholics. This was an Angolan national event, rather than a mere denominational event. It was non-denominational, but also it was non-partisan in terms of political affiliation. Everyone was there with a sense of ownership, and the representation demonstrated the neutral political stance that João Matwawana has always adhered to. It was also a preview of the reconciliation ministries that would emerge later in his career.

8

ADDITIONAL RESPONSIBILITIES ACCUMULATE

A staggering accumulation of additional responsibilities were piled on Rev. João Matwawana's shoulders during the period he served as Chaplain of the IME medical complex. They constitute a recognition of unique gifts and abilities in a person who could be trusted—in one who could be expected to perform them well.

1. Deputy Superintendent of the hospital, IME

It was under Dr. Mandiangu that João was appointed as Deputy Superintendent of the hospital, IME. This was an added responsibility distinct from the chaplaincy. Not only was João perceived as a capable person, but also as a neutral person, something of a natural mediator. Beyond that, he was also a neutral person nationally, ethnically, and institutionally. The role of reconciler was born into his psyche, and there at Kimpese that role came to the fore. He and Dr. Mandiangu became a remarkable working team, facing many conundrums that at times seemed to be without solution. There was a trust between them, and a working harmony that was indeed admirable.

Hospital Director Mandiangu and his wife.

One of the successes of my ministry at IME lies in the special relationship between Mandiangu and me, at the friendship level.

They wanted a chaplain to minister to their souls. Dr. Mandiangu told me repeatedly that I came as the answer to their prayers. We went through a lot together over the years. He did a lot to facilitate my work. He knew my background as a refugee and he tried to protect me. He invested me with some power, deliberately, to avoid my being put down by people, so he named me his Deputy Superintendent. We had full mutual trust with no competition, no sense of rivalry.

As an illustration of this very special relationship, João cites an occasion when Director Mandiangu was called to Kinshasa by President Bokeleale of the ECZ to participate in a meeting with President Mobutu, a meeting called by the President of the Republic to deal with some church problem. In turn Mr. Mandiangu asked João to accompany him.

"But you could take someone else."
"I choose you. Do you have a problem with that?"

On arrival in Kinshasa, they were informed that their clothing was too old to be worthy for a meeting with the President. They would need to purchase new suits. Director Mandiangu informed João that he would purchase both suits from his own pocket, so that they could be well presented. He was aware that João's salary was such that to buy another suit would be a burden, so he carried that cost personally. "He was that kind of man. I was conscious of being respected, loved, protected by him."

The position of Deputy Superintendent meant that on those occasions when Director Mandiangu was travelling, the additional administrative weight of this vast institutional complex came to rest on João's shoulders.

I did not immediately grasp the measure of how this position as Deputy Superintendent would come to complicate my role as pastor and chaplain. I eventually learned how difficult it was to function as chaplain while holding a position of power. It made my work even more difficult.

2. General Secretary for the Protestant Churches of Angola in Exile: (Église Chrétienne Unie de l' Angola—ECUA)

Among the 300,000 or more Angolan refugees who had arrived in the province of Bas-Congo in 1961 and the years immediately following, there were clusters of Christian believers who continued regular worship in the most informal of settings and without organization as such. In some instances there were some lay leaders from the villages back in Angola. Looking at the larger picture, however, they were, indeed, sheep without a shepherd, and it fell on Rev. João Matwawana to fulfil the shepherd role while also serving as full-time chaplain at IME.

The post of General Secretary of the Angolan Churches in Exile was created under pressure from Congo's President Mobutu Sese-Seko. Certain enterprising Angolans from around Maquela do Zombo were exercising their initiative by creating new medical dispensaries, with the potential for notable income. The problem was that Congo had established strict regulations governing clinics. They could not be opened by private individuals. Apart from state-run clinics, only the churches could operate medical clinics. So these creative and innovative persons were founding new religious sects, and opening clinics, using the sects as a front. This angered the country's president, who insisted that there be an Angolan chosen who would be accountable to the President of the Republic for any misdemeanors undertaken in the name of Angolan churches. João heard via radio that he was being called to Kinshasa the very next day for a meeting of Angolan church leaders, to choose this General Secretary for the Angolan Churches in Exile. Someone had proposed his name as a participant in the meetings and as a candidate for the office. There was general agreement that President Mobutu's wish must be honored to avoid the nasty alternative of having all Angolan churches banned and proscribed. The meetings lasted for about one week, and were held in a series of church buildings and halls.

The initiative was entirely that of President Mobutu. "There must be one protestant church for all Angolans in my country and I need to know who to call when I hear of a problem." The refugee congregations were guests in President Mobutu's country and they bowed to his will in order to survive. The name became *Église Chrétienne Unie de l'Angola*, ECUA.

There were three names under consideration for the position of General Secretary—Rev. João Matwawana was duly elected, his appointment then confirmed. The result was that João was now saddled with an additional weighty responsibility that carried with it no salary and no operating budget.

The Angolan church leaders were consequently obliged to draw up a constitution under which the organization and its General Secretary would function. This was eventually accomplished, though not easily, and it was approved by President Mobutu. João was required at times to spend a whole week in Kinshasa dealing with matters relating to the Angolan churches in exile.

Had resources been available to support the General Secretary of the Angolan Churches in Exile, this assignment could well have been a full-time calling, and, indeed, merited full-time attention. The general attitude was, "Why should we look for another full-time person when João could do it? And why would he expect to be paid?" Pastors within the refugee family were serving without pay, and João was known to be already salaried at IME.

As is often the case, important tasks are placed upon busy people. In João's words, "I was expected to lead my (Angolan) people and to organize the future church of Angola in exile." He acted as a bridge between congregations of worshiping Angolan refugees and the churches which were already in existence in the Congo. Precise statistics are not available, but 100 worshiping congregations seems to be a conservative estimate.

There was no identifiable office-headquarters established for this leadership role. It happened from wherever João was located at a given moment. The sense of responsibility that accompanied this office never left him. He was an important symbol for the entire community, contributing to their dignity and sense of worth. He was their own great man in a position of high responsibility. He was their Joseph in Egypt.

Because of the responsibility assigned to me, I was able to say that certain denominations did not have enough ordained clergy to function well. This is a recognition of pastors who have already functioned in that capacity for so many years. I compared procedure with what was operating within the Maiombe churches within Congo. There is no difference. They were ordained in recognition of their experience and their work in the church.

Ordination of IEA pastors arranged by Rev. João Matwawana

Sometimes João undertook road tours in his capacity as General Secretary of ECUA, visiting Angolans wherever their settlements and camps were located These visits could last for a month at a time:

Everywhere the people expressed their faith in songs, in a way which I never imagined.
Every small church gathered with refugees would announce that "today the choir is going to sing a song they just composed last week for your arrival."

3. Coordinator for Evangelism, Province of Bas-Congo

There was another complication to being pastor of the Church at IME. Because we were a church, we necessarily formed part of The Church of Christ in Zaïre—ECZ, an organization which loaded still more responsibility on me.

In 1969, João was appointed Coordinator of Evangelism for the Province of Bas-Congo, then in 1971 he was taken into Congo's National Committee of Evangelism. These were official ECZ appointments, and it would have been difficult to resist them, although João was successful in resisting efforts applied over several months by Dr. Bokeleale to have him moved to Kinshasa for a national appointment with the ECZ.

So the appointment of João Matwawana as Provincial Coordinator of Evangelism for the ECZ was scarcely one which he could decline, despite his responsibilities at IME which were already very heavy. And not a penny of budget with which to do the work! The area for which he was responsible stretched from Kinshasa to the Atlantic Ocean. Due to the condition of the roads, a distance measured in miles or kilometres would not be meaningful. One could not travel the east-west range of that responsibility in one full day's travel by car.

"How will I do the work without money?" I asked, and the response was "Debrouillez-vous," which was a standard response in the society. "Make out as best you can."

I had to use the meager resources of my chaplaincy office: paper, typewriter, stencils. Mostly I was reduced to tabulating the number of meetings held and recording the numbers of conversions, doing this by correspondence.

This became a very heavy load, but at the same time it was very rewarding. I was able to touch many lives.

All across Congo society in that era there was an idealism that showed itself in appointments and assignments that were not accompanied by a budget—often without salary at all. With this there grew a vocabulary which reflected the phenomenon:

"Debrouillez-vous"	Make out as best you can.
"Article 15"	Every man for himself (there were only 14 articles in the Congolese constitution).
"Pas moyen"	No way, or It can't be done.

4. Committee Membership, Angolan Memorial Scholarship Fund

João also took on membership in the Gilchrist Angola Memorial Student Fund. This *ad hoc* committee came into being following a tragic highway accident that took the lives of three Canadian family members who had come to Kimpese from central Angola, and were serving at IME because of the presence of so many Angolan refugees in the area. Dr. Sidney Gilchrist was a surgeon appointed by the United Church of Canada. From his base at Dondi, his name had become a legend all over Angola. Mrs. Gilchrist and daughter Betty were also killed in the accident.

The United Church of Canada established the Gilchrist Scholarship in their memory, to benefit Angolan students through programs of education and training. The fund later became the Angolan Memorial Scholarship Fund. At first a preference was shown for scholarships to those in medical training, but the restrictions were later relaxed.

The task of the committee was to identify appropriate recipients, and track their progress. Beneficiaries were chosen on the basis of merit. Those who worked with João on the committee were Dr. Allen Knight (United Church of Canada), Rev. Bob Malcolm (Canadian Baptist Ministries), and sometimes Rev. Wendell Golden (Methodist Mission) or Rev. Jim Grenfell (Baptist Missionary Society—U.K.).

An additional fund, of which João was chairman, was the *Committee of Angolan Student Scholarship Fund*. This was established under the ECZ, and the scholarships were disbursed through the Protestant Church of Angola in Exile.

5. Director of Angolan Refugee Primary Schools

There were those among the Angolans in Congo to whom João refers as "the politicians." Once he was installed as chaplain at IME, they began to bring pressure to bear on him to do more to help "the cause." He pointed out that he was already selecting and sending students to Kinkonzi for pastoral training, but they had in mind something more than that. Specific mention was made of two nearby refugee villages, known as *kimbalas*. Reports had reached them that 80 percent of the children in these camps were without education because they could not afford local school fees, which were established at a fixed rate. They pressured João to open two new schools, one in Camp Sousa and the other in the *kimbala* at IME.

> *How could I say no? My own children were in school, and even taken on the hospital bus.*
> *I could not refuse. They made an announcement, and the parents of the children started making the sun-dried mud blocks that we call* adobes. *There were always masons to be found among the Angolans. The schools were built at low cost, requiring mostly just labour. They had mud walls, roofs of thatch, and open windows for ventilation and light, which were not graced with glass or shutters.*

They then instructed João to recruit from the refugee camps former teachers in Angola who would give the instruction. These were located and put in place, all without pay from anyone to anyone. This volunteer work was done out of a sense of social responsibility, and because of a certain amount of pressure from both elders and community. Each school building was built with two classrooms. Conditions in all such schools were primitive, children sitting on bamboo poles, with no flat writing surface. The standard teaching materials were a blackboard, a loud voice, and a piece of chalk, combined with the ability of a teacher to instruct the little ones using rote memory. A question about the number of students per class draws a chuckle from João, for the standard limit of forty students to a class which prevailed in Congolese schools was never enforced in refugee schools.

> *What I didn't know was that they were expecting me to be the director.*
> *They were adamant. "You just check on them once a week."*
> *So I came to be the director of two schools, without a salary. Fortunately a church somewhere in Canada presented me with a motorcycle. I don't even know what church. Eric MacKenzie saw what was happening and appealed to them for funding. That motorcycle did all the work of running those two schools. I would check this school, check that school, then rush back to the hospital.*

> *Here I was with a school project, and I didn't have a penny.*

CBM missionary Charles Harvey lived near the Matwawana family on the compound at IME, and comments on how he appreciated the wisdom with which this relatively young man handled difficult decisions and complex relationships. He also added, with a twinkle of the eye, some observations about those years:

> *I remember complimenting João for being the director of two schools without salary, and being the treasurer of three organizations, none of which had a penny. In fact, on one occasion I presented João with a contribution of 45 cents just so that his treasury would not be completely empty.*

I also remember that João had a dog with the potent name Tshombe *(Moïse Tshombe was one of Congo's former Prime Ministers). There was an occasion when we held a walkathon at IME, with sponsorship pledges, to raise funds to buy a set of picnic tables for the area where the staff gathered for our Saturday afternoon fellowship. João's dog, Tshombe, walked with us. So there is a plaque somewhere listing Tshombe Matwawana among the other contributors.*

6. Leadership training for ACEBAC

ACEBAC was the Association of Angolan Baptist Churches in the Congo. Rev. André Ntemo was its first General Secretary, and João was the Associate Secretary responsible for leadership training. The organization made a long-range impact in two ways. Through it, many young people were selected and sponsored for theological studies, and are presently serving as pastors in Angola. Furthermore, ACEBAC laid the foundations and prepared the way, in exile, for the official organization of IEBA, the *Igreja Evangélica Baptista em Angola*.

THE OVERWORKED CHAPLAIN

Across the entire range of experiences, João testifies to how the grace of God sustained him through work loads that went beyond his human capacity. He regularly turned for strength to rich resources from Scripture, and these sustained him. Among his favorites were:

> *Those who hope in the Lord*
> *will renew their strength.*
> *They will soar on wings like eagles;*
> *they will run and not grow weary,*
> *they will walk and not be faint.*
> (Isaiah 40:31)

> *I know what it is to be in need, and I know what it is to have plenty. I have learned the secret of being content in*

any and every situation, whether well fed or hungry, whether living in plenty or in want. I can do everything through him who gives me strength.
 (Philippians 4:12-13)

While acknowledging the strength and sustenance he received from the Lord through these very special verses of Scripture, he acknowledges that he was neither wise nor prudent in pushing himself to such extremes of exertion. He was attempting tasks which were beyond reason and beyond human capacity to endure, and he paid the price for that.

My family suffered. I didn't know how to give proper time to them. I sensed that, but didn't know how to change it. I was driven by my agenda.

One day the Lord stopped me. I arrived at a point of total fatigue. Even to sit like this I would need pillows around me. I was unable to sleep. I was so tired, and my back was painful. And then my voice failed me.

João was attended by Dr. Swain from Holland. He commented that he had been watching João's hustle and bustle, running from ward to ward, from ward to classroom, from classroom to meetings. He had anticipated trouble, and wondered how long João could continue without collapse.

"Then why didn't you stop me?"
"It is difficult to instruct a pastor. He thinks that the Holy Spirit is driving him this way. Now I think you have learned your lesson. Now you are my patient, you must listen to me."
"OK, I'm listening. What do you want?"
"I'm telling your wife to put pyjamas and a toothbrush in a suitcase. We will take you where nobody will call you, nobody will talk with you."

João was taken in the hospital car and placed in one of the missionary residences located near the Leprosarium, a house which was temporarily vacant, its occupants on home assignment abroad. Nobody else knew where he was, not even Nora. João was to have total bed rest for a week, with no reading material on hand, no radio, no visitors. He was not to speak even a word. If there was a need, he was to write it down. The house had a caretaker, and that lady was instructed to feed him, nothing else. There was to be no conversation.

So I learned my first lesson.
After a week I was OK
But after a year I forgot. I was on the go again.

I was so busy with extra assignments, especially dealing with Angolan affairs. It seems I had to be in Kinshasa every week. I forgot my lesson. Again, I collapsed.
It was the same doctor.
"So you didn't learn!"

So it was back to the suitcase with pyjamas and toothbrush again, but this time Dr. Swain decided that the distance would be greater, and that Nora should accompany her husband. The isolation instructions were the same—no radio, no reading, no speech of any sort. This was a punishment for not listening to his doctor!

This time the hospital car took us to the Swedish Mission Guest House in Matadi and left us there for one week. No medication was necessary, only the rest.

Assistance for the Chaplain

By the time the car came back to Matadi for João and Nora, the Executive Committee at IME had decided that provision would be made for the chaplain to have an assistant. João himself returned to Kinkonzi, where he had studied earlier, to look for the pick of the class to be his helper:

There are many challenges in having an assistant—I had to train him. I had to sort out what would be his work and what would be mine. I discovered that this gave me more work than before. It was a headache to me.

Three months later that assistant was complaining that there was too much work, and that the nature of that work was not in harmony with what he envisaged as assistant to the chaplain. He was doing too much social work, not perceived as his role. So the matter went back to the Executive Committee who proceeded to hire an additional social worker, part time:

So the work of my assistant was divided again. (Chuckle.) Mandiangu asked me how I did all those things alone. "That's why I collapsed."

9

BRIEF RETURN TO ANGOLA

JOÃO AND NORA MATWAWANA GO TO INDIA

While working and living at Kimpese, João was surprised by a message from Canadian Baptist Ministries in Toronto:

> "...You are invited to participate in exchange ministries between India and Canada."

In 1974, a special program was being set up to celebrate 100 years of work of Canadian Baptist involvement in India. That work began in Andhra state and then expanded into Orissa. As part of that celebration, there would be a three-way interchange of special speakers, to celebrate the diverse ethnicity within the Christian family. Dr. Masilamani from India would be doing rounds in Canada. João was invited to tour and preach in India. A Canadian Baptist pastor, Rev. Georges Rocher from Quebec City, would proceed to Kimpese to carry a portion of João's responsibilities at the hospital.

CBM personnel working at Kimpese suggested to their Toronto office that by all means Nora should accompany João, and their recommendation was approved.

So it was that in January, 1974, Rev. João and Mrs. Nora Matwawana went to India for three months of ministry under the sponsorship of Canadian Baptist Ministries.

COMPLICATIONS WITH TRAVEL DOCUMENTS

Because João's status in Congo was still that of refugee, how would he secure the necessary travel documents?

Well, I had to go to Kinshasa, to FNLA, to get a letter of recommendation from their Foreign Affairs Division, addressed to the Ministry of Foreign Affairs in the Congolese government. Because these documents would be issued by the Democratic Republic of the Congo, which was operating under strict authenticity *measures, a Christian name like João or Samuel could not be used.*

General Joseph Désiré Mobutu came to power as President of the Democratic Republic of Congo in 1965, in a military coup. He then mounted a campaign which he dubbed *autenticité*, emphasizing a return to African "authenticity," including names that were authentically African. He himself became Mobutu Sese Seko Kuku Ngbendu wa za Banga. In its official translation this was rendered as, *The all-powerful warrior who, because of his endurance and inflexible will to win, will go from conquest to conquest leaving fire in his wake.*

Under this authenticity thrust, Christian names were prohibited. All citizens took on a new identity. He changed the name of the country's principal river from the Congo to Zaïre, an approximation to its earlier name *Nzadi*, in certain indigenous languages. He changed the name of the Republic to match the new name of the river. Léopoldville became Kinshasa, and the major cities carrying foreign names were all re-named. He insisted on the abolition of the necktie, for which many were profoundly grateful, especially in the high humidity of Kinshasa where temperatures often exceed 40 degrees Celsius. In 1973, under his Zairianization policy, some 2,000 foreign-owned businesses were seized and nationalized.

We were forced to find appropriate alternative names. João as a Christian name was taboo, so they asked me if I could remember any family name applied to me back in Angola when I was small. I remembered that my grandfather used the name Kulwa. *So I would go to India as Matwawana Kulwa. That in itself would create complications at times, for the person they were expecting at airports in India was João Matwawana.*

But there in Kinshasa I had to work through getting Nora's documents too. Her case was slightly different from mine, since Nora was not considered a Christian name, and so it was allowed. I remembered that somewhere along the line Nora was called Maleko. *So they issued us a* Travel Document for Non-Political Refugees, *and we would travel to India as Nora Maleko and Matwawana Kulwa.*

The Matwawana children, however, were to remain at Kimpese.

We got our travel documents, the required injections, and then we were faced with the task of telling Raymond, age 3, that we were going away for an extended time. How could we manage that?

We told him we were going to buy candies for him in Kinshasa, so we got a very friendly farewell from Raymond. The memory of that promise lasted three months and it turned out that the time span was not a problem for Raymond. People would ask him where his parents were. Consistently his answer was that they had gone to buy him candies. Our absence seems not to have been a problem for the older children.

INDIA

The experience of India was a very good one for us because it gave us another view of the world. We had good fellowship with the missionaries there, and rich opportunities to share experiences with Indian pastors. The new perspective helped us to identify weaknesses and strengths in our own Angolan churches, and we were able to evaluate both the strengths and the weaknesses we observed in the Indian churches.

João with pastors, in India

Nora's emergence as a person in ministry on this India trip began slowly. She comments that at first she was just accompanying João. In the long run, the India experience would be a help to her in her mastery of English, for it was in India that she began to study it seriously. Nora had previously worked in Kikongo, Portuguese, Lingala, and French, so languages, as such, were not a problem for her. At the beginning of the India assignment she still understood little of English, and couldn't follow the flow of conversation. She comments that she felt like a child, dependent on a parent for everything. With a twinkle in his eye, João comments on the positive side of that deficiency:

That wasn't bad either. When I was repeating a sermon in some places, Nora didn't know the difference.

Nora's first English language helpers were CBM colleagues Audrey Manuel and Muriel Bent:

I started asking them language questions, and it helped me a lot. From the India visit I got so I could follow what João was saying, even though I still couldn't speak.

Our itinerary took us from Kinshasa through Nairobi to Bombay, and on to Hyderabad. From there the Carders put us on a train to Kakinada, where we would join the centennial celebrations.

KAKINADA AND BEYOND

At Kakinada we stayed with Gordon and Rolanda Barss, and had a fine time with them. I addressed the students and staff at the Theological Seminary, and spoke in some of the churches.

We travelled with Mildred Law to Tuni. In one of the churches there, we met soldiers who had served in the Congo with the United Nations as peacekeepers, which led to shared experiences with them. Some private conversations during this India assignment could be carried on in English, depending on the education and experience of the people involved, but most of the sermons for the general public were translated into Telugu.

From Tuni, Mildred drove the Matwawanas to Akividu, to Pithapuram, and to Visakhapatnam, generally called "Vizag." In addition to preaching engagements, João addressed pastors about his chaplaincy experiences at Kimpese.

From Visakhapatnam, they remember their time with Ken and Shirley Knight, but they also remember the vigorous little preacher with the big voice, Rev. G. Peter. He would come to wake João at five in the morning. "Brother, you will be busy today, so I came for prayer."

We found a good insistence on prayer. They were more inclined to pray than our African people. We never forgot that.

When I think back on this India experience, one of my strongest memories is that the food was just too hot for me. It upset my stomach right at the beginning, and I never really stabilized. It was very different for us eating meals while sitting cross-legged on the ground and being served food on those large leaves. At the end of the meal they are just folded up and given to the animals, rather than having to wash the dishes. That was interesting!

Nora was delighted to find familiar tropical foods, those which also grow naturally in both Congo and in Angola, especially fruit such as guava.

EVALUATION OF THE INDIA EXPERIENCE

Nora shares these observations:

The time spent in India strengthened our sense of partnership with the workers of Canadian Baptist Ministries. It taught me a lot personally about having self-confidence in relating to missionaries as friends and colleagues. We had missionaries as friends in Africa, but the nature of this trip lifted our sense of partnership with them to a new level. We stayed with them in their homes, and I myself came to feel at home. From that time I knew that I could receive missionaries as my guests without discomfort. I had a new confidence at mixing. I felt at home with them and I didn't sense any difference.

That trip helped me a lot. Another part was just the experience of travel. Seeing how people manage things when they travel gave me the ability, later, to be able to travel from Congo to Canada alone with our four children to join João at Acadia Divinity College.

João also points out the value of certain ministry contacts with Angolans living in India:

God's coincidences permitted remarkable encounters along the way. When we flew to Bombay we met and ministered to people with whom we had direct connections from Angola. They had been sent by the revolutionary government to do studies in India. Women had been sent for medical studies, men for military training. One of the young women had been in second and third class with Nora at Mbanza-Kongo. The girl's parent at Kimpese had informed us that her daughter was in India, and had given us the address. And the son of António Fernandes, our classmate at Calambata, was among the young men doing military studies.

These reunions half a world away from Angola were a very emotional experience. The young people had never expected to see anyone from home. It was a total surprise, and we were able to encourage them. They sent messages back to Africa with us.

Nora as treasurer of the women's work at IME

While in India, Nora received a letter from Kimpese asking that on their return she accept the responsibility of treasurer for the women's work, which had suffered from a lack of careful records and the absence of financial control. Her studies at Kinkonzi had included the rudiments of bookkeeping and accounting. Based on that, she accepted the challenge, setting up careful records and insisting that no funds be drawn by women at random without her direct approval.

Wars Are Never Enough

Changes within Angola

In 1975, news reached the Congo of a cease-fire in Angola, but details were still lacking. Angolan refugees had experienced fourteen years of exile in the Congo, and when word circulated that it was now safe to make visits back to Angola, this was met with a lot of fear and considerable suspicion. A certain Costa, who had studied with João, was very business-oriented. He insisted that he must hurry back to Mbanza-Kongo immediately to see where he would set up his store. Costa turned out to be among the very first of the Congo refugees to return, and he later recounted the details of how he approached the town with fear and trembling after having been away for fourteen years. He met those who had survived the war. Among the first of those he met was Francisco, who had been João Matwawana's close friend at Buela when João was teacher and Francisco the storekeeper there.

> *Oh Costa ... you're back—you're not dead.*
> *Francisco ... And you're still alive!*
> *I had a friend, João Matwawana, is he alive?*
> *Yes, he's alive.*
> *Where does he live, and will you see him?*
> *He's at Kimpese, and I will see him.*
> *Okay. He may not remember me, he may not even like to hear from me. When there is a war you never know. I want to send him these things. Please tell him that his friend sent them, and I think he will understand.*

The gift was a certain kind of Portuguese sausage, *chauriço*, which Francisco was sending to João, and when Costa passed through Kimpese on his way back to Kinshasa, he stopped there to deliver it.

> "I'm just back from Mbanza-Kongo, and I bring some chauriço for you, as a gift."
> "Chauriço—*Francisco is alive?*"

"Yes, but how did you know it would be from Francisco?"
"I bought chauriço *every week in Francisco's store, and he would know it is my favorite."*

João insists that such a friendship was only possible because of his Christian experience. Those who were not Christians were hurting, and definitely in a bad mood.

> *Now that I look back on the early years when I was a teacher I see that the kind of life I was living, with Portuguese as close friends, put me under a lot of suspicion by our Angolan elders who knew the history of conflict with Portuguese colonial officials, and all the betrayals by them that our people had experienced. When I was teaching at Buela, Francisco the storekeeper became such a close friend. He would often sleep at my house if a storm came up, or I at his house. I know that a lot of people were not happy about that, but I do believe that such friendships diminished the tensions a little.*

THE ALVOR ACCORD, PAVING THE WAY FOR A TRANSITIONAL GOVERNMENT IN ANGOLA

Angola reached a transitional stage with a ceasefire in 1975. Details of what was happening at an international level did not always reach all the people profoundly affected, like refugees in the Congo. Events had been unfolding in Portugal which carried an impact on the colonies. In 1974 a left-wing government came to power in Lisbon, paving the way for the dismantling of Portugal's centuries-old colonial empire. Angola's three resistance movements were invited to a negotiating table.

On January 15, 1975, the historic Alvor Accord was signed, providing a democratic framework to end the 500 years of colonization of Angola. This agreement gave MPLA, UNITA, and FNLA equal shares in a transitional government.

To Luanda, Angola, leading a delegation of the AACC

In this time of uncertainty João was called upon, in his capacity as General Secretary of ECUA, the churches in exile, to lead a delegation of the All Africa Christian Council. They were eager to lay strong foundations for the reunification of the Protestant churches that had continued to operate within Angola and those that functioned in exile in the Congo. Meetings were planned for Luanda, with subsequent visits to Angola's provinces. The Congolese representative in this delegation was Rev. Jean Massamba. By now Angola was forming a transitional government, and plans were being made for the country's first elections.

Independence from Portugal was finally granted that year, after fourteen years of armed conflict, and following the change in government in Lisbon. Angola now had three competing political parties at the national level, parties which had emerged from the three armies which had been struggling against the Portuguese colonial administration. Although there was a measure of ethnic and regional basis for each of these armies and their parties, there was also a wider following for each. Elections were on the horizon, and there was a general euphoria that a new era had dawned.

The three principal political parties were still identified by their combat names, MPLA, UNITA, and FNLA, each with its candidates. The AACC delegation that João was leading visited with various departments of the transitional government. The most powerful voice for the churches inside Angola was that of Methodist Bishop Emilio de Carvalho, who had never ceased to function from his base in Luanda.

During these Luanda meetings in July of 1975, hostilities broke out between the armed forces of each of the three competing political parties. This open conflict resulted in the eventual demise of any plans for elections.

João advised the delegation immediately that they should return to Kinshasa from where they had flown in. They wished to visit the provinces if possible, but in the end they could not. The delegation, in general, was not in danger, but because he was perceived as being a leader from Angola's north, the danger to João Matwawana was acute. He departed at once, and as it turned out there were tense moments even on the way to the airport. With road blocks, inspections, and gunfire, it became evident to the taxi driver that João was in danger, and he instructed João to lay low across the back seat, below window level. "They know me, but they don't know you." They got through safely to the airport and João was able to return to Kinshasa, then on to Kimpese and his family, where decisions and action awaited.

Resignation from IME

Nora and João discussed plans for their return to Mbanza-Kongo. Angolans had lived on hope for decades and they did not abandon hope now just because hostilities had started in and around Luanda. There was still optimism that solutions could be found.

As a perceived leader, João wanted to set an example to Angolan church members and to other Christian leaders by being willing to suffer hardship, deliberately laying aside the security of the salary, residence, and other privileges he enjoyed as hospital chaplain at IME Kimpese. Staying at Kimpese on full salary would not be an acceptable example. Nora also wanted to return, but the children found it hard to leave the friendships they had formed in the Congo.

In his capacity as General Secretary of the Protestant Churches of Angola in Exile, ECUA, João commissioned Alvaro Rodrigues to proceed to Mbanza-Kongo as an advance scout to check out the general situation including living conditions. From there, Alvaro was to proceed on to Luanda to confer with Methodist Bishop Emilio Carvalho.

The Matwawana family then crossed into Angola to take up residence again in Mbanza-Kongo. They moved into what had been the Nearn house on the BMS mission compound, and plunged into service for their Lord and His church. João's early tasks included repairs to a house which would make it possible for Jim and Pep Grenfell to join them there. His own role was to be that of spiritual leader, not responsible for administration. It was his plan that Alvaro Rodrigues would be the administrative person, leaving João free to preaching, tending to pastoral care, and counselling, as the spiritual leader of the flock.

João set out to lower tensions between Protestants and Catholics, based on his experiences in the Congo. He established an open air prayer meeting to include both Protestants and Catholics. They arranged an ecumenical service to signal that times had changed.

Much of the population came to know "Pastor João". During this time of instability there was a period of intense church involvement by nearly everyone, and João preached to thousands of people. The thrust of his preaching at that time continued to be distinctly non-political. He was, however, able to have a very low-key role as a secret advisor to both the governor and the commander of the army. New roles were emerging.

The Cuban presence in Angola

The unforseen change in the balance of power within Angola came with MPLA's appeal to Cuba for help, and the arrival of Cuban troops. The MPLA party, assisted by the Communist Party of Portugal, pulled a coup by inviting Cuba into Angola's political mix. Cuban troops on the streets of Luanda and moving out into the countryside overwhelmed FNLA, though UNITA struggled on for years.

The MPLA, in conjunction with Cuban and Russian influence, sabotaged Angola's march toward democracy. They took over much of the country with lightning speed. The population and also the military movements of FNLA and UNITA were taken by surprise. The north of Angola and the southern areas were special targets; only the centre of the country was safe.

Soon there was a retreat of populations from Luanda to Mbanza-Kongo, because of the takeover of Luanda by the MPLA, assisted by the Cuban army. The town became full to overflowing.

> *Elections across Angola were not permitted to happen. The Cuban army entered the fray in support of one of the three parties, which then came to power in Luanda, and has remained in office as the government of Angola. The struggle for autonomy, independence, and peace did not, in fact, end at fourteen years, but continued on until the declaration of a cease fire followed by a Protocol of Agreement signed in April, 2002. Opposition to the government persisted until 2002. The government was*

> *able to fund its conflict from its petroleum resources, the dissidents through sales of diamonds.*
>
> (Matwawana archives)

The Matwawanas had been in Angola only six months when the area, like their nation as a whole, was plunged into chaos once more. Edward, now fourteen, had often been reminded that he was born at Mbanza-Kongo on March 15, 1961, when the war started. Here they were as a family in Mbanza-Kongo once more, with rumors of war building, and Nora was expecting the birth of their last child, Isabel. Edward asked, "Mom, is it because you are pregnant again?"

Refugees again to the Congo

As Cuban troops approached Mbanza-Kongo, the church elders, in consultation with senior pastor Rev. João Matwawana, decided that it was best to ask missionary Jim Grenfell to leave, because he was in danger and his presence brought danger to them. He should cross into Congo before the arrival of the Cubans, otherwise he risked being taken hostage or even a prisoner of war if the Cubans suspected him of being a mercenary.

Jim accepted graciously, pointing out that since Nora's pregnancy was advancing it might be well for her and for the three smallest children to proceed with him to Kimpese. They crossed the border together.

On arrival at Kimpese Nora was greeted warmly. Hospital director Mandiangu found Nora a tiny house on the nurses' campus where she could stay with her children both before and after the birth of the baby.

Nora gave birth to Isabel, as news broke of the civil conflict in Angola. João, crossing the border with Samuel and Edward, as well as nephews and nieces, arrived at Kimpese, where they now numbered about fifteen, living in a single room.

> *Tata Mandiangu came to visit us. His friendship was evident, but the staff at IME was against him. His was not an easy problem to solve. One could see that he was struggling with the issue "What do I now do for my friend, João?"*

We stayed there maybe up to one month. I spotted a little two or three-room house beside the highway, at Kimbala. For the first time in their lives my family had to go to Kimpese to carry water to Kimbala like everybody else. There was scorn, jeering, a lot of laughing. "He didn't listen to us. How the mighty are fallen."

Jim Grenfell wanted me to work along with him in assisting this new influx of refugees, and I did, but he had insufficient resources to offer the support needed for my family. His budget was inadequate. He negotiated for a month or so, trying to find a place at Kimpese for our Matwawana extended family, which was rather large.

A certain Monsieur Adrien arrived at my door, a Belgian. He was working with the United Nations, in touch with the High Commission for Refugees in Kinshasa (UNHCR), and was also getting advice from Église du Christ au Zaïre (ECZ). *He was looking for an assistant to help him in his new work among the 25,000 refugees newly arrived from Angola, fleeing from the communist regime there. In his journal he found a note written in Geneva. Someone in the committee at Geneva had mentioned Matwawana. "In case he runs back to Congo, he would be a key person to help you." Adrien drove to Kimpese, inquired, got directions, and stopped in front of this little house, asking for me by name.*

Adrien described his work to João. He would be distributing food to the 25,000 new refugees between Songololo and Mbanza-Ngungu and in this task he needed João's help.

João to Adrien: "I'm working with Jim Grenfell, talk with him."
Jim to Adrien: "I'm looking for a house for João."
Adrien to Jim: "If you can find the house I'll pay the rent."

Two days later we moved out of the Kimbala house and moved into a house of the Centre de Développement Communautaire

(CEDECO), right there at Kimpese. This was the house in which the CBM family, MacKenzies, had been living. Life returned as if from the dead. Our children were able to sleep in beds with mattresses, we had a refrigerator again. It was like a gift from heaven.

João and Nora with the Grenfells, decades later

Adrien engaged João as his assistant for a one-year period. It was Dr. Mandiangu of IME, always compassionate, who arranged the CEDECO housing for the family. They now had housing and were assured of some salary and transportation. Although João was working with Adrien, there was room for him to work closely with Jim Grenfell, as well, in the care of refugee needs. Sometimes he would travel with Jim to visit refugees along the Angolan border, sometimes with Adrien to Songololo.

From the very first day of my second arrival as a refugee in Zaïre, I worked with all the relief agencies as a co-ordinator, organizing the necessary help to meet the needs of 25,000 new refugees.

Dangers building

Soon, evidence began to mount that João's life might be in danger. Security elements of the Mobutu government, working with the FNLA movement, learned that the MPLA government of Angola had sent sixty-three informers to mingle among refugees in Bas-Congo Province of the Congo. One of these was identified as a person who had appeared at the Matwawana household. He was, in fact, a relative, cashing in on the family link, and posing his questions ever so skilfully.

"Are you still opposed to the government of Angola?"
"It's not that I'm opposed to the government. I oppose the way they are lying to the people."

Someone came running to the Matwawana home after this guest's departure, indicating that the person they had fed was not a genuine friend.

In the middle of that experience, João received a note from the person who had been his secretary in ACEBAC, the Association of Angolan Baptist Churches in the Congo. This person was not comfortable with the fact that João was frequently around Kimpese town, which was located too close to the Angolan frontier, making him an easy target for assassination. After all, he had become the most prominent civilian leader within the refugee community. He was popular, well known, easily identified, and highly influential. "It would be better to be farther from the border." With that message, the one who warned him also sent a proverb indicating that he should move beyond the range of the bullet.

Considering Options

Correspondence from João Matwawana to Jim Grenfell at the end of November, 1976, listed a number of perils that he and Nora were aware of. There had been assassinations in the prison at Mbanza-Kongo. João's brother, Lambourne, had been arrested in Luanika. Luanda authorities were keeping an eye on João's activities in bringing humanitarian relief to refugees, and more. The family were considering all options, including an offer that had come to them from Fuller Theological seminary in California.

> ...I was advised that I should leave Zaïre as quickly as possible. My name was on a black list in Angola because of my position as Co-ordinator of Relief Services to Refugees. I was looked on as a supporter of rebels by helping the refugees. Also my record of leadership among the refugees for fourteen years made the government afraid that I would use my popularity to work against it.

And another account:

> Angola's new Communist government soon began to regard Rev. João Matwawana as an insurgent because of his continuing efforts to help his fellow countrymen fleeing Angola and that new regime....
> (*Halifax Mail-Star*, Friday, September 21, 1984, p.31)

João informed Canadian missionaries Charles Harvey and Bob Malcolm, along with BMS missionary Jim Grenfell, that his life might be in danger. They contacted John Keith, who by then was General Secretary of Canadian Baptist Ministries.

One of the options considered was for João and his family to move to Brazil and minister there in the BMS missionary framework, with their Brazilian partner churches, or perhaps continue studies in one of their seminaries. CBM was prepared to send money to BMS to facilitate the Brazil appointment, but that arrangement failed to materialize.

The Nova Scotia Option

Dr. Abner Langley, Principal of Acadia Divinity College in Wolfville, Nova Scotia, and one of the directors of CBM, was contacted. He agreed that a move to Canada, to Acadia Divinity College, was the best option available.

Nairobi conference

In the midst of these tensions building up after returning to Kimpese from Mbanza-Kongo, João was invited to participate in a conference at Nairobi. This was the Pan African Christian Leadership Conference, sponsored by a number of organizations, including the Billy Graham Association.

At that time, André Massaki was working at Daystar communications in Nairobi. He was the one who perceived the importance of including church representatives from inside Angola as well as representatives of the church in exile, even though the country was at war. There would be twenty Angolans in all, ten from each side of the divide. At his insistence, sponsorship was provided for both groups. João attended in his capacity as General Secretary of the Churches in Exile. The conference ran for about ten days, on the campus of a technical college.

We were so enthusiastic when we learned that our brothers were coming from Angola. For us in the Congo this represented an opportunity and an open window to communicate with them. But when we got there we found we were all wrong. Those from Angola dared not even look at us, they were so afraid. Anything they did might backfire on them on returning to Angola if it were reported that they were in contact with Angolan pastors in exile.

One of the first things I noticed was that although I knew many pastors from various parts of Angola, Methodists and others, there was not a single pastor in their delegation that I could recognize. We were disappointed but not surprised. We knew the culture, and we knew the culture of repressive dictatorships such as we had experienced under the secret police of the colonial era, PIDE. We continued to pray for God's intervention so that we could really communicate with our brothers. This barrier to communication was not their fault.

THE DEMOCRATIC REPUBLIC OF THE CONGO

On the third day of the conference, one of the delegates from inside Angola developed a severe stomach problem. There was a clinic on site, its services available to the conference, but none from their group spoke English well enough to communicate with a doctor. Someone approached João asking that he assist as translator. This was the answer to prayer that he and his colleagues were looking for. As soon as they were alone in the privacy of the elevator this pastor fell on João with an embrace. João found him to be a genuine, loving person, but very afraid, not knowing who was the government/police informer in his group, what that person might choose to report back in Angola, and with what results. They agreed that the two groups of Angolan pastors would sing a hymn together. It would be *Mestre, o mar se revolte...* (Master, the Tempest is Raging).

We knew that we were crossing a kind of stormy ocean. We knew Jesus was in control. We chose this without discussion. It was so appropriate for the situation. It was like a message in body language, to which both sides agreed without fear. We were making a point that we were together, united.

We had peace in our hearts after we sang. We didn't speak much but our eyes spoke to each other. They were not yet in a free country. Our conviction that it was right to still remain in exile was strengthened.

It was when João returned to Kimpese from this conference that he found the telegram from CBM, opening the way for his move to Canada. Its content, complete with typos, was as follows:

ZCZC/52/223
TORONTO ONT 67 12-23 1405 EST PAG 1/50

LT
GRENFELL CARE HARVEY KIMPESE
AMBAPTIST
KINSHASA ZAIRE

RECEIVED OCTOBER NOTE TODAY INDICATED WHY MATUAWANA NOT STUDYING BRAZIL STOP ACADIA DIVINITY COLLEGE NOVA SCOTIA WILLING TO RECEIVE FAMILY IMMEDIATELY STOP COURSES BEGIN JANUARY THIRD
IF CANADA AN ACCEPTABLE OPTION STOP LETER OF SUPPORT ON WAY WHICH WOULD FACILITATE IMMEDIATE VISA SECURAL

G048 GRENFELL PAGE 2/17

STOP AIRPORT OF ARIVAL HALIFAX STOP FACILITIES FOR FAMILY AVAILABLE SECURE FINANCES FROM ROBERT MALCOLM GREETINGS
KEITH

COLL 52/223+

Part Three

Canada

10

ARRIVAL IN CANADA, STUDIES AT ACADIA DIVINITY COLLEGE

PREPARING FOR DEPARTURE TO CANADA

Leaving Congo on the basis of a message received by telegram, without a visa, was scarcely standard practice. João approached Immigration Canada at the Canadian Embassy at Kinshasa to get a visa. From the embassy he could secure only a letter classified as a *Titre de Voyage*, issued to a non-political refugee. It indicated that he was travelling to Canada at his own risk, which meant that if he were refused entry he would be responsible to pay his own return fare. On that basis, João Matwawana came to Canada, ahead of his family.

João Matwawana took the Sabena flight from Kinshasa to Brussels, where he connected with Air Canada to Montreal. It was February 8, 1977. As the pilot brought the flight into Canada across Labrador, he took the plane down to a lower level so his passengers could get a look at the snow. This, he said, was for the benefit of people who were visiting Canada for the first time. The impression João gained was less than reassuring. He remembers having experienced what he thought was snow in England, and describing it to friends and family back home in Africa. In retrospect, what he saw in the U.K. was really only frost. What he was now looking at over Labrador was an infinity of very real snow, magnified by the pilot's comments on how one could travel for days on end without meeting people, or fly for a whole hour without spotting signs of human life. The pilot didn't call it Labrador, he called it Canada. This is Canada? Where are the people? Where and how do they live? How could one survive in such an environment?

I thought, Oh boy, I'm in trouble. Maybe I've made a bad decision to come here.

Even the approach to Mirabel, out in the country north of Montreal, was not really reassuring for someone who had heard that Montreal was a city. Where were the buildings, the homes?

Immigration Canada—Montreal

Immigration at Mirabel airport was the first hurdle to be crossed. The *Titre de Voyage*, issued by a Canadian embassy official in Kinshasa, indicated that he was coming for studies at Acadia University, but without any University documentation to support the process. He was travelling at his own risk. The haste was partly to get him safely out of the Congo, and partly to get him into classes at Acadia that were already underway.

A letter guaranteeing support had been sent by CBM, Toronto, for presentation to immigration in Kinshasa. João had requested that the Kinshasa immigration officer make mention of Mission sponsorship, but that request was not granted. Now, at Montreal immigration, he was paying the price because of ambiguity.

Seeing his documentation from Congo (Zaïre at that time), the officials assumed João spoke only French. Commenting to one another on his status, they conversed in English, but of course João could understand it all. They concluded that this man must go back on the return flight to Brussels. He seemed to have no sponsorship. His documentation was vague. There was no supporting evidence that he was admitted to a university in Canada. A student without a dossier? Improbable. "When people like this arrive in Canada without knowing anybody they don't know where to go." They concluded that this man posed a risk.

The immigration officers were under no pressure to deal with João's case for a few hours, since the plane was going on to Mexico first. They would put him on the return flight to Brussels when it came back.

"Please sit over here, Sir, while we handle the documentation of the other passengers. Your case is complicated. We don't see this kind of document very often. We will come back to you later."
"Thank you."

The response in English surprised them. Then João sat to one side and watched as they processed other documentation. In the midst of that process, a voice over the intercom inquired for Rev. João Matwawana. That came as a real surprise to the officials.

"Do you know someone here?"
"It is possible."
"You can't go outside, you have not been admitted. One of us will go and see about this."

The inquirer was Dr. Maurice Boillat, General Secretary of *L'Union d'Églises Baptistes Françaises au Canada*. John Keith had alerted him to Rev. Matwawana's arrival, and he was delighted to go to the airport to meet João, for he had been a guest in the Matwawana home at Kimpese during an event sponsored by Canadian Baptist Ministries, called *The Flying Seminar*. He and two others had shared a meal at the Matwawana table, and been entertained by their three sons with songs from Sunday School. During farewells at Kimpese, the comment was made that they would only meet again in heaven, for Matwawanas did not have money to travel to Canada and the *Flying Seminar* was a one-time event. Now here was an opportunity to meet in Montreal, even though the snows of Labrador had not in any sense suggested heaven.

Dr. Boillat convinced the immigration official that João was a Baptist pastor, known to Canadian Baptists, highly esteemed; that Dr. Langley, Principal at Acadia Divinity College was both colleague and personal friend. Yes, Dr. Langley had made arrangements for Pastor Matwawana to take additional studies at Acadia. In fact, Maurice Boillat and Abner Langley often sat together as directors of Canadian Baptist Ministries (CBM), at meetings convened twice each year. He convinced the official to grant João admission, with ten days in which to regulate his status at the Halifax office of Immigration Canada. Dr. Boillat was the key to solving the entire situation in Mirabel.

Cleared by immigration, Dr. Maurice Boillat drove João hastily to his connecting flight at Montreal's other airport, Dorval. His ticket from Kinshasa had been issued with Halifax as the final destination.

Establishing status as a student of Acadia Divinity College

On the Acadia campus at Wolfville, NS, there was a family in residence at the CBM mission house who were hungry for every possible contact with Angola. Karl and Kathy Janzen were, themselves, preparing to serve in Angola. It was the Janzens who met João at the Halifax airport and took him to Wolfville. They and their three children made room for João in the mission house, and he lived with them for his first four months in Canada. The house is only a stone's throw from the Divinity College.

Studies began immediately, but João was very conscious of that worrying matter of needing to face immigration officials in Halifax within ten days. He needed the status as an approved student, granting the right of residence in Canada, allowing the family to be reunited in Wolfville. Days two, three, four, and five rolled by with no action. Finally, João went to Dr. Langley with a plea for his assistance in settling the matter. The Janzens were also jittery. Kathy fasted and prayed in the face of her fear that João would be deported. Deportation was, indeed, a real possibility. Dr. Langley wrote a letter for João to take to Immigration Canada.

If Dr. Maurice Boillat was the key to the solution at Mirabel, then it was his friend and colleague Dr. Abner Langley who held the key for immigration Canada in Halifax. João presented the Principal's letter at the reception desk. The immigration person was immediately at ease with the document, commenting that Dr. Langley was her mother's pastor, and a person of integrity. The ten-day limitation was removed, João was granted official status as a student, and the long weeks of uncertainty came to an end. He would face the next major decision when his studies ended. Perhaps by then Angola would offer a stable environment for safe return to ministry there. For the present, he was a student in Canada and could now bring his family from Kimpese.

Getting established in studies at Acadia

João Matwawana was accepted at Acadia Divinity College as a mature student. The Registrar and the Dean were appropriately cautious until such time as they were able to base their final decisions on courses successfully completed and marks assigned. Several factors had weighed in João's full admission. Dr. Abner Langley, as Principal, had been able to determine that his diploma in Theology from EPI Kimpese would gain him admission to second year at the Faculty of Theology in Strasbourg, France. At the end of April 1977, the Westhill College of Education, part of the Selly Oaks cluster of colleges in Birmingham, U.K., forwarded their transcript of João's studies undertaken with them. Based on these factors, Dr. Cherry, as Dean of Studies, pronounced that the faculty was prepared to base everything on the results of João's trial year of studies. "Since João has been chaplain at IME Kimpese we will let him work on the Post-Baccalaureate Diploma in Pastoral Care." There was a trial period of six weeks, followed by a trial period of one year.

Although he was now a student, João was not able to escape all other expectations. Another participant in the *Flying Seminar* who had visited Kimpese was Gerald Phillips of Woodstock, New Brunswick. Gerald was one of those who had shared the meal with Dr. Boillat at the Matwawanas' table in Kimpese. Nothing short of a preaching assignment for João in the large Baptist church at Woodstock would now satisfy Gerald. Tickets were arranged for a flight to Fredericton. When João appeared first before a Sunday School class, it was so large that he was prepared to preach his sermon, thinking it was the main congregation, but the full worship service still awaited. The church's pastor rushed him to the airport on Monday morning so he could fly back to classes.

THE FAMILY REUNITED

Nora arrived in Halifax with Ambrose, Julie, Raymond, and Isabel on September 9, 1977. They came by the same sequence of flights through Brussels and Montreal that João had used, but without the immigration problems at Mirabel. It was very difficult to leave Samuel and Edward at Kimpese to finish their high school studies, but at least this allowed them, as teenagers, to remain among friends.

CBM arranged family housing for the Matwawanas at Port Williams, a few kilometres from Wolfville, in a house owned by one of CBM's board members, Rev. Gordon Delong. This became the Matwawana residence until João's graduation.

With Dr. Gilchrist and family shortly after
Nora and children arrived in Canada

First Canadian Christmas

By the end of September, the Matwawanas were settled into the house rented for them beside the Baptist church in Port Williams. João was the only family member who spoke much English at that stage. He was away at Acadia University campus in Wolfville much of the time. He also took little Isabel along with him and put her in school on campus. Thus Isabel grew up as the most Canadian, by culture, of all the Matwawana children.

A friend of the family reports an occasion when little Isabel had this exchange with her father:

"*Daddy, you were the only black person in the room today.*"
"*Go look in the mirror, Isa.*"
"*Oh ... I'm black too.*"

It fell to Nora to sort out household procedures and adapt to the strange Canadian customs, with the help of several new friendships. She and her friends were heavily dependent on signs, symbols, demonstrations, and pointing. The conversations below, as reported by Nora as she looks back on that first Christmas, were not carried on in complete sentences.

A week or two before Christmas, people started bringing us Christmas gifts. We were living in Port Williams. Without knowing the culture, we started opening the Christmas presents immediately and of course the children then went outside to show their friends, and to play with the items. Lorena my friend came and noticed we needed help in order to know how to do things correctly.
"*You need a Christmas tree, and you put the presents underneath. You open them on Christmas day in the morning.*"
"*Oh, where do we get a Christmas tree?*"
"*Tell Ambrose to go with Chris and Craig to cut a tree then you will decorate it.*"
"*What will we use for decoration?*"

The other neighbour, Blanche, gave us some of her spare decorations and ornaments, balls, and all that. It made no sense to us. We just did it. We wondered how to keep this Christmas tree standing upright.
"Get a big board, nail the tree to it." (Lorena failed to mention putting stones on the board.)

Whenever we tried to put the tree up it would fall. Perhaps someone could hold the tree while others decorate. We kept discussing how to succeed. We got some rope, tied one end to a window, the other end in a corner. Now we bring the presents and put them under the tree. More suggestions from our neighbour take us to the next step.

"Nora, Santa Claus will come. Tell the kids to hang socks on the mantel."
The kids take that day's socks off their feet and hang them up, dirty socks, and maybe with some holes in the toes. It didn't make sense, but we did it.

"João, you are the one to put presents in the socks." Everybody who visited us saw these socks with holes! We woke up in the morning to find the tree on the floor, things broken. We got more specific help after the fact.
"Oh you should have put the tree in a pail with some stones to hold it, and some water...."

That was our first Christmas. We only knew about how to do a Christian Christmas. We didn't know about the Canadian traditional Christmas.

Recounting the Christmas events reminded Nora that their family initially had trouble remembering Canadian names. Within the family, they identified their neighbours and acquaintances by code names or by their activities. One lady who had sung for the children was identified as Mrs. Jingle Bells. One lady became Mrs. Mansanga because she reminded them of Mama Mansanga in Africa.

Nora learns to snowshoe

STUDIES AT ACADIA

Chaplaincy experience at IME Kimpese, and the desire to fortify those experiences with the best of whatever was available in formal training, led João to look at Acadia's *Post-Baccalaureate Diploma in the Practice of Ministry* with special interest. His instructor and mentor was Dr. Charles Taylor, and a special relationship developed with Dr. Taylor, who incidentally later was awarded the Order of Canada.

He gained a Diploma in the Practice of Ministry in the first two years, concurrent with his degree work. Transcripts of achievement reveal that João did solid academic work, with good marks.

It was with joy that João received a letter from the registrar, dated May 11, 1979:

On the basis of the studies that you have completed during the past two years, and your previous educational records, I offer you admission to the Master of Divinity Program.

With admission to that program, which João accepted, the requirements of an additional year of course work plus a thesis were spelled out.

The Master of Divinity thesis work was done under Dr. Oliver Ohsberg, who had identified with João's needs and followed his academic progress attentively. Early in life Dr. Ohsberg's own sense of calling to pursue a missionary career had proven to be a door which was closed to him, but he sustained his desire to foster the training of Christian leadership in African countries. One practical outworking of this came as he assisted João.

The title of the thesis for the Master of Divinity degree was *Team Ministry in Cross-Cultural Setting, with Particular Reference to Angola and Zaïre*. The thrust of the thesis was to fortify the process of integrating expatriates and nationals into team ministry modules wherever the missionary movement goes into play.

João's thesis concludes that there are four vital factors important to the success of such cross-cultural team modules:

(1) awareness of the call of God in the lives of the individual team members, however different the experience or expression of that call may be in each case
(2) cultural adaptation, social identification and religious empathy on the part of team members
(3) elimination of every trace of dominance, competition, and individuality among team members, in the interest of team relationships
(4) identification and adoption of a common goal
(Matwawana 1980: 71 & 72)

Studies in Theology were particularly appreciated under Dr. Allison Trites. But never far away, and always sensitive to his needs of whatever nature, Dr. Abner Langley remained João's key supporter. That link carried past graduation into placement in a church. With the direct contributions and special attention given by these four men and others, the years at Acadia provided the academic foundation for the remainder of João's career, while contributing to the spiritual dimension of his life, as well.

SUPPORT GIVEN TO MATWAWANAS AT PORT WILLIAMS

When the Matwawana family arrived at Port Williams, Nova Scotia, they found that their neighbours had children the ages of Julie and Raymond. The caring pastor and his wife lived just down the hill, and were always attentive to the family's needs. One of the neighbours was Nora's age and became like a sister, another relationship grew to that of mother and daughter. These and other women of the church and community helped Nora through her period of adaptation to life in Canada, with the details of shopping, cooking, and more. They were all friendly, helpful, and considerate. These affirming relationships conveyed a strong sense of acceptance in Port Williams.

The result was that Nora found herself in a large caring family at a critical time when that support was vital to her, making the transition from the Congo where she spoke French, Kikongo, Lingala, and Portuguese fluently every day, into a setting where she was as limited as an infant with no means of verbal communication. Nora remembers, in particular, the help with baking, much of it given by pointing and showing, in those days when the language links were minimal. The little experiences are remembered along with more significant help. For example, Nora remembers going over to the home of her "sister" at the end of a day, when they would light a fire and toast marshmallows. Friendship does not always call for momentous events or occasions.

SAMUEL AND EDWARD, STILL IN CONGO

Separation from their older sons was very difficult for both João and Nora. Their original intention was to stay in Canada for something like two years. A separation for that length of time would not be too difficult. Sam and Ed were in high school at IPE Kimpese, and the jeans or the track shoes sent to them by their parents from Canada gave them a sense of being important people. Nora picked apples in the Annapolis Valley during apple season to be able to make these expensive purchases to send to their sons in the Congo.

After two years, with the realization that they were staying in Canada longer, a visit was set up so Samuel and Edward could fly from Kinshasa to Halifax to spend Christmas with them in Nova Scotia. They bought Christmas presents, put them under the tree, and went to the airport on Christmas eve 1979 to await arrival of their flight. What a blow to discover that their visas to visit Canada had been denied. They were aware of snags in process, relating to dates of birth and ambiguity of documents, but concluded that it was just a matter of working out the details. Immigration Canada had not informed them that visas were being refused. The shock hit them all at once, and at the last minute, on Christmas Eve. This is when Nora started developing high blood pressure. She became increasingly worried that she would be permanently separated from their sons. Soon, Nora was threatened with hospitalization to deal with the extremely high blood pressure. Friendship and care for Isabel provided by the ladies of Port Williams, was a priceless and uplifting gift. Concern about her older boys would shadow all of Nora's decisions and feelings for the next several years.

THE IMMIGRATION HEARING

The critical immigration hearing on whether to grant João refugee status in Canada was held at the Canada Employment Centre on the campus of Acadia University, from 10:00 a.m., May 22, 1980, until 3:55 in the afternoon.

There were several serious preoccupations as preparations were made for this hearing. Of primary concern, would immigrant status be granted? Without that status, the entire family would face deportation as João's studies drew to a close, and this would happen imminently. The second concern was to draw together and present in logical order the various pieces of evidence and conditions that would place this family clearly and legitimately within the provisions of *Convention refugee* as defined by Canada's Immigration Act.

The third concern was how they should handle the troubling divided situation under which the two older boys, Samuel and Edward, continued to pursue their high school studies at Kimpese, in the Democratic Republic of Congo, while the four younger children were with their parents in Nova Scotia. The status of the sons in the Congo was further complicated by the fact that on the date of the hearing, Edward, in the Congo, was still a minor, whereas Samuel, born in 1959, did not fall in that privileged category. Canada's immigration process is complicated enough, without introducing such twists as this.

The hearing, though stressful, went well. The immigration officer's report lists solicitor Steele as representing the Matwawanas and John Keith, as a contributor at the hearing, with Rev. Dr. Abner Langley and Mrs. Virginia Keith present as observers.

News that they were granted refugee status was received on September 4, 1980.

Appointment by CBM to missionary service in Kivu Province of Congo

Canadian Baptist Ministries had a long-standing pledge to the Baptist Community of Kivu, in the Congo, that missionary families would be provided to work with them in leadership development. CBM therefore encouraged the Matwawanas to undertake this assignment. João was readied for this invitation by the impact on his life of the Missionfest event in Calgary in 1978, which featured Brazil's Dr. Nilson Fanini as special speaker. João acknowledged the hand of God on his life, in a special sense of being called to missionary service. João and Nora followed the process of interviews and appointment procedures established by Canadian Baptist Ministries and were appointed for service in Kivu in October 1979, which was prior to João's graduation. There was a brick residence awaiting them on a hilltop at Bwatsinge, north of Goma.

João's prayer at the time of their appointment, registered in the permanent records of CBM, was:

"I pray that God may use me to be a real agent of reconciliation, so that where there is hatred, love may be found in the name of our Lord Jesus Christ."

Kivu service with CBM was not the only option open to the Matwawanas in 1980. There were other options and invitations, but it was the African option that appealed, and seemed to offer João and Nora the promise of fulfilling God's will and purpose, leading back to their native Africa.

Seeing Ontario

After appointment to Kivu, CBM asked João to undertake a tour of speaking engagements involving specific churches in Ontario. A schedule for this tour had been established for a certain missionary couple who had served in Kenya. Faced with their resignation, the ideal solution would be for João to take over these engagements rather than cancelling them all. After all, Matwawanas were headed to Africa, and the "tour of deputation," as it is called, would serve the purpose of establishing the Matwawana's network of prayer support and financial undergirding.

On one leg of that tour, João was flying on a small plane from Fort William to Thunder Bay. He was aware that there would be an onward connection to Sault Saint Marie, but had not fixed the timetable in his head:

It was a very bumpy ride in the small plane and as we approached Thunder Bay. I was disoriented, afraid we were going to crash. When I got out of the plane there was a young lady there who obviously mistook me for someone else she was there to meet. She approached me and told me to come with her to the other plane. I said to myself, "These people know what they are doing," so I just followed with my luggage, without asking questions.

This was another small plane. We were only in the air maybe fifteen minutes when we landed, some people got off and oth-

ers got on. They delivered some packages. But again we were in the air no more than fifteen or twenty minutes, people got off, others got on, and some packages were delivered.

I asked myself "What's going on here?" but I still didn't say anything. Then the co-pilot turned around and asked if I'm not getting off somewhere.
"Why should I get off?
"Where are you going?"
"I'm going to the Sault.
"Oh, I don't think you're on the right plane. We're going to the Sault, too, but it will be a long while."

The short flights continued, many of them, for João had been put on the mail plane by mistake. He was getting to see many of the little mining towns of northern Ontario—without a ticket. He stayed with the little mail plane to the end of the day's run in Sault Saint Marie.

Maybe I got to know this part of the country better than Prime Minister Trudeau. Along the way the pilot commented that I must be hungry, having nothing to eat. I was famished. He pointed out a corner store in one of those little towns so I ran over and bought some chocolate bars. I don't know how many times we stopped, I lost count, but we did arrive in the Sault.

At the airport in the Sault I didn't know whether I was ahead of the regular Air Canada flight I was supposed to be on, or behind it, so I thought I'd just sit down and wait. When the scheduled flight came in, I was watching. The passengers came off. A man nearby spoke to the person near him, and he solved my dilemma.
"Oh no! Mr. Matwawana must have missed his plane."
"I'm Mr. Matwawana."
"How did you get here?"
"At the moment I'm too tired and too hungry to tell you the story. Later please, when I've had something to eat."

The pastor and João had a good time, with lots of laughs over the travel experience. The pastor admitted he had not known how to introduce the evening's speaker, but finally he had a worthy story to tell.

Matwawanas return to Africa

Their appointment process was complete, farewells were said and goods were disposed of. The Matwawana family found itself Africa bound, on their way back to the continent of their birth, even though Angola was still not accessible to them. The date was September 4, 1981, and the airport of destination was Nairobi, Kenya. They were to study Kiswahili in Nairobi, then proceed on to their destined post of service, Bwatsinge in Kivu Province, Democratic Republic of the Congo.

Documentation proved to be the snag at Nairobi. The immigration officer was suspicious of this family travelling on what he considered irregular documentation, and adamant that this family must not be admitted to Kenya. The risk was too high. He judged that he was dealing with a suspicious case, probably espionage on the part of Communist Angola.

The Matwawana family could not believe what was happening to them. The fact that CBM colleagues Elwood Bannister and Hans Van Nie came to meet them at Nairobi airport and actually gained entrance to communicate with them and with the Kenyan immigration officers carried no weight at all. This news was devastating! They were being sent back to Canada!

The British Airways flight that brought them to Nairobi proceeded on to Johannesburg and returned. Immigration would not allow it to depart for London until this family was settled on board. João comments that the immigration officer was convinced that he was dealing with a dangerous species of humanity.

Since the return flight to London on which they were to be deported was fully booked, it meant that immigration officers and the airline were deadlocked, but with immigration holding the trump card. Immigration could withhold permission for the aircraft to leave and they did. An irate load of passengers were pressuring for departure. One way or another, places for Nora and the children were found in the economy cabin, but nothing for João. Immigration was still adamant that this flight would not leave without him. The delay ran on to an hour. The irony of João's situation, which he was quite unable to appreciate at the time, was that in the end he was deported as a first class passenger—small comfort. It was not a happy flight.

The dejected Matwawana family flew back to Canada from Nairobi, arriving at Toronto's Pearson airport after their unpleasant deportation from Kenya. They did not know what their future held or where they should go. Dr. Cherry of Acadia Divinity College offered them the use of his house until Thanksgiving time, since it was his habit to stay at his cottage late each year. That was a great help, and they moved in without knowing what would be next.

Nora found it difficult to handle the phone calls of people wanting to offer their condolences. She was constantly breaking down in sobs. In order to avoid the calls, she decided that she would use apple picking as her device to get away from people. It would also provide the funds to help buy winter clothing for the family. They had given all winter clothing away when they set off for Africa, and they numbered six here in Canada, even without the two older boys. But mostly she wanted the opportunity to be by herself, always asking God, "Why?"

> *I called Blair Embree at the orchard where I previously picked apples. I was his best picker. He said, "Nora, you are very welcome." God gave me no answers to my "Why" at that time, but I have seen the answer later.*

11

THE PASTORATE AT LOCKEPORT AND RAGGED ISLAND

DISCOVERIES ABOUT FINDING AND DOING THE WILL OF GOD

Looking back on those difficult days, João concludes that although he wanted to work in Africa immediately after graduation from Acadia Divinity School, rather than in Canada, the time was not right. He and his family were not ready.

> *I was offered so many churches after my graduation, but I said "I can't work in Canada—you are too complicated." ... I didn't want to work in Canada at all! Anyway, I was warned that I didn't have valid documents to be able to work. I had entered as a student and they said that I couldn't change my status. I wanted to go back to Africa. Since I couldn't go back to Angola, I asked Canadian Baptist Ministries if they could find something for me to do. Their assignment for me was as a teacher in Kivu Province in Eastern Zaire ... instead of going straight to Zaire, I should go to Kenya, learn Swahili, and then enter Zaire from there....*

We were deported back to Canada that same night.

I discovered that it was God's will that I should not go back to Africa at that time.
First of all, I didn't know the life of the Canadian church, so I was not yet equipped to represent them well overseas. I was just a student, and to go overseas without knowing the churches who were supporting me was wrong. Secondly, the fact that I was just coming out from college meant that I had a very high agenda of things that could damage my work—even in Africa, so when I was returned to Canada, I could see I was a modern Jonah....

I came back and waited upon the Lord because I was a rebel. I should never have said, "I cannot work in Canada." It was not my right to say that. I remember the story of Peter when he said, "No, Lord." One of my teachers told me that every time you make a decision, waiting for God's will, you have to decide to discard that "No," because otherwise the Lord is not Lord any more.
(Matwawana: 2002)

Nora's assessment is that when they were setting out to undertake mission in East Africa in 1981, the timing was premature. She had not yet worked through the grief associated with Immigration Canada's refusal to allow Edward and Samuel to join them in Canada. The lads were still stuck in Kinshasa, feeling a sense of abandonment and rejection.

I was thinking that if I could get to Africa I would be able, some way, to meet my two sons. The deportation from Kenya became the lowest point of my entire life. I was asking myself when I would ever get to see my sons again. I was not really concentrating on the mission task that lay before me.

The Invitation to Lockeport

Dr. Abner Langley, former Principal of Acadia Divinity College, began checking to see what churches were looking for pastors. He spoke with

Robert Humble in Lockeport, NS, his friend, and chairman of their pulpit committee:

"You're looking for a pastor? Well, I have one. He's a missionary."
"Maybe that's the one we need."
"They're just back from Nairobi and waiting for a call to some church. They're ready."
"OK, have them come for a visit."

João recalls:

Remember now, that when we left Port Williams we sold everything in a yard sale. We were headed for Africa, convinced we would need none of these things for the next four years. Everything was gone, and that included winter clothes, bicycles for the children, boots and all that. I had sold our car so cheap, it was like a gift. Now after four days we're back, we need our things, but of course we can't get them back.

When Robert Humble invited us to Lockeport, Dr. Langley remembered that we had no car. "If you had a car you could go preach for a call. See me in two days."

During those two days Dr. Langley called some people, including the pastor at Bayers Road Baptist Church in Halifax:

"João is in difficulties. Do you have a car dealer in your congregation?"
"I have a few."
"Who is the best one who will agree to bargain? João is in desperate shape. He doesn't need an expensive car, maybe something about twelve hundred dollars."
They found something, so I went to Halifax by bus. It was a big Dodge station wagon. I could easily take all my family, or the youth group at church.

Wars Are Never Enough

What may have seemed like a simple operation for Canadians, accustomed to getting around and using our road maps, was less than simple for João and Nora at that stage in their experience.

We drove down, Nora and I, without any clue about where Lockeport was. We turned off the highway at Liverpool looking for a map.
"Why are you looking for a map?"
"We want to go to Lockeport."
"You don't need a map to go to Lockeport, just keep driving, look for the sign."

When João and Nora spotted the sign for Lockeport they failed to notice that it also indicated a distance of 28 kilometres.

Having seen a sign for Lockeport and also seeing a church up ahead, we needed to change our clothes. There was a little hut nearby.
"Nora, you change and I'll watch, then we'll switch and you can watch as I change."

But having changed our clothes we were still not at Lockeport, as we discovered. When we arrived there, what fun! There were street names, but no house numbers. How would we find our destination? And the first person we stopped to ask was mentally challenged.

With the next contact, my question was, "Do you know where we can find a Baptist church deacon or an elder?"
"Oh, I'm the wrong person for that, I don't go to church."

Finally someone told us to check with "Penney over there." That was our introduction to Lockeport. We concluded that Lockeport was a tough place to find our way around, but of course that was because we didn't know the town or the people yet. We went to check with Fred Penney.

> "Can I help you?"
> "I'm the person who came to preach at your church for a call."
> "Oh, that's my wife's business. I don't deal with church things... Pauline... Someone here to see you."
>
> "Hi. Can I help you?"
> "We came here to preach for a call. Maybe you got a letter from Dr. Langley?"
> "Oh, there must be a mistake. Dr. Langley wrote that it would be a missionary."
> "I am a missionary." (Maybe she thought I was the driver for a missionary?)
> "I'm so sorry for this misunderstanding—but you're so young."
> "Well, that's what they always tell me, but I'm not so young."

João asked to see a deacon and the lady directed them to Tom Whiteway's house. They found Tom Whiteway, informed him of who they were, and all was well.

> He was so excited. We felt warmly welcomed. Only a couple of people really knew who we were. After supper we went to church and I preached. They voted to accept us.

Before João preached Nora was already confident they would be invited, based on how they had been shown the parsonage before going to the service.

Growth of the Two Congregations

At the beginning it was very depressing for João and Nora, with so few people attending such a large building. Nora remembers:

> After we went to Lockeport, I cried again on that first Sunday. I had never seen as big church as that with only ten or fifteen people, I had never seen even a Sunday School that was so small. It was a disaster. Our own family made up 50 percent of the Sunday School

"What is it you want from us Lord? Are we sent here to bury this church?" That assignment did not help my depression—until the time when growth began. Then God began to give his answer. First, we were there in Lockeport for growth of the church. Then, too, we were not ready for that overseas component of our ministry. We would have been going to Africa with only the Port Williams church as an example in our minds, and Port Williams was a healthy church. We needed the broader experience of what Canada and Canadian church life was like, or we would think that Canadian churches were ideal and perfect. We needed to know more in detail. I was always invited to the church groups at Port Williams, but without English I only knew I was attending a meeting, then coffee and tea. I didn't yet know enough English to understand the content of what was happening. At Lockeport I began to understand substance of how Canadians churches function.

Little by little the growth started. They began with an attendance of only seven at Lockeport, and just fifteen at Osborne, on Ragged Island. The parsonage was located in Lockeport, and Osborne was about ten minutes away by car. João was responsible for both churches.

I remembered what one of the professors from Acadia told me when he heard I was going to the Lockeport field. He said that would be the last church a pastor would want to go, to start his work.

I can hardly believe how this church, which was seen as a problem by Canadian pastors, accepted us so readily and within just a few months. I can say that we made a kind of different approach, which brought some success.

Lockeport is a fishing town and not very large. The families are all closely related to each other. It was different from Port Williams. The difference was good for us because it was more like our African culture, having so much family closeness.

So when João settled into his work, and especially into his pastoral visitation, he decided to forget about the church's list of forty resident members:

I started just visiting people. If I visited a Williams family I would continue all through the Williams family. Then to Buchanan, and I would visit Buchanans all that week. That worked. In a few weeks, everybody was talking about Pastor John. News of his visits might come from an uncle or maybe an in-law. They were asking "How come this man is visiting everybody? That's strange."

Someone would say "I'm an Anglican but he visited me, and he visited my uncle already."

By following the alphabetical order, I touched everybody directly or indirectly, and the news spread. When they asked me why I did that, I told them it is because I am a community pastor. I care for everybody. Those people who were members were so ashamed to see people from other churches coming to our worship that they themselves came back. I never had to go look for them; they came out of shame.

That led to some accusations from my colleagues that I was sheep-stealing. The Catholic priest had closed his church; he had no members left. But we still had Anglican, United Church of Canada, Independent Baptist, and Pentecostal churches, in a population of less than a thousand. That's not much population for five churches. In order to assure my pastoral colleagues of other denominations that I was not here to steal sheep, I organized a ministerial fellowship. Every Tuesday they would come to my house for tea. The good thing then was that I was the oldest of all the pastors. We started sharing. They agreed that in such a small community my method was better, to visit everybody. So they also learned from that approach. Instead of being against me, they accepted me and we worked closely together.

The result was that all the churches ended up working together. Everybody was feeling a little growth, and there was no jealousy. The people were saying, "This minister is open. How does he know me? When he came to visit, he talked about my uncle."

Then at one point tension arose between the two churches. Lockeport was conscious of being oldest and first. Osborne had a later start, but having some young couples, it was growing more quickly. There were more baptisms in Osborne than Lockeport. Was it because João was spending more time over there? In fact, he was not. But Lockeport was feeling bypassed and left out. João was careful to balance his time carefully, being conscious of their feelings. The two churches had a combined youth group, often meeting in the Matwawanas' home. That may have helped to unify the work. The youth promoted causes and undertook projects, such as raising funds for hunger relief. They did a fast for 30 hours. Theirs was the only youth work in town.

The following excerpts of a letter João sent to his congregations reveals something of the spirit in which he undertook his work:

Lockeport,
November 13, 1981
A LETTER FROM BROTHER JOHN

It is now over two weeks since our arrival. ...invitation to you all to attend a roll call of love....

I earnestly urge you to consider this invitation to attend this roll call of love, the first of its kind in our churches, to plan the necessary strategy to reach, strengthen, and comfort the suffering body of Christ in this community.

Love is the way.... God's tools are men and women.... The community will be changed by men and women.... Let us decide before God that we are going to be those men and women.

(Signed) Rev. João Matwawana

Once into the work, João noticed the absence of men in church. He introduced a men's breakfast and the Ragged Island people caught the vision for that. "It went like wildfire." Then others came in. The whole community accepted it, and it became a big thing. The men's breakfast was scheduled for the second Saturday morning of each month, and it continued long after his departure, as a community event.

Determined to break out of the perception that church-related events in Lockeport were a matter only for women, João put much thought into the situation. He came up with a personal conclusion as to who was the key man in the community, and before the men's breakfasts were initiated there, João paid him a visit:

"I think you're a leader."
"I think I'm a leader, too, but the church hasn't acknowledged that."
"I would like you to come to a meeting with some men. Please listen carefully in that meeting because I will have a special challenge for you, a task to undertake. If you come, I promise not to embarrass you by asking you to pray or anything like that."

In the meeting which this man attended, João spelled out his concept of the men's breakfast project. Then he asked for volunteers to help prepare the first breakfast in order to get this new project underway. As he did so, he looked straight at "Mr. Leader." The response was immediate, a pledge to help, and of course this was somewhat stunning to others there. It became part of the momentum that got the program of men's breakfasts off the ground.

The deacons complained we'd never find anyone to cook that much food. I knew that most of the retired cooks from the fishing boats were around, so all I needed was to ask them if they wanted to be cooks. And they did. Earlier the church had never asked them this, or to do anything for the church. We had so many cooks.... We even had a supervisor and organizer of cooks who lined up a list of who would cook each week. I didn't have to do anything. All they needed was to be challenged, and they enjoyed it.

People came from all over. It was not denominational. Those were specialists, professional cooks from the boats, and they made it a very special breakfast. From time to time they invited the women. The men paid their own costs and they always had a project for the offerings they received.

An example would be funding the summer camp expenses of children not able to pay their own way. They were creative. They also picked up on some of the church's projects to help out.

Church growth

The church at Osborne / Ragged Island, Nova Scotia

Church growth was first felt at Osborne. More people were coming, and parking space was inadequate. It might have been a year after our arrival that they had to expand the parking lot. There were other renovations like the fellowship hall, changes to the washrooms, and all that. This brought excitement. But there were some traditions difficult to change. For instance, people had always been baptized in Lockeport because it was the mother church. The baptismal tank there was cold, the heater was not working. After the first baptism, I got a cold.

One of the baptisms was revolutionary in its impact, the conversion of a lady whose life had not been good. When she became a Christian she became as active within the church as she had been outside. She said, "I was cold in that baptistry. I don't want my children and my grandchildren to be cold when they become Christians. Here's my twenty dollars, and we'll start a fund for a new tank in Osborne." People can get excited when there is a project. Everybody was donating. We got a warm tank, and sometimes even Lockeport people came there to be baptized.

THE CAR ACCIDENT

(There was) ...a couple who had lived near the Osborne church for decades but never attended. The church members avoided them because of their threats and their hostile attitude toward the church. The husband of the family was a fisherman. He hated everything to do with the church so much that each successive pastor was warned to avoid these people as if they were possessed. Previous ministers had accepted that.

Something led me to ask myself what Jesus would do about that situation if He came to Osborne. This plagued me.
"I think Jesus would go straight there to that family."
I recognized that I had been following a tradition that maybe should be broken, even if I got into trouble. The question was just how to do the right thing. One day I prayed about it and

concluded that I would just go to the house, out of the blue, and that is what I did.

"Greetings, can I come in?"
"You are lost!"
"No, I'm not lost."
"Doay's house is the other one over there." (Their abbreviation for Dorothy.)
"I know Doay's house, this is your house."
"You came to us?"
"Yes."
"Oh.... have a seat. But we never had a visit from a minister."
"Now you have one."
"This is different.... You know, they think we're bad...."
"I don't think so."

Conversation ranged over a number of topics. Where João came from, the size of his family, comments about his own history, with no discussion relating to the church. They established that João was a community pastor visiting everybody, regardless of who they were.

"Can you come back when my husband is here?"
"Sure."

She told him the day her husband's ship would be back in port and said that if João were to return on that day, he would be able to meet them both together. Nothing of this was mentioned to the deacons, but João noted it in his book, thought and prayed about it all week.

The day indicated was the day when João placed his weekly announcements in the newspaper in Shelburne. He rushed to Shelburne first to do that errand.

That visit was on my mind as I was driving back from Shelburne. It's even possible that I went to sleep driving. My car left the road, broke off two successive trees, then struck a telephone pole, breaking it off and dragging it along on top of the car. The car kept on until it struck rocks, which burst the tires.

I looked out and could see a big pole on the roof of my car. The steering wheel was all broken. I tried doors on both sides—they were stuck. I crawled into the back seat, both those were jammed as well. Because it was a station wagon, it had a back door which was thrown open by the impact. I went out the back.

A vehicle had been following João, a member of the Pentecostal church. He stopped and assumed that "Brother John" must be dead in that wreck. He was there trembling when he saw João staggering toward the road.

"You are alive?"
"I think so."
"That's a miracle."
"I believe in miracles."
"Come to my car, I'll take you to the hospital. "

João asked the man not to take him to the hospital, because he didn't feel anything broken. Rather, he just wanted to go to see one of his deacons, because he had an important appointment.

So he drove me to the gas station of my deacon. I told him I had an accident, that the car stayed there by the roadside, and I needed his car. The deacon recommended that I go to the doctor first, but I told him, "Later. This is very important." I was feeling that this accident was like an attack from the devil to keep me from visiting that couple. He didn't believe that, but he agreed that I could take his car.

It didn't take long until reports began reaching Nora. The Pastor from the United Church was first:

"Nora, is Brother John home?"
"No, he went to Shelburne"

Then another called, asking if João were home. Nora concluded that something unusual was afoot. She then called the deacon at the garage where João had borrowed the car:

"Ralph, where's João?"
"He's visiting."
"Why are people calling me?"
"Well, Brother John had a little bit of an accident—but he's OK."
"Can you tell me where he is?"
"I don't know where he is."

Then Nora called the church caretaker:

"Doris, do you know where João is?"
"No, I don't know."

At this point Nora phoned the doctor to make an appointment for João saying he might actually be on his way right now.

In spite of the car accident which had shaken him up badly, João went to visit Elmer and Florence, making no mention of the accident:

"I have come."
"We were waiting for you."
"Do you have anything to tell me? I have just come for a visit."
"You said you would visit us. Tell us more of your life."
So I told them more of my story, my experiences.
"What a life. What kept you having that kind of faith?"
"Because I trust in God."
"I wish we could have that kind of faith."
"You can have it."
"How?"
"By accepting Jesus as your Lord and Saviour."
"That is exactly what we want to do," said the wife. Then aside to her husband—*"You don't think so?"*
"I think so."
"If you are ready we can have a prayer, and you give your lives to the Lord."
"Yes."

So João had prayer with them and they discussed what would happen next. All three of them knew that the entire community would find it hard to believe that this change had come over the couple. They concluded that husband and wife should be baptized together, both going down into the baptismal tank at the same time, as if it were another wedding. "We have been in bondage together. Our testimony of faith in Jesus will be together. We want the community to know that we are free."

I was so relieved.
I told them, "I have to go now because my family is waiting for me for a special appointment."

João went home. Nora sent him on to his appointment with the doctor. The next morning he announced to the deacons that a couple had just accepted the Lord. The deacons had no idea who, and when they saw that it was Elmer and Florence, they couldn't believe it.

"Brother John, we will not say no to your suggestions any more."
"We've discovered that your approach is not the Canadian one and it may be useful to our area."
"We'll give you that freedom to make mistakes if you need to, and we will not oppose you."

From that time on, João sensed total freedom to conduct his visitation in any way he wanted. They refrained from warning him off with stories of people's backgrounds.

There was another outcome of that car accident that brought blessing. The Lockeport congregation was growing increasingly impatient about the question of inequality in growth between the two churches. There had been tension, even if some of it was expressed in a joking way, such as comments on how many friends their pastor had in the other church:

I didn't answer to the jokes. I was thinking that God will reveal to them that these things were not true. He will fix this situation, we just pray about that.

When the accident came, we discovered I didn't have collision coverage at all. The little insurance I had was recommended by the dealer. All it paid for was the telephone pole I broke off. He said that because the car was so old I didn't need heavy coverage. When the church checked out the situation they asked me, "Pastor you have very little insurance coverage and your car is gone. What will you do for visitation?"

My idea was that the junk man would pay me 200 dollars for the wreck. With that I would get a good mountain bike and do my work without any problem. I know I can't afford a car because I must pay off the rest of the old one that was wrecked. I will not even dream of having a car any more.

The deacons were devastated. They called a secret emergency meeting to which João was not invited. They could not imagine, with five churches in town, allowing a situation to develop whereby their Baptist pastor would be doing his visitation on a bicycle. The embarrassment would be too much:

"This man doesn't understand Canadian culture. The minister is the representative of the church. We must show him we care for him, we respect him. He can't travel on a bike. We will buy a car."

At this emergency meeting, they zeroed in on a certain car left by a fisherman who had just died, having driven it only six months. They resolved to get it. They negotiated with the widow. It was a Ford LTD, and the lady's response was generous:

"Because of Brother John, I'm selling this car just like a gift. I'll sell it for 5,000 dollars. The rest is my gift. I want my minister to have a car."

The 5,000 dollars represented no more than half the value of the car. They started collecting funds.

I had been driving Mr. Humble's car for that week, and took it to the Sunday service. When giving the announcements, I fol-

lowed my regular practice of asking whether someone had an additional announcement which did not figure in the bulletin. A deacon raised his hand for an announcement, then he called a young teenager from the back and she came to the pulpit. "I'm the youngest member of this church and I'm presenting you the key to your new car."

João was unable to hold back his tears. The people applauded. The church insured the car this time.

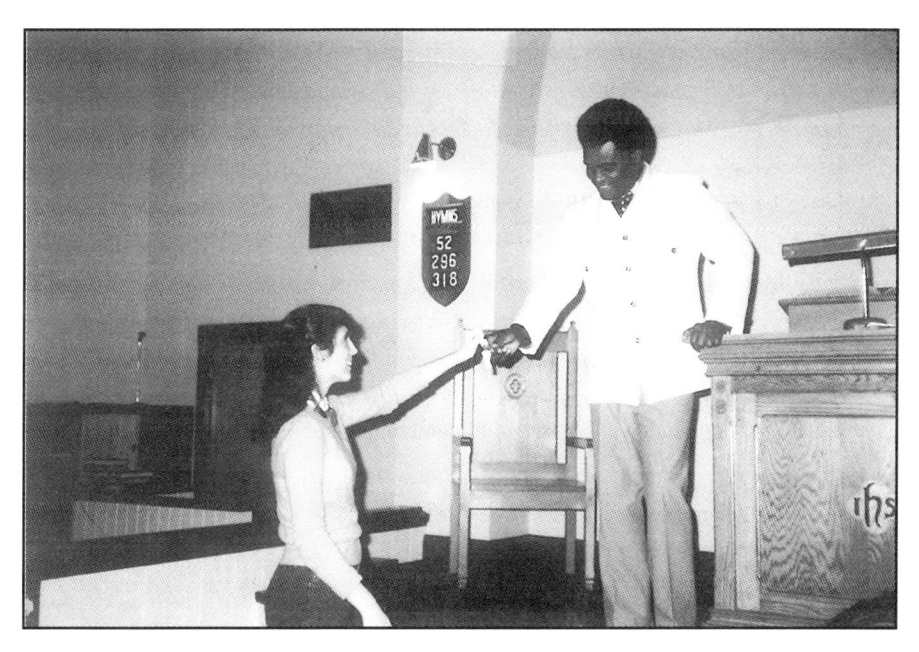

The keys to Brother John's new car

This car project was something which united the two congregations, as they undertook it together. Lockeport had fewer members but they felt compelled to participate, and they contributed almost 900 dollars. They said in Lockeport that I was working like a horse, but how could I work less with such manifestations of love?

Services to the Community

Because of João's work load, there were fellow pastors who said he would have a heart attack. The car didn't change his patterns or his undertakings. There was a certain commitment that he had already begun before his accident, a practical way that he had worked out of caring for the elderly.

The seacoast area had many widows whose husbands had died in fishing disasters. They were living there alone, often in big houses, their children having gone away to work. I discovered that this is a place where preaching is not the pastor's only duty. I have to take care of these ladies and some elderly people, to monitor how they are doing. I discovered that they needed some attention. First they are given a lot of medications, which need to be sorted out. There were medications in bottles that were hard for them to open. When I asked people what bothers them in the course of a day, the first answer I often got was that they had difficulty opening their medication containers. So I spoke to the doctors not to use these bottles.

The second thing I discovered was that all these ladies were keeping their money at home, not in a bank.
"The banks steal money," (a reference to service charges).
"They have to steal a little, but you are safer using banks."

It's as though I became a counsellor and advisor to them. I also discovered that many old people died in Lockeport not because of complicated diseases, but just because they never got to a specialist. I asked why they didn't see a specialist.
"The specialists are always in Halifax."
"What's wrong with Halifax?"
"Nobody was ever taken to Halifax who came back alive."

They had all been waiting too long. People were being taken there for strokes when it was too late, and Halifax was three hours dis-

tance by car. I explained that if the one who had the stroke had been to a specialist, the stroke could have been avoided.
"If you'll go with us, Brother John, we'll go."

What I did was meet with two Lockeport doctors. I explained how I had many elderly people in my pastoral care. I asked them to co-ordinate the specialists' appointments. Whenever five or so appointments could be made together, I would take them all at the same time with one trip.

There are things that maybe a pastor doesn't need to do, but I knew it was part of my ministry to check in on the well-being of these elderly people. When I took them to Halifax, I also had to make sure they didn't leave the premises. If I left one group at the Victoria General Hospital, I would instruct them to wait there for my return. Some would also go to the infirmary, some to Dartmouth General Hospital, some to the Medical Professional Building, then I must collect each of them. The LTD was doing its job. Other pastors wondered why I gave myself this kind of trouble when it was unrelated to my work. I knew it was related.

These older people were happy with the help and the attention. There came a time when I could not leave the house before 8 a.m., for I would need to have my calls from all these people telling me they were OK this morning. They were so close that they felt I should know. I told the children not to touch the phone before 8 a.m. I would have a half-dozen calls or more each morning. Most of them were just saying, "I'm OK today." "Now we don't care about our children, they can stay in Alberta."

God can reveal ministries we don't learn about in theological school, by observing the needs, having initiative, and putting faith into practice.

In January, 1983, João presented to Lockeport's town council a proposal to offer free counselling service to its citizens. The letter of proposal cited his training and fifteen years' experience in the field of counselling—to hospital staff, students and patients; the aged; divorcees; emotionally disturbed persons; the mentally ill and retarded; the lonely; parents; gangs; juvenile offenders; runaway youth; retired persons and single adults; widows and widowers. This proposal was greeted with enthusiasm, accepted, and appreciated. Those who took advantage of the service included persons with other church affiliations and others with no links to church life at all.

The unique environment of a fishing village

Most fishermen of this pastorate did not attend church. The Sunday before the opening of the fishing season for lobster, their Pastor, Brother John, issued a special invitation for all lobster fishermen to come to church. They would hold a special service. For this occasion he secured a suit of oilskins, and that was the garb in which he preached. It had never been done before. This pastor's identifying with the fishermen was genuine rather than artificial, and through the identification he established his credibility.

Getting Samuel and Edward out of the Congo

During this period in Lockeport, the Matwawana family in Canada was chasing down all options in their desire to reunite with Samuel and Edward, still in the Congo. They were even giving consideration to dividing the family, with Nora going to Congo to be with the older sons, João remaining in Canada with the younger children. However, in 1983, Edward was successful in coming to Canada as a landed immigrant. Samuel was refused because he was over twenty-one. He could not understand, "Edward is chosen over me." Samuel felt rejected.

The son of Pastor Mavungu, a prominent Congolese Baptist leader, was in the United States. Edward wrote him on Samuel's behalf, inquiring whether Sam might get admission to the USA as a student.

Sam was losing weight. The parents were alarmed—convinced that weight loss came from anxiety and a sense of rejection by his family. The Matwawanas continued exploring possibilities. One day, in the middle of this, a packet of papers arrived from the USA, application forms from a school there, with various requirements, including the need to obtain a letter of recommendation from someone resident in the States.

João and Nora had known Dr. Steve and Stella Price in Nova Scotia. In fact, João's first contact with them, through Baptist churches, was even before Nora arrived in Canada. Having moved to the USA, they were now working in the Boston area. "Out of the blue," (João's words), a letter came announcing that Dr. Price would be coming to Yarmouth, NS, to conduct a seminar and workshop on abortion. Could they meet?

"How are you?"
"Not well, we have all this anxiety over Samuel, still in the Congo."
"What's the nature of your problem?"
"We have nobody to do a recommendation letter for Sam's admission to study in Boston."

Dr. Steve Price assumed that responsibility. He returned to Massachusetts, and in a very short time Samuel had his visa to the United States. Now that he had his visa and his admission, the question to be faced was where he would stay, for he knew nobody in Boston, or so he thought.

In July, the assistant clerk in their church in Lockeport received two visitors from Massachusetts who came to worship. João greeted them, and said:

"Our son, Samuel, will soon be coming to Boston and I will go there to welcome him, but I don't know where to put him."
"You will find him at our place."

When Sam arrived in Boston, that whole family welcomed him at Logan airport and kept him until João arrived from Lockeport. With little latitude on how long he could stay in Boston, and with no connections, João had to settle for placing Samuel in a very expensive apartment for one month. Samuel began with studies to improve his English.

When Samuel arrived in Boston, he carried a letter to Paulo Tuba, a relative of João's, from his wife in the Congo, who was facing a caesarean section for the delivery of their child. Samuel didn't know Paulo Tuba, and wondered how he would be able to locate him in Boston. After inquiries, he located the address, delivered the letter, and met Paulo Tuba, who recognized the rather unique family name Matwawana.

"Your father has been here in Boston?"
"Yes, he was here this month."
"I know your father. My own father and his father, your grandfather, Zakuadia, are cousins. If I had known you were here, we could have arranged more reasonable housing for you."

"He's coming back again in August...."

At the end of August, João and Nora planned to drive to Boston. The church at Lockeport heard they were driving and took exception to so much time on the highway. They chipped in for tickets so Nora, Isabel, and João could fly to Boston. They arrived and stayed with Sam, who was, at that point, still in the expensive apartment.

João knew Paulo Tuba well but they had lost touch. Neither knew the other was in North America. That trip made the connection. Tuba remembered that when his father was dying at IME Kimpese, all his family lived in the Matwawana house there. He also knew his father was a cousin to João's father. This implied a certain responsibility to help Sam. "If we knew you were struggling we would have helped earlier."

Costa lived in the same apartment building with Paulo Tuba. He was an Angolan who had been in Kinshasa. Paulo Tuba arranged for Samuel to rent space with Costa, who had fewer children and more space. Beginning the following month, Samuel slept in Costa's apartment but ate meals in the Paulo Tuba apartment. Step by step, the concerns relating to Samuel and Edward were being diminished, lifting loads from the shoulders of their parents in Nova Scotia.

Paulo was working in Boston as a supply teacher but also carried a watchman's job at night. He arranged for Samuel to work as a watchman, as well. This meant that Samuel could pay part of his rent and school fees.

Samuel Matwawana was one of the students who benefited, in two separate years, from assistance through the Angola Memorial Scholarship Fund, for which he and his parents were most grateful. While in Massachusetts on that occasion, João and Nora met with Dr. Steve Price, as well. He offered to oversee Samuel's medical needs and in their generosity, Steve and Stella also contributed toward Samuel's expenses, recognizing that he was serious in his studies and headed toward a degree program.

After that first month of language study, Samuel advanced to Roxbury College, which in one year, prepared him for his serious studies. The following year, he advanced to the Wentworth Institute of Technology, where he earned his Bachelor of Science degree, specializing in electronics.

The Matwawanas were very aware that God had opened door after door, and lifted many of the loads they had been carrying.

Edward's Bond with a Kindly Deacon

Edward arrived in Canada from the Congo in 1983, and at Lockeport he was still struggling to master English. Deacon Hamilton of the Ragged Island congregation was a dedicated person, kindly and helpful in all matters, and it seemed that he was always around the church, helping in one way or another. A special bond developed between Edward and the deacon, who was patient in listening to whatever he was trying to say. Edward came to consider Deacon Hamilton his Canadian grandfather.

In this context, prominent visitors arrived from Angola. Pastor José Agostinho of Cabinda and Pastor Daniel Zau of Soyo were in Canada to confer with Canadian Baptist Ministries, and they paid a visit to the Matwawana family in Lockeport. A younger helper was travelling with them. Charles Harvey of CBM was accompanying these special guests. An opportunity like this was not to be missed. With so much to talk about, they would be up much of the night, so all invitations to have the guests hosted with congregation members were declined. Mattresses would be spread on the floor, to extend visiting time to its maximum.

A pot luck supper in honor of the visitors was held in the Ragged Island church. João and Nora hurried away afterward to set up sleeping arrangements, while one group of young people continued discussions with Daniel Zau, another group with José Agostinho. When Charles and the guests arrived back at the parsonage, the parents discovered that Edward was still missing, so they phoned the church:

"Don't worry about Edward, we saw him talking with his grandfather. He will certainly bring Ed home to you later."

The following morning, Charles Harvey and the guests continued their travels, and João and Nora were mulling over all the Angolan news they had heard, when another deacon phoned with shocking news. Deacon Hamilton had just passed away in the night from a massive heart attack. The last person he had been speaking with was Edward.

At the funeral I was unable to control the flow of tears over the passing of this beloved man who had become a surrogate grandfather to our own son, and Edward had been with him at the very end.

That visit by the Angolan elders to Lockeport was especially significant to João, because Daniel Zau had been his colleague at Calambata. Daniel and José were prominent leaders in CBM's partner denomination, *Igreja Evangélica de Angola*. Shortly thereafter a telegram from Angola informed him, and the Lockeport churches, of the tragic drowning of Pastor Daniel Zau along with other pastors, crossing the river to a conference. The dangerous eddies and whirlpools created by the mighty Zaire River where it empties into the Atlantic trapped and sank their motorized launch. The loss of such valued leadership was a staggering blow to Angolan churches.

Resignation from Pastoral Ministry at Lockeport

The overriding family concern which led Rev. João Matwawana's to resign from the pastorate at Lockeport and Ragged Island was clearly a concern for their children's education. They would need to live near an urban centre where the children could live at home and pursue their studies. The churches João was pastoring clearly wished for a continuation of his loving and productive ministry in their midst. During his time with them, the attendance at Lockeport went from fifteen to over fifty, and at Osborne, from twenty-five to eighty or ninety. However, it was time to move on:

I said to the people that it was time for them and time for us to make a move...and we did.

12

PRISON CHAPLAINCY AT THE HALIFAX CORRECTIONAL CENTRE

FAMILY DECISION TIME

The move from Lockeport to a larger urban centre was a difficult emotional struggle for João and Nora, as it was for the two congregations. The Matwawana family was facing a time of transition in 1984. Their children were approaching college age. It would be important to live near Universities, otherwise costs would be prohibitive. They deliberated whether they should move to Montreal or Halifax.

One day I was called and given information that there was an opening for a new chaplain's position for the Metropolitan Halifax Authority, sponsored by the inter-faith committee. Dr. Charles Taylor of Acadia was aware of this and Rev. Jim Chang of Dartmouth, as well. Both were aware of our need to move from Lockeport. They also noticed that the requirements fit well for me. They wanted a clergyman with pastoral experience and experience as a chaplain, with some course work in pas-

toral care. They encouraged me to apply. I sent an application and a day was set for interviews. When I went there I discovered that we were twelve applying and I was the only black. They asked some questions. One of the questions was, "How can you feel the suffering of an inmate? Have you experienced suffering in your life?"

I am an inmate myself. I'm not in my own country and I cannot go back to my country, otherwise I might be shot in the head. For twenty years I have been cut off from my people. I feel like an inmate. I have been made a refugee twice.

"What kind of experience have you had with inmates?"
João gave them the story of his practical work at the prison in Springhill, while studying at Acadia. He noticed that the team interviewing him were looking at each other indicating maybe he was the right person. Before he left the interview he said:

"Excuse me. If you have any answer to me, I have a big family I need to move. I have to know in advance."
"You can't tell us what to do."
"Sorry."

Immediately, worry set in. Had he been too aggressive, spoiling this good opportunity? Probably he should not have mentioned his personal family deadline. He came out of the interview very disappointed, kicking himself:

I got to Bridgewater all uptight. I stopped to eat something. When I arrived home, Nora asked how the interview went.
"Terrible."
"Why?"
"The interview went well, but at the end I made a stupid move, pressing them to decide quickly. I think that turned them off, and I think I lost the job."
Nora was smiling.

"You got the job."
"What?"
"They called here asking for you. I told them you were still on the road. They asked for your social insurance number and told me that my husband got the job."
I couldn't believe it.

HALIFAX CORRECTIONAL CENTRE

The Halifax Correctional Centre is a provincial institution for prisoners serving terms up to a maximum of two years less one day. Those with longer terms are sent to Federal institutions. The prison population used to be weighted toward the younger set, but with the *Young Offenders' Act* the younger ones have been separated and placed in different institutions. As a result, this particular prison had inmates from eighteen to thirty and older.

An overwhelming number of inmates are alcoholics and drug abusers. Many started drinking at about eleven years of age. Some of these kids are the product of unstable families, some are victims of a series of placements in foster homes, and they are often people with a poor education. They try to get a job, they are unsuccessful, they get frustrated and they attach themselves to groups.

There were those who came to my chaplaincy office seeking an interview, and it would turn out that what they really wanted was help in filling out a job application, because they were unable to do it on their own. They might try, but would find it hard, never having been through that experience. One could see how low their level of education was, and how difficult it would be for them to get a job if they couldn't fill out a simple application. One could sense that this person should be treated differently, even in the process of finding a job.

Female offenders made up another category. The Halifax Correctional Centre was the only prison in Nova Scotia that provided a facility for women. João served as chaplain to both men and women. Women made up about 4 percent of the inmates, and they were held in a separate part of the prison, with no communication between the two parts.

> *Unfortunately the women in prison are difficult to minister to. After long incarceration they get lazy, sitting around, playing cards, watching TV and mostly doing nothing. They get in the habit of sleeping through the day and they reject anything that requires some element of self-discipline. This would include education or religious attendance, or even social activities. "I'm not interested." Then they sit back.*

Origins of this chaplaincy ministry

In Halifax, Baptists, Anglicans, the United Church of Canada, and Roman Catholics work together in certain projects through the Metropolitan Halifax Inter-Faith Committee. They persuaded the Halifax Metro authority to hire a full-time chaplain for a period of three years. As a result of that request, João was hired by the Metro authority as the first full-time, paid chaplain in that institution. The takeover of all prisons by the province of Nova Scotia in April, 1986, meant that the chaplain's position became a permanent position under the new structure:

> *So, after three years I automatically became an employee of the Province of Nova Scotia, even prior to the three-year evaluation established by the Metro Commission to evaluate whether to continue the chaplaincy project.*

There was clearly trauma involved in the switch from the pastoral responsibility that João had carried in Lockeport to the prison chaplaincy. First, he had lost his support system. Studies indicate that within five years, chaplains who do not have a support system either fall sick or deteriorate spiritually. He also sensed a vulnerability in being a provincial employee, without any measure of job security, especially at the outset. Then there were the frustrations of working within the framework of a government bureaucracy.

At the outset João was on church support, even though he was serving with a provincial institution. It was arranged with the two cities of Halifax and Dartmouth and they were monitoring all his work, but with no assurance that the chaplaincy would continue. It was a trial project. When the Province of Nova Scotia assumed responsibility for his salary, this came as a solid affirmation of the work he had been doing. His position became a permanent one, but it fell short of providing the sense of security that had been associated with the support of his inter-faith committee. He was not a member of the union that protected employment security for the guards. His position was vulnerable, because the government would be free to cut that service at any time if they found the need to save some budget money. He also discovered that a chaplain's freedom is limited. When serving under the Metro committee, João reported straight to the prison superintendent. Under the new provincial arrangement, he found much red tape. He could not reach the Superintendent. He had to go instead to a coordinator of programs appointed by the Department of Justice or the Department of Correctional Services.

Then he discovered that this coordinator of programs was a young woman who didn't even attend church. How could such a person coordinate the chaplain's work, if she knows nothing about church or about religion? She got the job and she had to do it. To João this seemed like an insult to his training and his experience, "but that is how the government works." The only thing assured was his salary. João did not care for the new structure. After some friction, he sat down with the new coordinator:

"Please defer to me," she requested.
"You have to be honest and acknowledge that they put you in a difficult situation, asking you to supervise something which you don't know about. I know how you feel."
She admitted that.
"Look João, I don't know what you are doing. As long as you give me your report, I will not be harsh on you." In the end that arrangement worked out OK.

João Matwawana's role as chaplain

The first component of João's role as chaplain was to provide the daily presence of Christian witness, and that included bringing in standards of morality. The second was to provide pastoral care to the staff as well as to the inmates of the Halifax Correctional Centre. A wide variety of circumstances could lead to calls for his services. These might include the illness of a prisoner, the illness of relatives, which of course could be upsetting to one who was not free to visit them, or perhaps a death in the family. In those situations, he undertook to comfort the inmate in relation to the loved one outside. There were also emergency situations such as suicide attempts.

Chaplaincy work cannot be sectarian. Sometimes the inmate of a family member desires to see a clergy person of the inmates's own faith. Someone else might mention being a Roman Catholic, and that although João's ministry was appreciated, they would like to see a priest. João would arrange for that, setting up a time, and clearing security with the prison authorities so that clergy could come in for purposes of ministry. He coordinated all religious activities, including both worship and Bible Study inside, but also including pastoral care coming from outside. Rabbis came in to minister to Jewish inmates.

The 1984 Matwawana family letter of Christmas greetings sheds light on João's perception of his role as chaplain:

Every day I am reminded of the truth that counselling is not really the handing out of advice. It requires listening, accepting, and guiding the person to their own solution of a problem. I also realize that the more patiently a chaplain can listen without directing, the more able he will be to understand. When it is clear that he accepts people as they are, loving and caring for them, they will seek him out.

Why should churches be involved in chaplaincy ministries? The church is biblically called to a ministry of reconciliation (2 Corinthians 5:18), and Jesus specifically refers to caring for those in prison (Matthew 25:39-40). He indicates that by caring for them *is how we minister to* Him.

GETTING TO KNOW INDIVIDUALS AND THEIR NEEDS

How would he get to know the need of each individual inmate? The process started with an initial interview. Every new inmate would be interviewed by the chaplain right after registration, picture taking, and the issuing of a uniform, even before getting to see his cell:

When he comes to me (and you'll remember my comments on being asked to help fill out a job application), his conversation will indicate to me the kind of need he has. That initial interview was a time of great tension. Many inmates told me after going through much humiliation that the only thing they heard along the way was cursing. Sometimes the guards are less than human, seeing no human side to inmates. They treat them like animals, without respect. So the victims of this treatment lose hope.
"I'm in hell. I've never met anything good since coming through that door."
Inmates are frequently cursed as they enter, cursed as they get their number and their picture taken. Suddenly they are sent to the chaplain.

Each newly arrived inmate received a personal message from the chaplain:

"My name is João Matwawana
I would like to extend my friendly welcome to you.
If you wish to talk with someone who cares, please do not hesitate to come and see me.
My office is located near the chapel.
Although I am the chaplain for the Halifax Country Correctional Centre, and wish to help your spiritual life, I am also available as a friend."

Initiating change in prison policy

Initially I was told that the door to my office must remain open, and that the guard had to stay beside the inmate during the interview.

This was a regulation that had to be changed. The regulation militated against any relationship of trust. He insisted that he would not allow a guard to be in his office while conducting these interviews:

My ministry is different from that of other officers. I have to be alone. The individuality and privacy of the inmate has to be respected.

This insistence was not welcomed with grace. João found that he also was being cursed. "You will be killed there, and we won't care. On the day you are stabbed or taken hostage, don't call!"

No matter, that is my job. But I want to be sure that the inmate is given the freedom to share. No matter what crime has been committed, this person is a human being.

This door to his chaplain's office was a solid door, without a window. The guard could not see in. Authorities finally accepted, and agreed that guards would not intervene. The conclusion reached by inmates was that during their entire ordeal, the only time they were allowed to be human beings was when they came to João's office, where they were treated as a person. In that context, to hear someone say, "*Please* sit down," was like a miracle. They no longer expected to hear *please*. This had a calming effect and a conversation would begin. The story would come out about what led to this imprisonment. Invariably the inmate's life story would unfold.

I felt that I was always able to get through to the real situation.

They trusted me that I would not reveal their confidences.

After having held the interview and completing the forms, I knew the need of the individual and I would follow through accordingly.

From time to time João gave out literature or assigned a study or set up courses.

Prison Atmosphere and the Chaplain's Influence

The men and women I encountered were hurting, depressed, lonely, and frustrated with the system. They were in pain. A chaplain in the prison, especially one on a full-time basis, spending all day there, reduces the tensions and reduces the level of violence. The chaplain is seen as a father. When he is there, they feel safer. The chaplain is perceived as a witness, reducing the degree of abuse by the guards.

Most of the time, when I would return after an absence, there would be the report of some fights. Sometimes the guards allow them to fight, thinking that the more prisoners hate each other, the safer it will be for them.

The chaplain is the one person who can approach an inmate with no hidden agenda. Everyone else has an agenda. The chaplain needs to assure inmates that they are not forgotten. This is especially true for the many who are innocent. Only the chaplain knows how many are innocent in a prison. Some people are arrested not because they commit a crime but because they were in the wrong place at the wrong time. That is particularly true of those who have a criminal record. The police just pick them up.
"We know you, don't say anything. We're looking a for a suspect here."
They have no need to go farther. Many people are picked up like that because they have a bad record and are found at the wrong time in the wrong place.

At the beginning a chaplain can be fooled, deceived. As the years go by, one gains experience and they know they can no longer deceive you. Prisoners feel that they are victims of injustice. One of the weaknesses of prisoners is that only a few can accept personal responsibility for what they have done.

One has to work hard to get the prisoner to accept responsibility for a crime committed. The prisoner needs a close friend. Normally that is to be found only in the chaplain or the prison volunteer. A listener is needed, one who can wisely and lovingly question without a judgmental attitude. I discovered that it would only be a very rare occurrence where a term in prison actually changed anybody. Prisoners were so ill-treated that they became more hardened and more angry. If the person didn't really accept the Lord in prison and have his life changed, then this person is worse than when he came in, because the prison facility, the prison experience, does not rehabilitate. Rather, prisons recycle criminals and produce more educated criminals.
Even those who are not confirmed criminals, once they get into prison, come into contact with the hard core inmates. The penal system does not accomplish what it is established to do. It trains people to be worse.

The delegation from Block D

João was surprised one day by the arrival at his Chaplain's office of an unsolicited committee of prisoners from Block D:

"We want to steal a car for you."
"We're tired of seeing our chaplain drive around in a junky old LTD."
"All we need is your licence plate, you pay nothing."
"We have the car picked out, and we're ready to move."

Some projects do not have a long life. João just kicked them out of his office, and did not report the incident to the officials.

Canada

Volunteers

After some time it became evident that the ministry was growing and that João could not do all that needed to be done alone, so he contacted the local churches for assistance, especially those in Bedford, Dartmouth, Halifax, and Sackville. The churches responded. Volunteers participated in a visitation program that provided an opportunity to translate their faith into concrete actions of love. These volunteers were mature people, both men and women. Because the prison atmosphere is radically different from that of society at large, it was necessary to set up an intense training program to orient them. João organized courses for prison volunteers who, after six months of training, would be able to give him practical assistance. He ran these courses right there in the prison setting, because of the importance of exposing the trainees to the realities of prison life. They came once or twice weekly for six months, and for this they were given a certificate. They would then lead group discussions and conduct counselling. These trained volunteers filled the gap. João perceived them as an extension of himself and his activities in the area of pastoral care, expanding his possibilities for providing personalized listening and compassion to individual inmates.

Prison chaplains become painfully aware that they are working alone. They lack an appropriate consultation network, and João was very aware of his need for a prayer support network, which does not readily appear for most chaplains. There is a lack of feedback to shape one's ideas.

In my case it was Dr. Charlie Taylor of Acadia who modified my situation by suggesting that the use of volunteers would bring me a breath of fresh air. He impressed on me the importance of their assistance, even though their orientation and preparation would be time-consuming. They would make mistakes and they would break some of the rules, but he insisted that I needed volunteers at a time when I didn't think that I did. He was right.

The Range of Demands and Expectations

Being the only chaplain, João was expected to serve people of all faiths. It was important to note that the volunteers who trained to help him were drawn from several denominations in the Metro Halifax area. João worked in co-operation with all the clergy who wished to minister to their own members who were incarcerated. The Halifax County United Baptist Association of Churches was the only denomination which financially sponsored a part of the volunteer training program They did this through their Social Action Committee.

I discovered there were a lot of limitations which forced the chaplain to be humble, flexible, and cooperative with the captain on duty.

Prison administrative ranks included the Superintendent, the Captain, the Sergeant, and below them, the wards. The Captain would readily cancel the chapel service or change the time of it because of security reasons. When he chooses to do so, the chaplain has no recourse to appeal.

That demands a lot of humility. You put your announcement at the central. "Chapel time in five minutes" will be announced over the public address system. Then two minutes later the P.A. system announces: "Chapel service is cancelled. Chapel service is cancelled." The authorities may come and explain to the chaplain about the situation, but it is a shock nevertheless when one is all ready with a sermon.

Or then it might happen that I would leave everything and go to see the Captain.
"What's wrong?"
"Apparently someone from one block was going to attack a prisoner from another block at chapel time."

The administration have their security people and their informers. Instead of instructing one or two inmates not to go to chapel, and to avoid the need to tell them why, the chapel service is simply cancelled. And then they undertake an interrogation....

The prison chaplain must be extremely flexible to operate under circumstances where snap decisions must be accepted and cannot be questioned. The chaplain must trust the captain on duty and maintain a friendly stance toward him. Security being the number one concern in a prison, the chaplain ranks at the very bottom of the hierarchy. The prison's attitude is that security is definitely top priority. If something shows signs of going wrong, they don't care if a communion service or a marriage is cancelled. The chaplain and his work are tolerated but they don't come first. In secret, however, the officials may admit that tensions are lower when the chaplain is around.

Evaluating those years of chaplaincy ministry, João feels satisfied and fulfilled as he considers the degree to which his objectives were reached. He was able to offer pastoral care. He was able to announce the good news of Christ's gospel. He found joy in seeing some inmates make a decision for Christ and in witnessing the changes in their lives. Some have been released, some remain inside.

The Metro volunteer program in retrospect was a very real asset. When people were released and went out, I could be sure that they would meet somebody who would help them in follow-up. The chaplaincy program and the volunteer program both continue to the present.

A Roman Catholic deacon came to be João's assistant. He took over from João and continues until the present. He was very helpful, and João recommended his appointment.

Launching the Matwawana Peace Manifesto

It was during his period of chaplaincy service that João Matwawana, always conscious of responsibility for the well-being of Angola as the country of his birth, launched his peace manifesto. His struggle at the time was to create an interest in and an acceptance of the manifesto, without compromising himself with one or another of the conflicting parties in Angola's internal struggles.

The manifesto was the embodiment of João's hopes for how the process of reconciliation and nation-building might begin. The document was forwarded to a number of recipients, emphasizing the author's neutral stance. He was approached by each of the major political parties, in turn, with overtures asking that he commit himself to their party, their program. Without exception he declined each of these opportunities. The most frequent requests came from Holden Roberto and his FNLA party, but he was also approached by the others.

Shortly after these approaches to João were made by MPLA and UNITA, the two parties undertook discussions that led to the signing of an accord in Bicesse, Portugal, in May 1991. On hearing this news, João wrote letters of congratulations to both parties, reasserting his neutral stance. It emerged that João's manifesto was destined not to go anywhere at that time, for it could not be implemented as long as a state of war prevailed. Its requirements included peace and the ability to travel about in Angola. João chose to remain consistent with his own ideals rather than make changes in the manifesto to adapt to the circumstances. In striving to reach out to the spectrum of Angolan society, his proposal exists in Portuguese, French, English, Umbundu, and Kikongo. It appears as an appendix to this book in its original form.

COMMUNICATIONS FROM ANGOLAN POLITICIANS WHILE SERVING AS PRISON CHAPLAIN

Life holds many surprises. Among those João experienced at Halifax was a series of contacts with Angolans. From France, Johnny Edward Pinnock wrote asking if he could locate a hymnal in Kikongo.

Then there were a series of long-distance phone calls to him at his work number in care of the Halifax Correctional Services.

The first long distance call from Holden Roberto to Nova Scotia had actually come while they were still at Lockeport. Nora took one such call when João was away. Holden, the leader of Angola's FNLA party was calling from France. A second call came through to João in person. João wondered whether it was even appropriate for them to be in phone contact, in the light of his deliberate resolve to maintain a political neutrality that would allow access to all Angolans when the time became right. "Did you hear what is happening in Angola? Maybe the time is right for you to take part." Holden was laying plans for a leadership congress.

Remember, I have a full time job, I'm not a refugee receiving rations. I'm salaried, and working as a prison chaplain. I would need to request time off even to make a short visit. What would you think of my son, Edward, going to represent me?

That did not work out. Although João declined the invitation, Holden maintained the contact and called from time to time.

He was also contacted by each of the other political entities in Angola, which by this time had eclipsed Holden and his FNLA. It was vital to the integrity of his Peace Manifesto that João remain entirely neutral of any political party affiliation.

Each of the three major political parties made serious attempts to recruit João Matwawana to its ranks and to its cause, especially when there were prospects of elections on the horizon in 1992. MPLA and UNITA each carried the firm conviction that he could only be effective if he were to link up with them, and each told him so. He resisted that temptation, and in the long run was proven right in his conviction and in his unflinching neutral stand.

After UNITA representatives in Washington received his peace manifesto, in October of 1990, João received a direct phone call at the prison from Ernesto Mulato, on behalf of Jonas Savimbi and UNITA. "I really think you should be in UNITA...." He implied that no other context would offer João a comparable platform for pursuing his peace initiatives. This is the person who was appointed in 2004 to the post of Vice President of UNITA. Ernesto Joaquim Mulato was born near the BMS mission at Bembe. In that phone conversation, the content of João's manifesto was part of the discussion. Mulatto pointed out some of the articles in the manifesto that he thought needed to be changed. He did not appreciate part three of the rationale segment, feeling it did not give appropriate respect to partisans. Furthermore, he was unable to really believe João's affirmation of neutrality:

"Why do you question my neutrality?"
"We find it hard to believe that you are not in league with Holden."

This specific representative of Savimbi was from Northern Angola and even spoke with João in Kikongo.

"When the revolution started it was OK to follow Holden, but now a man like you must think in the bigger picture. Elections are coming. Remember that we appreciate you and we know that now all the missionaries are gone, you are our Reverend."

Those calls created a lot of stress for me. They were something like contraband in the prison setting, calls from people unrelated to my assignment.

Sometimes Holden called for advice on various matters, especially relating to his international contacts. This was becoming stressful. How could I put a stop to it? Everybody wanted to recruit me. Both MPLA and UNITA contacted me officially as well as other small parties that were forming, who wished to have me on board as one of their elders.

That's when I was invited to go to Angola. Ambassador Pedro Pacavira called me on behalf of the MPLA government. I had just recently launched my peace manifesto. He was Angola's ambassador to the United Nations in New York. Visitors were being received at a house in New Jersey. The MPLA party was recruiting the best elements of FNLA for insertion into MPLA. They included me in that list, the very purpose for them calling me.

I had doubts and did not accept the invitation. There was a confusion of voices calling me, each to accept their cause. Had I accepted any one of the invitations, it would have prejudiced the *work that I am doing these days following my retirement. It was attractive at the time to link up with somebody, but I did not.*

It was especially tempting during the lead-up to that first election. The peace had been signed at Bicesse, in Portugal, on May 31, 1991. It seemed that nothing could go wrong. The appeals to me at that time were very attractive, but would have turned out to be a snare. The date was set for holding elections. At that time the Cubans were still a significant force in Angola, but everything was in place for elections. There was no reason to suspect that anything would go wrong. Everybody knew UNITA would win because they had more people. But the way it was set up, it wasn't a case of the number of who could gain a majority of votes, rather the winner was determined by the number of seats in Parliament.

MPLA wanted João to boost their campaign. "We need ten days from you of intensive campaigning in the north." It was all presented to him in a plan. He should fly to New York:

"From New York all is paid. You will be cared for by the Government of Angola. You fly via Portugal to Luanda, where a hotel is reserved. You travel by presidential jet to northern Angola. We want you to speak about peace and UNITY the way you do it. The people will listen to you because they know you. After ten days, if you want to return, we bring you back to Nova Scotia by the same route."

One of the hitches was that João inquired about taking Nora. On that topic he was turned down immediately and abruptly, which raised questions in his mind. Was something not right? Nothing developed.

SOCIAL AWARENESS WITH RESPECT TO NOVA SCOTIA'S BLACK COMMUNITY

During his time of life and ministry in Nova Scotia, Rev. João Matwawana was socially aware of the Canadian context in which he lived while still carrying an emotional burden for his beloved Angola. That awareness later expanded even more when retirement provided the time and the opportunity. His memberships over the years have included:

- His position as a board member of ALARM, African Leadership Reconciliation Ministries.
- His role as founder of NFRA, National Fellowship for the Reconciliation of Angola.
- SAANS, Southern African Association of Nova Scotia.
- CDVS, Centre for Diverse Visible Cultures, Halifax.

An Exploratory Visit to Africa

During his chaplaincy at Halifax, João remained in contact with Canadian Baptist Ministries, and in conversation with its executives, considering an eventual CBM assignment for them in Kivu. After all, the Matwawanas had already been through the formal appointment process prior to their fateful, abortive trip to Nairobi when they were deported for inadequate documentation. This time they would be able to travel on Canadian passports.

The advice of CBM's General Secretary, Bob Berry, was that João and Nora should not proceed with any firm plans until João had made an exploratory visit to both Kivu and to Kenya. Such a visit would give him a realistic look at prevailing conditions and help the family to assess conditions, as well as all the realities involved should their family move there to serve. That exploratory visit was set up for 1986. The itinerary included passage through Kinshasa en route to Kivu. From Goma in Kivu he would move on eastward to Nairobi and the homeward flight would be from there. When passing through Kinshasa he did a visit to Kimpese where he had served as Pastor and chaplain. When in Goma he was taken for a visit to Bwatsinge, their place of assignment.

Dramatic Events at Kimpese

Upon his arrival in the Congo, João was met in Kinshasa by Charles Harvey, CBM missionary. João cashed a forty-dollar traveller's cheque, but could never have guessed the use to which the money would be applied. With Charles he travelled the three or so hours by road to Kimpese, territory so familiar to João.

At Kimpese a vast gathering was arranged to welcome the return of the pastor who had been their hospital chaplain and so much more. Hospital director Mandiangu's preparations had insured that this became an important event. When the service finished, a crowd of people followed João and the Harveys back to the CBM residence which is on the same IME compound. Friends, family, and visitors extended the conversations well into the night.

Frances Harvey had retired for the night. Charles was in his office. João was in the front room counselling his nephew and fiancée who were preparing for marriage. The screen door was unlocked and the main door was open.

I saw two young men at the door, and although I did not recognize them I called to them, "Come on in, join the party." They did. Although the two I had first seen carried no guns, the masked group that rushed in with them were armed and aggressive. We found ourselves in a situation that invited panic, but that's when certain training received at Halifax Correctional Services came into play. They had taught us how to react under hostage-taking conditions, which are not uncommon in prison experience. So I began to smile.
"Why are you smiling?"
"I know you are desperate and need money."
"Yes. So?"
"I have some money to give you."
"Since you promise us money we will leave you alone."

At that point they turned their focus on the others in the house. We noted that they spoke very good French, at least one of them, but they might not speak English. I called out in English to Frances in her bedroom, saying there were thieves, but that she should remain there, quiet.

The bandits were convinced that the cash offering from the large service at the church would have come back with us to this house, even though that was not the case. It's that cash that they were after.
"Where do you keep the church money?"
They insisted on a search of the house. Charlie told them he had just come back from Kinshasa, and his briefcase was there at hand. They could open it to see, and take everything.
"We're not stupid, how would we cash those cheques? We want cash."

So the search of the house continued. They took cash that the Harveys had on hand, some was personal, some for paying workers and some for refugee relief. We had been copying music from one cassette player to another, they took both machines. I had a good camera of my own for slides, and had borrowed one to take the black and white photos CBM had requested. Both cameras were taken, and a dozen films. They gathered some other items. They brought Frances out of the bedroom and forced her to give them the gold wedding ring from her finger.
"You yourself promised us money."
"Yes, and I didn't forget." I gave them the forty dollars I had cashed in Kinshasa.

At this point João slipped off his own wedding ring and slid it along the floor to a place where it would not be seen. The intruders turned their attention to wristwatches, and João said, "Here, take my watch."

"We don't want your watch, we want the white man's watch."

Obviously these people did not know Charles Harvey, who comments with glee that he had never paid more than 20 or 30 dollars for a watch in his life. They would have done far better to go with João's good Seiko!

Fortunately these entrepreneurs did not concentrate on the guest room where João's suitcase had been slipped, providentially, under the bed. It contained his passport, money, and other documentation. They missed it entirely. He would not have welcomed a second attempt at entering Kenya with temporary documentation!

The sentinel left at the door had doubts about João. Why did he keep on smiling? Was he armed? He had his colleagues frisk this person who behaved so differently from what they expected, but they found nothing. As the uninvited visitors wound down their activities they focussed on getaway plans. They cut the telephone line.

"We have a lot of stuff here, we need a vehicle."

Both sets of keys were there in evidence. They decided to take the Land Rover rather than the little car. Then they forced the five adults into the master bedroom, planning to lock them in, and warning them not to make a rumpus.

"Where is the room key?" (It hadn't been seen for years, but the bedroom doorknob had a pushbutton lock on the inside).

"We have no key in here, but the door is locked, you can try it." (This with a smile.)

Even after the sound of the vehicle's departure they dared not come out for a while, not knowing if someone was left behind to insure that they were not trailed. After an interval the hospital compound sentinels (unarmed of course) made their appearance. "The thieves have gone." They were dispatched to inform hospital superintendent Mandiangu.

The Land Rover was eventually found by the roadside in the Matadi area, stripped of its wheels and more. Fortunately it was reported to the police, and was eventually returned to its owner. It had been used in a bold and successful armed robbery of a church-related credit union, pulled off in broad daylight.

"That was my first experience in Congo after ten years in Canada." Welcome back to the realities of suffering Africa, João.

The Outcome of that Exploratory Visit to Africa

The results of João's exploratory visit to Africa in 1986 were positive, but not felt immediately. They still needed time to prepare themselves spiritually for their African service, and a time in which he prepared the Correctional Services for that move which they were convinced would never happen. Why would one take a cut in salary to become a missionary? How could someone miss a solid opportunity to top off his pension plan? There were dynamics at work and there was a call to return to Africa which officials in the Nova Scotia Correctional Services were not equipped to understand.

PART FOUR

The Great Lakes Region of Central Africa

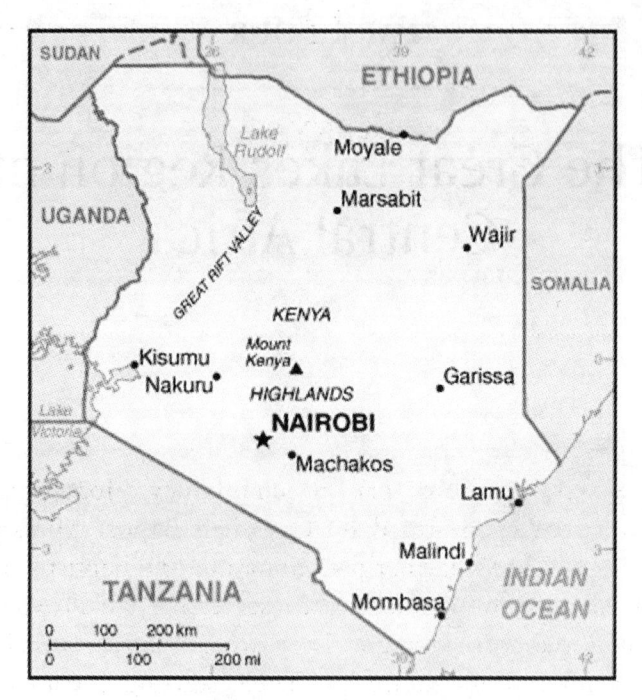

Kenya

13

KENYA

After resigning from prison chaplaincy, João and Nora Matwawana were reconfirmed by Canadian Baptist Ministries, and appointed (with CBM's partner denomination, the Baptist Community in Central Africa), as missionaries to serve in Kivu Province of the Democratic Republic of Congo. They were finally on their way in August 1991, but only indirectly. Their starting point was to be Nairobi, Kenya, to learn yet another language.

Nora notes that by then she had a much clearer focus and purpose. She was ready to really enter into ministry, no longer carrying her concern about her sons. By then the children were mostly on their own, except Isabel, their youngest, who travelled to Kenya with them.

That delay prepared me a lot in many ways. I also continued to gather experience which prepared me well for the things that I was called to teach in the Congo. I can see, looking back, that even my employment, cleaning for the sisters at Mount Saint Vincent Mother House, was a useful part of that preparation.

Their beginnings in Nairobi, to gain proficiency in Kiswahili, allowed them, as well, to be in the same country as Isabel, enrolled at Rift Valley Academy, where she would finish her high school studies. By the end of that year, they were ready to move on into Kivu Province of the Democratic Republic of the Congo.

Teaching at the ABC Seminary in Mitaboni

Unable to proceed to Kivu due to political instability there, the Matwawanas accepted the invitation of Bishop Nathan Ngala and the African Brotherhood Church to teach at their Divinity School in Mitaboni. That compound is located an hour east of Nairobi, in Machakos District. Because Canadians had taught there previously, housing was available for the Matwawanas. They went right to work, with João teaching seminary students.

At first the Matwawanas were disappointed, which is natural. The goal of working in Kivu had been before them through the fall months of language study in Nairobi, and their faces were set toward their destination at Bwatsinge, which was their assigned residence in Kivu. In those fall months of 1991, language was mastered with much more facility than many other students experience, for two reasons. Kiswahili was the sixth working language for both João and Nora, and language acquisition skills are cumulative. Furthermore, Kiswahili (also referred to as Swahili) is a trade language, which developed from a combination of Arabic and African Bantu languages. Their mother tongue, Kikongo, belongs to that Bantu group of languages.

That disappointment appears to have disappeared early. Nora comments:

> *Our first five months at the Divinity School in Mitaboni will be unforgettable to both students and ourselves.... During our study of the thirteenth chapter of the Gospel of John, João asked the class what is the closest act a teacher should do to his Kenyan students, in place of washing their feet. Their answer was, "Make us a cup of tea this evening...."* That should be easy, João thought. However, he was very wrong. He didn't

know that to make tea for Kenyan students was a real job, as it is made differently, or that some students would drink more than three cups. But at the end we all enjoyed a wonderful evening. We will miss their smiles, friendship, prayers, and the beautiful singing.

Whereas João or Nora may have experienced disappointment over this assignment, which did not place them in Congo, neither the ABC leadership nor the students sensed any such disappointment. Their skills, experience, and gifts were welcomed with open arms. The immediate demands of the classroom provided an excellent context in which their recently acquired language found opportunity to gel and become part of their normal patterns of thinking and expression.

In May of '92, João and Nora were able to move on to Goma and then to their destination, Bwatsinge.

14

KIVU PROVINCE, DEMOCRATIC REPUBLIC OF THE CONGO

FIRST ARRIVAL AT BWATSINGE, KIVU PROVINCE

Travelling north from Goma to Bwatsinge, our friends moved through the tropical rainforest of the Ruwenzori mountains, referred to as "The Mountains of the Moon", in country popularized by Jane Goodall and her work with chimpanzees. En route, they passed through savanna grasslands that included Virunga National Park, and wound their way up the switchback roads above Virunga to Kanyabayonga, with its dense population. The road northward from Kanyabayonga to Butembo gives one the impression of winding along the rooftop of the world. At one point, the road along this narrow ridge is literally the watershed between two extensive catchment basins. Water from the west side of the road flows off to the left into tropical forests that stretch as far as the eye can see and beyond. This is the vast Congo basin, with its streams and rivers draining into the Atlantic. Rain falling on the other side of the road drains down to the watershed of the White Nile. This water winds northward, emptying into the Mediterranean. The region is strikingly beautiful, dense in human population as well as dense with wildlife, a recipe for conflict and ecological tragedy. The greatest concentration of hippopotamus in the world is found here in Kivu, in the headwaters of the Nile.

For approximately eight years, the pastoral leadership at Bwatsinge and the church members of the area had been praying specifically, by name, for the arrival of the Matwawanas.

On May 30 we started our historic trip to Bwatsinge. The roads were bad. On one occasion the truck went so slow that it took us two hours to travel only 15 kilometres. However, the road troubles were all forgotten by 3 p.m., when we saw a crowd of over 2,000 people waiting for our arrival. Many carried big banners printed with the welcome messages in three languages: French, Kiswahili, and Kinandi.

The welcome program lasted more than two hours. At the entrance of Bwatsinge we were asked to walk a half kilometre to the big musical program prepared for the occasion of our arrival. Different church groups presented dramas based on their particular ministries. These were followed by singing and speeches. We were given gifts of eggs, a goat, fruits, and much more. And flowers covered everything as a sign of warm welcome.... It was a royal welcome they gave us. To God be the glory.
(partners in mission Letter #16, Summer of 1992)

Once João and Nora arrived at Bwatsinge, they had little time for rest. Immediately in June they traveled north to Beni to attend the annual assembly of the *Communauté Baptiste au Centre de l'Afrique* (CBCA), where they were able to meet, among others, all of the fifteen pastors-at-large whose function was similar to that of bishops:

Our reception there was wonderful. After the Assembly we came back to settle into our home at Bwatsinge. But it didn't take long to realize how strange it was to be living in a rural setting. It was not easy to adjust to our extreme isolation. Our nearest shopping centre is Butembo, a drive of 4 to 5 hours. The other option is Goma, where our colleague [Connie Smith] works, and it takes between 6 and 7 hours to get there when the roads are dry. Mail arrives every three weeks, and it takes a month to reach us from Canada.

There are a number of advantages to living in Bwatsinge. First, it is so peaceful, which gives us an opportunity for study and meditation on the Word. We enjoy the fresh morning air and the wonderful mountain view. Our house sits on the highest point in the area, over 6,000 ft. above sea level. We are very comfortable with this new house and the final improvements are being made little by little.

(*partners in mission* Letter #16, Summer of 1992)

João and Nora plunged immediately into work, often travelling together in those early days, both of them as leaders in their own right, both with much to accomplish. That pattern of travel would only change when Nora began to expand her work with women. After that, João's travelling companion would be a Kivu colleague. From the outset, they experienced a high level of acceptance. The seminars and workshops were popular, receiving accolades from participants that this was just the sort of content they had been needing. As the programs developed, certificates of achievement were drawn up and issued to those who completed specified components of training.

Their seminars and workshops were tightly scheduled and their goal was to eventually cover the length and breadth of the CBCA sphere of influence, which stretched some 500 kilometres from Bukavu in the south to Beni in the north. That was in reality a great distance, considering the condition of the roads. They shared certain leadership responsibilities between them. Nora was the featured speaker at the annual church conference for women held at Kirumba, where they had nearly 400 women in attendance, along with some men who were designated "counsellors."

Patterns of work

The most concise summary of João's undertaking would be to call it Church Leadership Development. In his systematic coverage of his field of responsibility, each segment of time would be devoted to one of the fifteen ecclesiastical areas, each of which had its own supervising pastor. It was vital to confer with them, getting to know the problems and anomalies as seen through the eyes of that supervising pastor. Specific lessons were never imposed. Rather, the content of lessons would arise from conversations with the leaders, related to their needs. He might make suggestions:

"Do you want me to prepare lessons on...?
"Yes, and could you add a segment covering...?

The range of material covered often looked like this:

- Dealing with sects and cults
- Handling moral problems
- Dealing with cases of mental illness
- Marriage
- Youth
- The converted polygamist
- Fetishes
- The pastor and his prayer life
- The pastor and his administrative responsibilities
- The pastor and his family
- The pastor's need of rest

In preparing these lessons, João cut a lot of stencils, for in that era the hand-cranked Gestetner was the most dependable method of duplication for lessons and resources. He was aware that the contents would be repeated again and again after his departure. It was hard work, setting up the material in French, from which translators would then transfer it into the KiNandi language, especially in the areas of Bwatsinge and Katwa where many did not master Kiswahili well.

Everybody wanted me to come to their area and teach. It was like a sort of competition.
Nobody held back.

João also held separate seminars for the regional pastors with supervisory responsibilities. They had very little literature on hand beyond their Bibles.

In a seminar at Bwatsinge João makes a point about the pastor's family life

The peaceful atmosphere they described on arrival at Bwatsinge was soon to evaporate. The main source of turmoil was the Congolese army, which was paid irregularly at best and which in recent months, had not been paid at all. The troops in their anger took to looting and by the Matwawanas' first Christmas in Kivu, the countryside was in turmoil. The proximity of the looting to Bwatsinge was most unsettling, and the violence moved closer by the day. They recorded the diminishing distance as the violence approached their home base:

Dec. 22	*Shops in Goma were looted*
Dec. 23	*Katale, Rubare, and Buturande looted (140 kms.)*
Dec. 24	*Vitshumbi (90 kms.) was looted in the morning.*
Rwindi (60 kms.)	*Soldiers were spotted in the afternoon.*
Dec. 25	*Soldiers arrived at the road construction camp (15 kms.)*
	(*partners in mission* Letter #17, February 1993)

The newsletter that reported these events carried the heading: "Safety is not the absence of danger, but the presence of God."

It was to be a season in which the newly arrived Canadians lived out the reality of that observation. A Christmas party had been planned with pastors and their spouses. Should they proceed with it? They decided to go ahead, and Nora pleased the participants with special Christmas baking. "Our guests were very happy. We sang Christmas carols and prayed together for the country." During these days, the following portions of Psalms were very much in their minds:

> *The Lord is my light and my salvation—*
> *whom shall I fear?*
> *The Lord is the stronghold of my life—*
> *of whom shall I be afraid?*
> *When evil men advance against me*
> *to devour my flesh,*
> *when my enemies and my foes attack me,*
> *they will stumble and fall.*

> *Though and army besiege me,*
> *my heart will not fear;*
> *though war break out against me,*
> *even then will I be confident.*
> (Psalm 27:1-3)

> *I will lie down and sleep in peace,*
> *for you alone, O Lord,*
> *make me dwell in safety.*
> (Psalm 4:8)

Previous experience involving situations of violence in Angola and western Congo equipped João and Nora for their task of strengthening, encouraging, and advising their colleagues and fellow church members throughout the times of turbulence in Kivu. They drew upon resources they had tested earlier and found adequate. João's sermon preached on Christmas Day of 1992 is a good example. He chose as his text, "Do not be afraid" (Luke 2:10). He brought his hearers a powerful word of comfort from the Scriptures, confirmed from his own personal experience, highly relevant to the moment. His observation on that morning was, "Nobody expected that we would end the service without seeing guns pointing at us, but there were none."

Local church leaders around Bwatsinge were preoccupied that the CBM Land Cruiser, vital to the Matwawanas' work, would prove an attractive target to the looters. On December 24 they recommended taking it to the camp of the Brazilian road construction crews. This proved to be sound advice. Interaction with the Brazilians was easy and natural, as they spoke Portuguese, the language of all João's early education in Angola. Rather than have their equipment pillaged, the Brazilians reasoned and negotiated with the rampant troops, pacifying them with money.

How reconciliation ministries began in Kivu

During March of 1993, valuable training sessions at Katwa were proving productive, followed by a pastors' retreat. Toward the end of that month, inter-tribal violence erupted at Masisi, claiming many hundreds of lives. Masisi is some 50 kilometres northwest of Goma. João was called in by the CBCA to help in the search for peaceful solutions.

Thus, the beginnings of the reconciliation ministry that became the highlight of all the Matwawanas accomplished in Kivu actually began during these initial months of their teaching and training work with the Baptist Community of Kivu. João learned that the churches were experiencing conflict among six different tribes that made up their membership. The economy of some was based on agriculture, others were dependent on their herds. Conflict and tension relating to land for both agriculture and for grazing was spilling over into church life and damaging the sense of fellowship.

These tensions involved Wanandi, Hutu, Hunde, Tutsi, Nyanga, Mashi, and Banyamulenge ethnic groups. All resided in North and South Kivu. The ethnic mixture of the population living in this fertile and densely-settled area resulted from Belgian practices in the colonial era, when a single Governor ruled Congo, Rwanda, and Burundi, and ruled them as one territory rather than as the three countries they represent today. The Belgian Governor was entirely at liberty to shuffle groups of people around from area to area according to what he saw as a solution, and for whatever reason. For such activities his authority was supreme. His word was law.

> *Within these conflicts I knew that people were fighting for more land for their crops and their herds. So really we were finding our churches and schools full of refugees coming from within this very same province, Kivu. It was becoming too dangerous for them to stay in their villages because of these conflicts. We knew we had to do something, so the CBCA took the initiative to mediate between these tribes and villages. They asked me if I could lead their reconciliation team because I was more credible, not belonging to any of the conflicting tribes. That was the beginning.*
>
> *We went to Masisi. We talked with the chiefs. Things were settled and it was decided the people can go back to their homes*

and their villages.... The beginnings at Masisi were after we had been in Kivu for about one year. It seems that God sent me there for that purpose without my knowing it. These reconciliation ministries started quite early in our ministry to Kivu. It was just necessary that they have somebody there with the experience of being a refugee and with the experience of having struggled with concepts of hatred against people who have taken over your land and your home.

João and Nora Matwawana served in Kivu during highly turbulent times, and they did so as ministers of reconciliation, even though that had not been the original purpose behind their appointment. It was also a fulfillment of a mandate from the Scriptures, expressed in these terms.

Christ's love compels us...
He died for all, that those who live should no longer live for themselves
but for him who died for them and was raised again.
...Therefore, if anyone is in Christ, he is a new creation;
the old has gone, the new has come!
All this is from God, who reconciled us to himself through Christ
and gave us the ministry of reconciliation:
that God was reconciling the world to himself in Christ,
not counting men's sins against them.
And he has committed to us the message of reconciliation.
We are therefore Christ's ambassadors,
as though God were making his appeal through us.
We implore you on Christ's behalf: Be reconciled to God.
God made him who had no sin to be sin for us,
so that in him we might become the righteousness of God.
(2 Corinthians 5:14-21)

THE CYCLE OF VIOLENCE CONTINUES TO ESCALATE

In April of 1993, violence continued in their area, and the escalation of violence took over as it does when retaliation is met and answered in turn with retaliation:

Soldiers entered a village 45 kilometres from here and stole some animals. Local youths lost patience and started fighting with them, resulting in one soldier being killed. The next day more soldiers returned for revenge. As they failed to find the youths, they killed two elders burned 136 houses and attempted to kill our pastor, Kasekera, and his two deacons, but they were saved miraculously by the commander. In spite of these troubles, the annual conference of women was held as planned in the village of Kanyabayonga where the soldiers had come from.

(*partners in mission* Letter #18, Spring of 1993)

Nora's workshop there at Kanyabayonga was called "The Identity of a Woman." The theme of continuing violence around them would now recur regularly in their letters to *partners in mission*. Due to the violence around Beni, where fighting had been going on for many months, that area was not considered safe enough to take Nora, so she would remain in Goma during João's ministry there. The Beni area was also infested with malaria.

DEATH OF NORA'S FATHER

Nora was able to return to Mbanza-Kongo for a visit with her parents in 1992. Then they heard nothing until February 1993, when news arrived that her father had died in December. The internal conflict in Angola made communication with them next to impossible, and they agonized that they were not able to travel there from Kivu. They lamented that Angola was still in the turmoil of war.

HEALTH COMPLICATIONS

The Matwawanas also experienced complications with their health. One of the earliest health problems surfaced when Nora experienced crippling arthritis and resulting surgery in September of 1993.

In December of 1993, a tense situation developed after João had finished preaching a sermon at a large open air rally in

> *Nyamilima. In the sermon he condemned looting, and word of this angered the military. After he returned to his hotel soldiers came to his room, and it appeared that they were about to shoot him:*

> *"Who was preaching today?"*
> *"I was."*
> *"Come and see our chief. He insists that you must drive some of our soldiers to a place 30 kilometres from here on the Uganda border. We have been stranded here for a week without transportation."*

This was the rampant Congolese army, and they were not slow to impose their will. Undisciplined, it seemed they were turning up everywhere. The atmosphere was tense in the room, and the soldiers were in an ugly mood. "We, the soldiers, are stranded here while you foreigners drive around with good cars."

João's Congolese colleague, a pastor, was bold. He realized the intense risk that his Canadian missionary would be kidnapped, would disappear, and would be heard from no more. He jumped forward and without a moment's hesitation broke into the conversation with a story which might be credible enough to get João off the hook, might even save his life:

> *"Our missionary cannot drive because he suffers from high blood pressure. After he preaches he must sleep two hours, otherwise he will die. I have my driver here with another pickup truck that belongs to the church."*

The pickup was brought around immediately. When they watched it drive away, it had more than twenty soldiers piled into such a small vehicle. The driver took them to the Ugandan border. It had been a very close call. It *was* true that João suffered from high blood pressure, a problem which peaked from time to time.

Then both João and Nora contracted malaria in mid-January of 1994. The cerebral malaria variety, which João suffered, is a perilous strain, and though he survived, it caused him dizzy spells. Together with fatigue and high blood pressure, it was a dangerous combination, to the point where João was unable to drive, and had to depend on a CBCA driver to take him first to Goma, then to Katwa for treatment.

By this time João and Nora were carrying a number of burdens, albeit without complaint.

Nora's father was not the only close relative lost. That whole year brought a succession of deaths. In April João's mother died, in May Nora's mother died. From 1994 to 1997, three of João's sisters and one nephew died, and later João's brother, Pastor Lambourne. They were carrying a heavy load of grief while ministering day-by-day to the needs of others.

Added to this was their own health issues, awareness of Congo's political instability, separation by distance from their children and grandchildren, as well as considerable inconvenience in trying to do significant work amid shortages of virtually every vital commodity, with less than ideal living conditions and a dearth of communications facilities. All this was accompanied by the uncertainties of living in the perils of a war zone where life was cheap and bloodshed was a daily occurrence. If the cumulative weight of it seems unfair and far too much for one family to bear, they saw it in the context of their role model, Jesus of Nazareth. His lot was to bear suffering and injustice without complaint.

João to a Chaplaincy Consultation in Pretoria

João was on the road much of this time, while Nora was ministering to the women (see chapter 15). Then, in co-operation with Medical Assistance Program, based in Nairobi, he was sponsored for travel to Pretoria, South Africa, to attend a consultation on medical and chaplaincy training in Africa. This was held at Medusa University, where he had an opportunity to share his chaplaincy experiences. João was invited to attend as a participant, but when conference organizers learned of his extensive experience, he was upgraded to a conference leader.

Those among whom the Matwawanas were working had suffered greatly in the local fighting with burning, pillaging, and the destruction of gardens. The Matwawanas were able to draw upon CBM's *Sharing*

Way grants to implement programs that equipped people to help themselves. Their frugal and innovative use of these grants brought comments from another internationally respected organization, as reported to them through the CBCA:

> One official of Oxfam U.K. said, "We are amazed at how you Baptists can manage to help so many people with such a small budget."

THE ONSET OF GENOCIDE IN RWANDA

In April of 1994, the media reported a suspicious plane crash that killed the presidents of both Rwanda and Burundi. Following that, a massacre was unleashed in Rwanda, in which thousands of Tutsis were liquidated by Hutus in systematic fashion. This was the reverse of what had taken place in Burundi. The tensions between minority Tutsis and majority Hutus in these two small but densely populated republics, which bordered on Kivu, were of long standing, and there was a history of periodic violence, considerable injustice, deep mistrust, mutual fear, and suspicion. Impressions of April events in Rwanda were reported in these terms from neighbouring Kivu:

> In one incident a mob of angry Hutus stormed a university near the border and killed all twenty-five students of Tutsi origin. In addition they found 300 other Tutsis who had taken refuge there and slaughtered them all. Witnesses said that some of the killers were between twelve and eighteen years old.

> A refugee woman from Rwanda who was in tears stopped João at the entrance of the CBCA office in Goma to tell him the story of how her husband and two children as well as her sister and brother were killed in their home because they were Tutsis. Her life was spared because she was away on a trip.

Because of all the violence, a conference on reconciliation which had been planned for Kigali (Rwanda) was cancelled, as the

Government of Rwanda and the Tutsi-led rebels were already at war. The same letter that carried this news contained an illustration that gives us a glimpse of how the Matwawanas were thinking and feeling as they were surrounded by these events:

> *We want to close this letter with the Scripture reference Mark 4:35-41. Working in Zaïre is like crossing a lake during a furious storm. When the going gets tough we start to feel like the disciples when they were rebuked by the Lord. But a great deal depends on how we perceive the storm. We can graduate from a fear of the storm to a fear of God, We can see the hand of God in Zaïre even in the midst of chaos. We know that crisis raises leaders, forges experience, and makes history. Instead of yielding to the temptation to abandon ship, we are learning to look to the One who stays in the boat with us.*
>
> (*partners in mission* Letter #20, April 1994)

To a different province of Congo

João and Nora spent the last three weeks of May 1994 with Canadian colleagues Doug and Carolyn Brown. They were working in another of CBM's Africa partnerships, this time with the Baptist Community of North Zaïre, a denomination working in Bas-Uele Province, which had its roots in work begun by Norwegian Baptist Missionaries. They flew to Buta, but also conducted workshops for church leadership at Likati, Bondo, and Monga. At Bondo, for instance, seventy pastoral couples participated. Both João and Nora contributed. The topics covered included:

- The pastor and his work, his family, his life of prayer, his preaching, his time, his rest
- How to improve communication
- How to solve marital problems
- The pastor's wife and her home

- The pastor's wife as a teacher, a counsellor, a nurse, a bookkeeper
- The pastor's wife as an unpaid inspector of her husband's work and his health

In a single morning at Likati, they met with seventeen couples who brought problems that really required much more time for discussion and counselling. "If only the pastors themselves were well trained for this ministry!"

The summer months of 1994, when they accompanied Isabel to university, provided a time in Canada with family, and a chance to meet with the Canadian support base. But before they left Congo, they participated in a week of open air meetings in Goma, designed by the CBCA to make a faith impact on the total community. Services and workshops were organized for youth, couples, singles, students, teachers, merchants, government officials, soldiers, police, prisoners, lawyers, and others. During this week, João was asked by the CBCA to minister specifically to soldiers, police, and prisoners of Goma. This put him into five different military camps, where over forty soldiers registered a new commitment to Jesus as Lord of their lives. Similarly, when speaking to 450 inmates in Goma's central prison, roughly eighty prisoners declared a conversion experience. Having served as prison chaplain in Halifax, João was at ease among prisoners. For all of these men, their world was already in turmoil, and destined to become still more difficult. One could only wish for some present-day word from these men, to grasp how a new beginning brought hope and stability in their lives.

REFUGEES ARRIVE FROM RWANDA

In July of 1994, before departure to Canada, the Matwawanas started their long-awaited training course for chaplains, which was held at Katwa. International developments that month would drastically change life for them and for all who worked with them. As they reported on that training course, they also chronicled the onset of the tide of refugees from Rwanda.

...The big event of the month, of course, was the greatest exodus of the late twentieth century, as more than a million Rwandan refugees spilled over the border, creating a human catastrophe in and around Goma, Zaïre. We do praise the international organizations that have come to Kigali and Goma to help. We also praise Zaïrean Christians in Goma and area who have taken refugee families into their homes and are supporting hundreds of orphaned children. (When they saw the mob, they just opened their homes, shared their food, and then opened their classrooms and sanctuaries (as places to sleep). The Baptist Church at Kako, a village near the Katale refugee camp, sacrificially gave over their huge fields of corn, which otherwise may have generated some income for their local church's budget. They reached out in every way and all of this because of Christ's love.

(*partners in mission* Letter #22, Fall of 1994)

THE INFLUX OF REFUGEES CHANGES MINISTRY EMPHASIS

Back in Kivu, after their short interval in Canada, João found that the tidal wave of refugees flowing from Rwanda into Kivu had radically changed the priorities of his ministry. This transformation, in late 1994, happened virtually overnight, a result of the genocide in Rwanda and ongoing hostilities there. This was the infamous massacre that Canada's United Nations Peacekeeper, General Romeo D'Allaire, attempted to forestall with the handful of troops at his disposal. The mandate he was given by the United Nations was inadequate in the face of the crisis that was developing. The United Nations failed to grant him the moral support, the minimal number of troops needed, or the other logistical resources required to avert the disaster he saw unfolding before his eyes, and which he faithfully reported with his cries of alarm and pleas for help. General D'Allaire repeatedly and vigorously reported to his United Nations superiors the developing crisis, but without effect. The massacre happened, carried to the eyes of the world by the media.

One of the results on the ground was this massive exodus of refugees across Rwanda's frontier and into the Congo, precisely into the region of Kivu Province where the Matwawanas were living. Gisenyi in Rwanda and Goma in Congo are neighbouring border cities like Detroit and Windsor, or Niagara Falls and Buffalo, except that they are not even separated by water. Tens of thousands, then hundreds of thousands of people flooded into the region around Goma, where the United Nations installed them in clusters that came to be known as the refugee camps of Mugunga, Katale, Kahindu, and Kibumba.

In Kivu, as in Rwanda, the sparse availability of United Nations resources added to problems that were building, as heavily-armed militia from Rwanda melted into and blended with civilian refugees. The UN contingent in Congo, echoing the shortage of troops in Rwanda, did not have the muscle to enforce any sort of disarming process. As militia arrived they proceeded, fully armed, into the refugee camps. That armament included a profusion of assault rifles. Many different adjectives are applicable to those camps. The civilians were vulnerable, the atmosphere was tense, the situation was an explosive tinder-box of humanity. This was clearly a perilous atmosphere in which to operate. The limited UN troops were deployed to protect the humanitarian agencies which mushroomed on site to deal with the massive need, to protect their workers and their supplies.

By Christmas of 1994, the Matwawanas were reporting that they were combining ministry to Congolese pastors with relief services among Rwandan refugees. Some members of the missionary community asked just who had directed João to focus on refugees, since that was not his mandate. Despite this query, his long-standing and profound sense of call to minister to people in this category kept him on track.

From refugees, as well as from Congolese, they heard many disturbing stories. João and Nora felt they needed to begin to work with a limited and specific segment of the newcomers. They began with the 7,000 refugees in the Katale camp near Kako who affected the Baptist congregation nearby. Among them they found 145 Rwandan pastors of eight denominations. The first plan was to equip those pastors to minister to their own people effectively, to respond to the need of healing and reconciliation. So João started to conduct workshops, planning one or two workshops a month. The sessions would deal with trauma, grief, anger, hatred, vengeance, forgiveness, and reconciliation. The pastors eagerly responded, affirming this to be the kind of help they needed: "Come back any time." They found it easy to put the Rwandan pastors together, thanks to the refugee committee in the camps. These workshops were successful. They accepted João because they knew he had been a refugee pastor himself.

WORK IN REFUGEE CAMPS—BUT ONLY AFTER 4 P.M.

It had been impossible to disarm the Rwandan refuges on arrival, so these very large camps with their concentrations of armed fighters were highly volatile. The stance of the United Nations was both realistic and understandable. They had only a small contingent of armed personnel, and all they were able to do was to protect in some measure their personnel who worked in the camps as well as a number of non-governmental humanitarian agencies, commonly known as NGOs. Regular hours were established during which the United Nations undertook to provide security for their own workers and those of approved humanitarian organizations. The UN would move in each morning at eight, and withdraw at four in the afternoon.

> *I went to the UN administration office to ask their permission to work in the camps. I was asked how much budget I had to work with. It would be necessary to participate in financing the administration costs of the UN security operation. (The levy was ten percent of budget payable to the United Nations.)*
> "My budget is five thousand dollars."
> "You are not qualified."
> "What is most important here?"
> "Security. It's dangerous. They can kill anybody at any time."
> "Suppose I have no need of your security?"
> "Then that's easy for us. It just means that you arrive after 4 p.m."
> "That's what I'm requesting."
> "No problem. You'll work alone, they'll kill you alone."

João thanked them for that permission and it was under those conditions that he began his work in the camps. There were no other organizations on hand while he was there, and he went about his work, teaching about the nature of peace and reconciliation. His focus was on working with the considerable number of pastors who were in the camp, preparing them to teach and help their people.

When it got to be 3:45, the agencies would begin their rush to exit the camps. They know that security is about to terminate. As I approached the camp it had to be with great care or I would get run over. Those people roared out with such speed, in their Land Rovers with the flags of their organizations.

It turned out that in my work at night in those camps I was unhurried, with lots of time to interact with the pastors and the camp leaders. I tried to calm them of their fears. A very great majority of those in the camps were innocent. But even those who were killers came to sense the power of God. At first they were suspicious of me. Then they began to reason it out:

"If everybody else is fleeing, why is this man continuing with us? He must have confidence in us. Maybe he loves us. For sure he can't have any money or he would not come in here alone."

There are times in ministry when a wealth of resources, instead of lightening the load, adds to the burden.

In the early days of my ministry in the camps we had not progressed far enough for anyone to come out of the camps with me when I left. Later, when we began programs like sewing for the women and carpentry for young men, then sometimes I was accompanied by people from the camps.

After four in the afternoon, when the UN forces had withdrawn for the day, the refugee camps around Goma functioned as the Republic of Rwanda until the following morning at eight, when the UN forces returned. They had their own police, and they were armed. At first it may have been only the militia who were armed, but inside the camp guns were sold in exchange for food, so it became impossible to predict just who was in possession of guns. The hierarchy was well established. They passed judgments and carried out executions. They had their own structure and organization with mayors, communes, and prefectures. One is led to wonder how João was able to work in the camps controlled as they were by the *Interhamwe*.

This *Interhamwe* force were originally the Rwandan Army's militia, trained militarily and armed with modern weapons, but not part of the formal army. They were supposedly on call to strengthen and reinforce the regular army if an emergency were to arise. But following the shooting down of the aircraft which carried their Hutu President, they swung into action full time, motivated by hatred, anger, and a spirit of vengeance. Whereas armies have rules and at least a modicum of discipline, the *Interhamwe* roared across Rwanda's countryside as an undisciplined mob, pressing into service those of Hutu ethnicity of all ages and both sexes.

> *In the Kinyarwanda language, the word* interhamwe *means those who work together. Their background springs from an era when the UN pressed the Rwandan government's President Habyarimana, a Hutu, to accept a power-sharing formula involving negotiations with the Rwanda Patriotic Front rebel movement, RPF, predominantly Tutsi. The Hutu component of the population was roughly 85 percent and that of the Tutsis about 14 percent. Hutu extremists prepared a genocide plan to eliminate all of the RPF's potential supporters. The plan started to unfold on April 6, 1994, following the shooting down of the presidential aircraft which killed President Habyarimana. A major role in the genocide was assigned to the* Interhamwe *militia, while the former Rwandan Armed Forces, FAR, who were predominantly Hutu, tried to fight the advancing RPF troops. The RPF succeeded in quickly conquering the country, and seized control of the powers of state before the end of July 1994. Within a few weeks the genocidal killings stopped.*

Among these 1.5 million refugees were some 40,000 defeated ex-FAR troops, along with over 500 *Interhamwe* militia. Despite the difference in numbers, the *Interhamwe* were the ones who held sway in the camps.

At first the *Interhamwe* in the camps looked on João with great skepticism, but the fact that he was not allowed to work under United Nations protection eventually worked in his favour. Working as he was in the camps alone, at night, and without protection, they apparently were led to ponder just how he was different from the other organizations and their workers. He could see that the camp leaders' attitude toward him was changing. They began to greet him, "Good evening, Reverend...."

As he began to search out the Rwandan pastors among the refugees, he found these Hutu pastors were guilt-ridden. They knew that they had lost their moral right to speak, they had lost their message because of association with the momentous evil which had taken place in the form of the genocide. There were only Hutu pastors in the camps, no Tutsis. To these he ministered both directly and prophetically:

> *"You must cry for the sins of your people like the Old Testament prophets."*
> *"We can't do that. We are afraid of these Interhamwe leaders who are looking over our shoulders."*
> *"You must do it."*
> *"But we will be killed."*
> *"Some of you may be killed, but others will survive. Have courage. Preach against sin, preach against killing. One day you will have to live with those you now call your enemies."*

The pastors listened. They began to gather spiritual strength as they reflected and acted inwardly on these things. João was working with all denominations inside the refugee camps. The pastors started to sort themselves out into the various denominations within which they had functioned in Rwanda.

The Graham Association Meetings

For many months, the Christian community in and around Goma were praying for a program being prepared by the Billy Graham Evangelistic Association, which would take place inside the refugee camps. They would be tuned in live to a worldwide program, lasting four nights, broadcast from Costa Rica, using state-of-the-art technology. The signal was to be transmitted to the camps directly by satellite link, and picked up by a number of special room-size dish antennae flown in on two aircraft for that purpose, complete with the technicians to do the installation. One technician was from Germany, two were from the United Kingdom, and there were two people from the Graham organization.

João was first contacted because of his potential to solve the security issues for this operation, which were monumental. The camps functioned by night as if they were the Republic of Rwanda in Exile, its *ad hoc* administration enforced by the multitude of assault rifles in the hands of individuals and militia far too powerful for the limited number of United Nations personnel to disarm. The broadcasts were to be at night.

Red tape had to be overcome to gain permission for the meetings in the camps. The arrival of so much equipment created suspicion. The Graham Association's leadership team recognized many obstacles to be overcome, and they came to João for orientation and for assistance, having learned of his extensive work in the camps, his understanding of the overall situation, and his credibility:

My orientation to them was actually quite brief. There were a series of God's coincidences, part of His plan, which established my credibility with them, and made the advice I offered totally acceptable. I related the story to them.

While I was in Birmingham, studying at Westhill College, I met a black American, William Thomas, who came to the UK and married an English girl, and got to know the English churches. The Baptist Missionary Society appointed him to serve in

Kinshasa. He wanted personal and first-hand information about the Congo. When he learned that I was living in the Congo, he invited me home to meet his wife, so that they could learn as much as possible about the Congo. During the meal he asked, "Do you know that Billy Graham is coming to England soon? He seems to be offering scholarships to foreign students who are Christians, as part of his plan for world evangelism." I asked Bill for more details.

A week later he was back with forms which would qualify me to travel to London at the Graham Association's expense. They were making available ten days at the Billy Graham School of Evangelism, all expenses paid. The requirements were that one attend evangelistic services in the evening after studying all day. I should also visit in the community during afternoons.

That was my introduction to the Graham Association—ten days in London on a scholarship.

"Enough news," the organizers said. "God sent you in advance. We were afraid we might not find anybody who could understand why we are here. Now we will depend on you for everything. You will be in front, you will be the door opener."

United Nations authorities, who held an overall responsibility for the camps, insisted that they could not assume responsibility for after-hours activities there, a repetition of their stance at the time when João himself had asked permission to work there in the evenings. If he could negotiate something with the camps' internal management which was run by the Hutu chiefs, it was not a UN concern. "You may be attacked or whatever, we will not be responsible, for it will be at night, and it is not our worry." In effect, the Graham Association program came to be looked upon by the United Nations authorities as an extension of the personal ministry that João pursued in the camps on a regular basis. Nobody else was attempting that kind of activity, which they considered both weird and frightening:

The organizers asked me how I would do it. I told them that getting permission is no big deal, the chiefs know me already. Security arrangements are a matter of money, and must be arranged through the camp chiefs who will hire their security agents. I started to negotiate with the chiefs, all the chiefs of the three camps for which I was organizer, the camps in which I had been working.

The chiefs know who are the bandits, but the bandits have to be paid. I got money from the Graham crew, and paid it to the chiefs who would disperse it. As long as they had the money, all was secure. There was no way anybody could attack us at night. The worst criminals had become our security team.

Katale, Kahindu, and Kibumba were my three camps. There was not a single incident in those three camps. We learned, after the fact, that one person wanted to steal equipment one night. "I came because I was attracted by the music. I saw the equipment and wanted to steal it. I was convicted and came forward to accept Christ as my Lord and Saviour."

There was a fourth camp, a large camp out past the University campus, where João was not in charge. At that camp, security was under the responsibility of World Vision's director, an American. He lacked the advantage of being known as João was known, and lacked the experience of knowing where and how to negotiate the security, assuming that United Nations permission to operate was sufficient. Stones were thrown there every night, and some people were hurt. Between that camp and the city of Goma there were three roadblocks. After the services, the bandits created seven additional roadblocks, to make a total of ten that the team needed to pass returning to the hotel after the services. Instead of making security payments through the chiefs, they were paying through the roadblocks.

The Great Lakes Region of Central Africa

Other Responsibilities at the Graham Program in the Refugee Camps

João also participated in the training programs leading up to the special meetings. When the actual program began, he was sometimes called on to lead the program, make announcements, or interpret. When the final evening arrived, his participation became much more crucial. For some technical reason, the entire setup failed. They could capture no voice from the Costa Rica transmission, no picture. The whole team gathered. They asked the choir to keep singing, and they all went to prayer. Mr. Kennedy of the Graham team finally told them that the time for prayer had passed, and now it was time for action. "We can't just send these people away, for this is the last night. João, you are a preacher. Go to the top of the truck." The attendance numbered in the thousands. João preached in French, translated into Kinyarwanda:

People listened. They knew me. The response was similar to the other nights when normally 500 to 1,000 people would respond. The technicians were almost crying. They felt they were a failure. "You were not a failure. Did you notice that people came forward anyway in similar numbers to the other nights? The technical side was not what brought people to Christ, it was the conviction of sin."

The Billy Graham organization did a good job of training counsellors all week. They knew what was happening and they continued their work after the campaign was over. After the campaign, I took the two co-ordinators to Bwatsinge with me to spend the weekend with us. It was a highlight for them, being in Africa, sitting in front of a fireplace near the equator at 6,000 feet above sea level.

Pastors began reporting that commanders were coming to them confessing their sins, for example, that they had incited young people to atrocities.

The following facsimile message as a follow-up was sent by João Matwawana to Bill Kennedy of the Billy Graham Organization, 1995:

Greetings in the name of our Lord and Saviour Jesus Christ.

Since we said good-bye in Goma, Zaïre, I have visited Katale, Kahindo, and Kibumba camps twice. There are large increases in attendance at their Sunday services and other weekly church activities. Pastors reported that some Hutu ex-military people confessed that they had killed Tutsis in Rwanda during the massacre. Many of these are coming forward to respond to the invitation to receive Christ as Saviour and Lord during Sunday worship services in the camps. Testimonies of the Katale camp chief say that the security situation has improved and that criminal activities have decreased tremendously since the Billy Graham mission.

The highlight was Easter Sunday. I was invited to preach by the refugee congregation of Katale camp. Over 1,000 attended the service. Even the Sunday School children refused to leave the sanctuary. These people sang hymns to praise the Lord in spite of the fact that they were seated on volcanic lava stone for more than three hours. Fifty-four people were baptized that morning; thirty of them adults who made their decision during the Billy Graham mission. All the pastors and evangelists in the camps are asking for your prayers as they try to nurture these many hundreds of new converts. Please pray for me as I plan to accept the second invitation to preach there on Pentecost Sunday, that the Lord may give me the correct message.

(partners in mission *Letter #24, Easter 1995*)

One of the realities of life is that our important priorities are often interrupted by other high-profile priorities. That was precisely the case with João. So what was the impact of the Rwanda refugee influx on the assignment to which Matwawanas had been appointed in Kivu Province? CBM works by well-considered policy under which its overseas partnership programs are conducted in response to the invitation and to the expressed needs of the overseas churches. The Matwawanas were in Kivu by church invitation, and for a specific task. Naturally such a momentous influx of refugees into one's own back yard changes everything. Flexibility and adaptability permitted João to adjust to two distinct tracks of ministry, one with refugees, the other with churches. The advantage was that the tasks were harmonious in nature, even though they posed conflicting demands on resources of his time and energy. Both priorities came to be met with remarkable success.

Dynamics begin to change in the refugee camps

There came a time when pastors in the camp came to João asking that he intervene on their behalf with the United Nations to grant them a place where they could put up a plastic-covered chapel for worship. That request was granted, and they began to clear a space, moving the chunks of volcanic rock into rows to serve as seats. After only one week, João found the place for worship prepared, the plastic stretched over poles that they had been able to come up with. Their place for regular worship was functional and in service.

> *The grace of God was evident there in the camp. And as I came into the camp repeatedly while the others were leaving, expatriates would comment "That fool Canadian pastor is going in there again."*

> *The reality was that when I was there, the atmosphere was different. The real reason why refugees attacked the humanitarian organizations was because the rations had been reduced. Officials were very cautious and were stockpiling significant reserves of supplies. It was their estimate that this food had to last for six months. But one cannot explain that need for prudence to an African who is suffering hunger. He cannot accept that "there is food on hand while I am hungry." He does not live by a budget. One eats what is on hand. For the future there is no problem—"we will plant and the food will grow, then we will eat." The UN, instead of arranging fields where refugees could plant, distributed food.*

I told the UN that before their arrival, we had distributed hoes and machetes to some who had come early as refugees, before the main influx. We didn't have much food to give, but after three months they were self-sufficient. They produced their own food. Organizations arrive with big budgets, they proceed to spend all their money, and still refugees die of hunger. With the little 5,000 dollars that I had, God permitted more things that were significant, and more things that remained behind, than were achieved through many big budgets.

CHOLERA IN THE UNITED NATIONS REFUGEE CAMPS

When cholera struck the camp they buried thousands of people per day, but it was hard to tell that there were so many dying. Instructions to the families were simple. When somebody dies, wrap the body in a blanket or a mat and put it by the side of the road. The Red Cross will come by in a few hours to pick them up. There were regular patrols assigned specifically to the task of picking up the corpses.

It was too late for vaccination. If there had been only small numbers, then immigration at the border might have had some control. But these refugees were too many, arriving by the thousands, and they were armed. We ourselves had been vaccinated.

There were problems in and around Goma, a very dangerous place at night because there were shootings and killings almost every week. The Katale camp was even more dangerous, under the control of bandits at night. After learning of the killing of twenty-seven people at Kako, with 105 more injured there and at Buturande and Katale, João and colleagues visited the area to bring a measure of comfort and pastoral care to both the Rwandan and Zaïrean families who lost loved ones.

Throughout this period they were never far removed from violence, but at times the contact was too intimate. On a certain day João was to come face to face with killers, locally known as *Wangilima*, as he was stopped by six armed men, two with arrows and four with loaded guns. They told him they were out hunting for Hutus born in Zaïre, to kill them. João was especially fearful for the lives of three orphan children in their local primary school who were of Hutu origin. After long and complicated negotiations, he persuaded these masked men to leave the village:

> *Even in the presence of these* Wangilima *we felt safe and at peace.... It is, we believe, the same ongoing of ethnic cleansing which started at Masisi area which we reported in June of 1993.*

In the middle of such turmoil, João reported his gratitude that there were many Christians in Kivu who were praying day and night with tears, asking God to stop these tribal wars in the area.

A STRATEGY FOR TRAINING EVANGELISTS

Looking at João's program as it had been developing prior to the refugee influx, he was aware that evangelization was given the highest priority by the CBCA and also by its pastors. For their evangelistic programs, they needed some new methodology, and he was there to provide it. That task marked the logical place to begin, so João requested that every church should send ten evangelists to be trained. Buturande was a centrally-located church post, and that is where the first sessions were held. Later some events were scheduled for Bwatsinge, where the Matwawanas had settled. Others took place at decentralized points convenient for gathering clusters of pastors together. Some sessions were scheduled to last a week, others ran for two weeks' duration.

> *When they came to that first event at Buturande, I expected 150 because of the fifteen church areas we served. But they like evangelism so much, they cheated on me. Some sent more than ten representatives and I ended up having more than 200 people for the first sessions. In terms of numbers and participation, they never turned back from that kind of enthusiastic response. But I didn't mind because I know that these are the people who*

will get the work done. But I would need to change my budget so all these people could be trained. They already knew how to evangelize. They eagerly took in new methods, and new material. They returned full of enthusiasm. The church and people of Buturande helped with the cooking, but I had to buy the food. The CBCA department of evangelism participated with some money along with my money.

The vehicle at João's disposal was always full. There would be a Kivu pastor with him, attached to the CBCA Department of Evangelism. The pastor might also bring a brother or a wife or a cousin or a helper, so he always expected a Land Cruiser full of people when he was travelling. Working in an area where transportation was a problem, he was constantly picking up people:

The moment you stop at a village the pastor may say his wife is in critical condition. You have to take his wife to Katwa. You have to make room. That was routine.

We trained those people, then we continued with retreats for pastors and their spouses, for nurses, and other church leaders. But then in the midst of that, the Rwanda crisis broke. That shifted our focus somewhat, but all the time, both in Kivu and with the Rwanda crisis, we felt they needed the message of reconciliation in the same way. They were already struggling with their internal problems in Kivu, then on top of that we experienced the big influx of refugees from Rwanda. Well, we knew that these pastors in Kivu have to be equipped too, for they are the ones who will continue to minister to the Rwandan people after we are gone. So in the end we did training in both countries.

So what kind of support did João receive from the pastors and from CBM leadership for the new emphases that he was introducing, namely ministries to refugees and the unfolding thrust on reconciliation—did they feel they were being cheated?

When we were dealing with the mediation inside Kivu itself, the support was 100 percent. When I started reconciliation in the camps, the support dropped to about 50 percent for a time. They felt that I was wasting too much energy among refugees because there were needs of their own that should be met. So it became difficult to help them understand. A pastor raised the issue pointedly.
"Do you know what those people did in Rwanda?"
"I know."
"So why are you so close to them?"
"I must give you more information when you have time. I can't answer you quickly like that."

The day came when João sat down with this pastor to tell him about his own life and to tell him that all people in Portugal consider Angolans to be the perpetrators of genocide, including João himself.

"That's the way you feel, too, because you don't know the people in the camps, but I know that it may have been as little as 300 who did most of the killing. In these camps you have a quarter of a million innocent people, so you have to know these factors before you judge. We are dealing with a lot of innocent people here. I don't even expect that the militia people will come to my seminars in the camp because they don't see the value of that, but there are some people who are happy to participate, people who are innocent."

"Okay, maybe you should continue."

So the people of Kivu began to understand, little by little, and to agree. One of the CBCA leaders told me I was giving too much time to the Rwandan people, that I had not come for that purpose. But I said, "This is an open door and that is why I want also to be teaching you, because you will be continuing this when I am gone." Little by little they understood and they were very cooperative afterwards, but it takes time for people to understand, especially where there is a possessive attitude that says "this missionary is ours, here to serve just us."

Back in Goma, which was now their base of operations, rather than Bwatsinge, violence continued unabated. Fatal shootings in Goma were happening every few days. Four people were shot dead across the street from where João's office was located. A bomb was thrown into the Baptist hospital. The Matwawana letter sent at Thanksgiving that year (#32) lists a series of their activities that one might deem possible only in a peaceful and normal environment. Ministry went on in the midst of turmoil. Twenty-six people completed a chaplaincy training program. João and Nora conducted a marriage enrichment weekend for pastors, elders, and spouses. João was travelling to give seminars on conflict management skills. He participated in a three-day theological consultation to revise the theological education program of the denomination. He travelled to Katwa and addressed the Bible Institute Graduation, and then gave a week-long training course for hospital chaplains.

> *Working in Goma was very stressful indeed. One encountered frequent harassments by hungry and unpaid soldiers, the sporadic shooting every night by armed gangs, and travelling on insecure roads due to the local fighters known as Mayi-Mayi, the many never-ending beggars on the streets of Goma, and trying to adjust to life in Goma without the moral and spiritual encouragement of other missionary colleagues.*

For more than three years, government forces of the Congo tried to suppress the militia movements without success. Commando troops were deployed one after another in the region. Instead of bringing relief to the population, the Mobutu military operations always added to their consternation. Government army reprisals made more victims and did more material damage than the attacks from the various militia groups. The inconvenience, confusion, mourning, and suffering at the hands of government troops became the common lot of everyone in the area, including expatriates. This suffering prepared the ground for the

The Great Lakes Region of Central Africa

Kabila rebellion, when that leader merged his troops with Zaïrian Tutsis to rebel against President Mobutu.

Multi-ethnic Youth Conference on Reconciliation

João Matwawana was given an invitation and a mandate by the Baptist Convention of Kivu to work toward the reconciliation of tensions among six different ethnic groups within their churches, people among whom there were serious problems arising from population pressure, land usage, conflicting identities, and varying expectations, all resulting in an explosive atmosphere. These were not church tensions, but rather ethnic and regional tensions that seethed throughout the area. Blood had been shed and lives had been lost. Because the problems also surfaced in the churches, João was asked to address the situation, asked to attempt some sort of solution and reconciliation. He proceeded to lay plans for a youth conference that would bring together a group of young people representing all those conflicting groups.

Discussion groups, as youth from six tribal groups sort out issues of conflict

The Provincial Governor, located in Goma, was not in favour. He considered that to plan such a conference would be a flagrant courting of disaster. He withheld permission to hold the conference. The Matwawana conclusion, when permission was withheld, was this: "If the door is closed, it will be necessary to enter by the window."

As he consulted with tribal elders on his vision for a conference, he found that he had their full support. It was their advice that he change the venue from Goma to the village of Sake, some 50 kilometres distant. The advice of the elders was, "Ignore the Governor's opinion on this. He doesn't understand our problems."

The conference went ahead. Within CBM's *The Sharing Way*, there was a Peace Building Committee. They made a grant of 5,000 dollars so that João could hold reconciliation seminars with young people from the region. The youth were helped to work through their differences and their prejudices. They found joy in living together and eating together. In view of the existing tensions, this was considered by all to be a virtual miracle.

As the conference drew to a successful close, the elders informed João of the danger he had been in. When the Governor learned of the event he put his secret agents in place. They were ready to pounce if any sort of conflict were to emerge, which he fully expected. If that had happened, João would have been imprisoned. He had dared to risk, he came out successful, and reconciliation was achieved.

The Governor and some of his delegates moved in to be part of the success story and to be included in the photo opportunity that was part of the closing exercises.

THE MATWAWANAS ARE LEFT BEHIND

As evidence mounted through 1996 that an invasion was being prepared in Rwanda, many expatriates left the area. There were some who remained behind, including the Matwawanas. The massive refugee camps around Goma contained thousands of fully armed men, both military and militia, and the invasion had as one of its main purposes to destroy and dismantle these camps. Some, among the foreigners who still remained, were personnel involved in the refugee camp programs.

In the countdown to the actual beginning of hostilities, the Matwawanas, like all other foreigners, were asked to keep a walkie-talkie unit by their side at all times, and even to sleep with it at their pillow. João and Nora were given a borrowed communications unit for this purpose, a unit with which they were unfamiliar.

One night, official announcements were made by radio with urgent instructions for everyone to form up in convoy and evacuate. The dozen or so vehicles of those that responded in this final convoy assembled hastily and then proceeded from Goma the short distance to the border at Gisenyi, where they crossed into Rwanda and safety. While all this was happening, and the call was issued for the Matwawanas to join them, João and Nora were sleeping peacefully and didn't hear it at all. They were unaware that the batteries had discharged, and that their radio unit was inoperable.

The next morning João took the car out to fill it at a service station, and noticed that people were looking at him strangely.

Why are you all looking at me like that, is something wrong? You're a muzungu, *you shouldn't be here. All the others have gone. You are the only one left.*

This term *"muzungu"* commonly denotes a white person, and João chuckles at the accusation, but then he clarifies that it also refers to foreigners or even to people fortunate enough to have a vehicle. The implications of the conversation were clear. The entire expatriate population of Goma and of Kivu had been evacuated. João and Nora were left behind.

"What's going on?"
"We will probably have war tomorrow."

At that point João purchased tickets for themselves and their assistant to fly out to the north.

The next morning, a pastor colleague from Goma drove João and Nora Matwawana to the airport. They were the last family from among the hundreds of expatriates who had been working with churches or with humanitarian organizations in the wake of the massacre in nearby Rwanda.

The Matwawanas were tense and anxious. They soon discovered that soldiers had set up a series of unofficial security checkpoints between the parking lot and the airport. The only two options were "pay" or "stay."

As João and Nora began to negotiate these impromptu hurdles one by one, they found the final tally of the checkpoints to be no less than eight. They had been forced to pay 120 American dollars just for the privilege of reaching the check-in counter. There at the check-in counter, their baggage was cleared and sent to the plane. Then a new problem emerged as the commanding officer of the military approached them.

"No more civilian flights now. Due to military priorities all civilian flights are cancelled."

"What will we do? We can't return to the house. It's too dangerous out there."

"Why should we be the only ones to die, and not you? You will stay and die with us here at the airport."

They quickly assessed the situation. Pastor Mauka, who had driven them to the airport, had already departed. (Later they learned that his vehicle was confiscated by soldiers as he made his way back to the city.) Taxis? Taxi drivers had abandoned their service for obvious reasons, given the level of peril. But there always seems to be someone ready to die for money, and they spotted one taxi. Before their eyes, a woman immediately engaged it. However, since she had too much luggage to fit in the taxi, and since the Matwawanas no longer had any luggage, it became available to them.

We didn't even stop to bargain over the price. We knew we would really have to pay, but we just wanted to get out of there and arrive at the guest house. It was a junky car in bad shape. We got into the back seat, and when we sat down it was like sitting in a bathtub. Windows were broken out and the seat was saturated from the rain. We just got in.

"Go. Go. Go."
He got us to the guest house and that is where we were when the war broke out.

Three days under bombardment

The shooting began after midnight, maybe at around one in the morning. By daybreak it eased off. Pastor Mauka came to assure us, "Don't worry, even though we don't know who is shooting." He told us that one of President Mobutu's generals has been given the responsibility for evacuating us in case of danger, so all is arranged. Kake came with another military person to assure us that nothing would happen to us. "If something happens we are here, don't worry."

Well, Kake left. He tried to return to his house, but before he got home gunfire broke out everywhere. The general who was supposed to evacuate us was the first to run. He got as far as the University, where his car was confiscated by the rebels, then he began walking. However, he was a big man. You know how those generals have large stomachs, they never do anything. He walked only 15 kilometres, then lay down, unable to continue. So when the other soldiers were running away, they carried their general.

At the guest house we were alone. Everybody was gone. Workers were gone. The manager just threw his keys inside the guest house and we picked them up. When the shooting was tense, a group of President Mobutu's government workers from Bukavu came to us. "Pastor, can we run away? Everybody else is going."

With the government people there before us, we looked at each other. It was pouring rain. "At this time we can't say whether you should go or not go, do what you want to do. But for us we don't know anywhere else to go. We feel safer here."

Those workers left but within 15 minutes they were back. "Goma is already captured by the rebels. All Mobutu's soldiers are gone."

Another lady came to us, trembling, "My husband works in the government. He gave me two soldiers to protect me and the children. We ran into rebels who said 'Lady, we don't have anything to do with you and the children. You can go.' Then there before my eyes, the two soldiers with us were shot." The lady was devastated. Her husband was somewhere in hiding. Because multitudes of Congolese children have been witnesses, often repeatedly, to this kind of violence, trauma is widespread among them.

For three days of shooting, we stayed there in the basement without going out. God has a purpose for everything. We were the only missionaries who stayed. At the end of the shooting, people relied on us. Counselling and comforting became a full-time job from morning to evening. We opened the storeroom at the guest house, where we found rice, beans, and other things. We began giving out food, and also cooking meals for those who were inside with us. All this was without permission of course, but people were starving and nobody else had remained there in charge.

We were detained for one additional month and five days, told not to leave the city. It was like a house arrest, except that it was a "City arrest." We were allowed to move around. Kabila's rebels were multi-national, including not only locals, but also soldiers from Uganda, Katanga, Angola, and Eritrea.

The extent of Kabila's influence before the rebellion seems not to have been widely known or published in the outside world. From the army he had gathered together in the forest over a period of time, he sent troops to help struggles in Eritrea, Uganda, and Rwanda. He had twice been arrested by Mobutu's soldiers, but since he could bribe them with more than Mobutu was paying them, he was released each time. When his rebellion came, it was pay-back time, and so these other countries he had helped sent him supporting troops.

This city arrest was imposed on João and Nora because of the Kabila army's need to clean up the evidence of the 300 or so civilian corpses that were in evidence on the streets. These were the corpses of Goma people killed by the rebel movement. The Matwawanas had unwittingly become international observers of events that were to be shielded from international scrutiny. João asked the newly-arrived military commander, General André Ngandu Kisase, why they were being detained:

"If we keep you here long enough, the things that you have seen will not be considered news by the CNN."

There was a general awareness that the CNN always wanted *fresh* news of what had been happening over the last few days. During the same month and five days of their detainment, the airport and frontiers were sealed as well, so that news reporters would not have access to the profusion of bodies on the streets. For the most part, João found General Kisase to be sympathetic, and helpful to them personally. He was the military commander, but not fully in charge. Behind him there was a Tutsi who carried higher authority. When the time of their release arrived, João asked General Kisase what had changed:

"You have no fresh news for CNN."

General Kabila declared himself president in 1997, and changed the name of the country from Zaïre back to the Democratic Republic of the Congo. In September of that year, President Mobutu Sese Seko died in exile in Morocco.

Post-war return to ministry in Goma, Kivu

In the early months of 1997 João held reconciliation conferences in Kigali, Rwanda. By May 1997, the situation in Congo seemed stable enough to permit a return to Goma.

Letters to their support network indicate that in June of 1997, João and his reconciliation team, which now contained Congolese colleagues, were given clearance to travel long distances from Goma to conduct seminars on conflict management skills. One of these was a week-long session at Kalungu, with more than thirty church leaders in attendance. In this same period a chaplaincy training program for twenty-six people was completed. In Goma, thirteen students completed the introductory chaplaincy program.

Travel on the roads continued, and violence on the roads continued. Seminars on peace and reconciliation, with components examining trauma, fear, and violence, to be countered by love and peace, were like a light shining in the midst of the darkness, the punctuation added by sporadic gunfire. Two days after João had travelled by road to Bwatsinge, two men were killed on that same road. He also reports that pastor Kibangiri of Masisi was killed by a spent bullet. Random acts of violence were interspersed with deliberate acts of love.

The Matwawanas concern with HIV/AIDS

A significant portion of the information in this part of our story has been gleaned from letters sent by João and Nora to their supporters in Canada. These letters regularly listed items of concern for which they requested specific prayer. HIV/AIDS as a plague and a crisis received consistent coverage. Not being connected with dramatic breakthrough events, AIDS has tended not to get mentioned in the ongoing events of their lives. However, João and Nora were certainly attentive to and grieved by this pandemic, which poses such an enormous threat to Africa and its people. In their teaching sessions, they were diligent in making their seminar and workshop participants alert to the problems, and motivated to face all of the issues squarely, whether pastors, denominational leaders, young people, church members, health workers, government officials, or the general public.

The Great Lakes Region of Central Africa

Assessing the Impact of Trauma

Trauma was not new to João and Nora, who had gone through repeated disasters and many resettlement adjustments to a variety of new environments.

Through their time in Kivu and in the months that followed, it was their spiritual orientation which served as the foundation for their lives. It served as their compass to orient them to circumstances, to people, and to opportunities for ministry. They were continually aware of God as their refuge and their strength. They could look to Him for guidance and care; their very presence in Kivu was to be a representative of Jesus Christ as Lord of their lives, to be messengers of reconciliation for Him.

Following their wrenching experiences in and around Goma, there was an opportunity for them to discuss what they had been through with a psychiatrist in Nairobi. The interview was set up for them by Doug Loden, who was CBM's Africa Representative. At first their inclination was to decline the opportunity, but they came to realize they had been through a lot, and the experiences had affected them. They remembered how jumpy they were during their days at the guest house in Goma, under bombardment. They were tense, and could not relate to each other in a relaxed and normal way. They remembered how the slightest noise triggered anxiety. Nora might drop her fork, and João would jump as though a bullet had been fired.

This counselling helped them to put their Kivu experiences in the past, and to move on in life, as they had done so often before.

Trauma counselling they received, and trauma counselling they would continue to give, both in East Africa and beyond, in the spirit of words written by St. Paul:

Praise be to the God and Father of our Lord Jesus Christ,
the Father of compassion and the God of all comfort,
who comforts us in all our troubles,
so that we can comfort those in any trouble
with the comfort we ourselves have received from God.

(2 Corinthians 1:3-4)

Bujumbura Conference

The year 1998 was a busy one, with a number of conferences and consultations. Following his May participation with the Association of Baptist Churches in Rwanda, working on Hutu-Tutsi reconciliation, João proceeded on to Bujumbura, Burundi, for an international event, the "Conference on Democracy, Good Governance and Development for a Lasting Peace in the Great Lakes region of Central Africa." Three regional universities arranged the program, backed by PNUD, *Program des Nations Unies pour le Développement*. Universities in Rwanda, Burundi, and the Congo were represented, with speakers invited from all over the world. Participants attended from Congo, Rwanda, Burundi, Uganda, Tanzania, France, Switzerland, Belgium, Sweden, and Italy. When João arrived, the representative of PNUD clarified that Canadian Baptist Ministries were *bona fide* participants in reconciliation. João was given full accreditation as a participant, and his expenses were paid by the United Nations.

Reconciliation Ministry report to CBCA churches, June 1998

Working as he did with CBM's partner denomination, the CBCA, João reported to them, interacted with them as a fellow-worker, and functioned as a partner with them:

Our partners, the CBCA, have suffered a great deal on account of wars. Many times some churches looked after more than 3,000 displaced persons running from war and kept them for many weeks before an organization reached them. As a consequence there is insufficient food and medication, with psychological trauma among the population. Some families are grieving for their young boys who were conscripted into one or another of the armies.

The Baptist Community in Central Africa (CBCA) made one of its priorities for 1998-99 teachings in the area of reconciliation. They have witnessed first-hand the destruction of hatred and war. Their objective has been to teach Christ's love and forgiveness, and to encourage living at peace with one another.

Our presence in their midst during war has been a great encouragement to CBCA people. This opened the doors for me to work with the CBCA pastors in teaching and reconciliation, with these objectives:
a) Holding healing and reconciliation workshops to build skills in conflict management for the local churches and communities in the DRC
b) To train trainers who will continue after the Matwawana departure
c) Teaching youth the culture of non-violence, the alternative of tolerance, encouraging each participant on returning to church or village to teach ten others on peacemaking and reconciliation
All this has been undertaken at the grass-roots level, targeting pastors, deacons, women, youth leaders, who can multiply these efforts in churches and villages.

Nora on self-support

When João was away at the Bujumbura conference in Burundi, Nora was left at home in Goma without resources. It seems that they were down to 300 dollars, and that money had to go with João to the conference. CBM's Doug Loden had earlier brought guava trees that had been planted and were just coming to fruit. Nora made an arrangement with one of the young women of the community. For 10 percent of their value, she would pick guavas and sell them in the market. The proceeds represented Nora's self-support.

There came a time when financial instability and insecurity in the province was such that merchants were reluctant to take the cheques which CBM's treasury had provided to the Matwawanas as a means of transferring funds. Since there were stocks of salt in their store room, which João and Nora had purchased to give out as gifts on special occasions, João took this salt and proceeded to the market, where he secured what he needed on a barter system: "Potatoes for salt anyone? Bananas for salt?"

João secures passage through a roadblock with bananas

TRADE SCHOOLS AND REFUGEE SELF-HELP PROJECTS ESTABLISHED

The trade school project involving refugee camps started small, evolving naturally in response to the local need. It all began when João discovered that there were complaints and murmurings because starving refugees, needing wood for cooking, were breaking up the furniture in schools and churches for that purpose. When refugees first arrived in such great numbers, they used up the available firewood quickly, but still needed fuel for cooking. One of the churches complained that their chairs, tables, and benches had been broken up for firewood. It became obvious that tensions would build between refugees and the local population unless something could be done. In the first program that João started, young men from the Katale camp began repairing chairs and tables.

When João began communicating with the refugee pastors, he found them expressing a number of concerns, all related to needs that could be filled by creating a trade school. Their youth were at loose ends. They were fearful of being recruited by the *Interhamwe* militia, who were after both boys and girls. They wanted their young people to be busy. The opening of a trade school met two distinct sets of concerns, those of the local churches in Congo and those of the refugee pastors from Rwanda. Trade school for girls would allow them to make dresses for themselves, and others for sale. This would be good for their own self-respect and would gain them respect from others. Boys would learn carpentry.

To get the trade school underway, they built simple adobe mud block buildings with sheet metal roofing, just outside the Katale refugee camp near Kako. The carpentry shop began as soon as they identified skilled carpenters among the refugees, competent to serve as instructors.

The first items made would be presented to the CBCA for reconciliation plus restoration. The first benches went to the church in Kako where the problem was first identified, and the response to this was jubilation on the part of that congregation. Later, the schools made benches for their chapel in the refugee camp. CBM's *Sharing Way* provided support in the form of materials for the girls' classes and tools for use by the young men.

Benches they produced in the trade school were sold to the United Nations. When the UN officials inquired where these things had come from, they found that it was from the Baptist Project:

"When did you do all this?" they asked.
"After four o'clock."

The management of the trade schools fell under a mixed committee of refugees and Congolese. They administered all facets of the operation of these trade schools. João simply asked them for their budget requirement and undertook to secure it for them. They showed a very high level of initiative. A food purchasing committee negotiated effectively for the cheapest prices. The attitude was that if they were skilful in their bargaining, money could be saved for unforeseen expenditures such as coffins for the dead and blankets for the sick.

Then we bought some sewing machines, engaged some teachers we located in the camps and the girls began to learn how to sew dresses, and even to sell children's clothing. There were semi-nude children in the camp. They sold clothing at a reasonable price.

The United Nations staff were surprised that our 5,000 dollars produced so much, when they had considered us poor, and unqualified to participate in their programs. They had said that they accepted only organizations with a budget of at least 100,000 dollars. Of this, 10 percent would be levied by the United Nations for administrative costs and security. Perhaps they were unaware of Jesus' miracle of the loaves and the fishes.

The United Nations undertakes programs for a fixed span of time and they have an established budget, which they proceed to spend, otherwise they will be judged as not having done their work well. We who have been living there in the country think differently, and it is possible for us to proceed differently.

The big organizations have expenses which we do not need to match. Supposing they arrive with a foreign staff of ten. Each will need his or her own Toyota Land Cruiser at 40,000 dollars, even though the distance to travel may be only 20 kilometres on paved roads. They come with contingency plans made to provide for every possibility. We who live there know the conditions and precisely what is required. Our budgets can be more realistic to the needs.

The remarkable part about our experience in the camps was that the people promised to do the right thing after they went home, and in fact they seem to have done that. We heard amazing stories when we were later called into Rwanda to repeat the same kinds of seminars. When the camps were dismantled, approximately 200,000 people returned home to Rwanda. We heard stories from pastors in Rwanda that con-

firmed the impact of the seminars we had conducted with them while they were in the camps near Goma. There were others who feared arrest if they were to return home. They ran away to the forests of Congo and those are the ones who are still in the Congo until today. They are making trouble there now.*

INTERNATIONAL INFLUENCE ON LOCAL CONFLICTS

Pausing for an overview of Central Africa and its persistent hostilities, João observes that the nature of problem solving and conflict resolution has been changing. Problems which once might have been solved locally are now beyond that kind of intervention. New strategies are required, intervention at a different level:

Reconciliation can be made to work at the grass roots level. The problem comes when you move up to working with the hierarchies, and those hierarchies function at several different levels. At that point you have problems, because the remote control moves into the hands of foreign capitals like Paris, London, Washington, and Bonn. When that happens, people on the ground can no longer do anything.

In support of that observation, João recounts a conversation with two young guerilla fighters that highlighted for him the foreign origins of these conflicts, together with the continuing stimulus of foreign money that kept the hostilities going:

"Who is your commander?"
"A mzee." (An elder)
"His name?"
"We don't know."
"Can you fight for a commander if you don't know his name? I certainly wouldn't."
"You're a missionary and you have money. We have no money. That mzee *pays us 20 dollars every Friday."*
"From where?"

That last question remains unanswered. There are big business interests involved in mining and resources, interests which profit from instability, from the arms trade, from human conflict. There are corporations with mines in Kivu whose representatives, because they have money, can come and go at will. Those who fight are fighting for money.

The natural wealth of the eastern provinces of the Congo make the country a target for a wide range of private profiteers, corporate giants, superpowers hungry for raw materials, warlords with private armies, and even neighbouring countries, which are less than anxious to remove their armies, glad for excuses to keep them active inside Congo's borders, greedy for the benefits. Mineral resources abound. The presence of significant reserves of gold and uranium have long been attractive, and cassiterite exploitation continues to grow. The importance of tantalite to the computer and cell phone industries puts it on the high-paying list. Congo's populations are the all-round losers. Not only do they fail to benefit from the wealth that is looted and exported, their country is kept in turmoil, denying them the benefits of an ordered society and a stable administration that would allow stable lifestyles, as can be seen from the following newspaper report:

> *Thousands of Rwandan troops were massed on the country's border with Congo this week as a scramble for mineral wealth risked fresh conflict in Africa's Great Lakes region.*
>
> *A network of plunder—illegally mining precious metals in the forests of the Democratic Republic of Congo—has pushed Rwanda to the brink of another invasion. On Tuesday Rwanda's president, Paul Kagame, said his troops may have already crossed the border to hunt Hutu militants, but there was evidence of another reason: to protect Rwanda's access to riches.*
>
> *Congolese troops who are loyal to Rwanda are trying to keep control of mineral-rich areas in North and South Kivu provinces, which provide a flow of lucrative income to the elite in Kigali, the Rwandan capital.*

In the towns of Walikale and Rubaya, soldiers of the Rassemblement Congolais pour la Démocratie *(RCD-Goma), Rwanda's proxy force in eastern Congo, transferred sacks of the valuable minerals cassiterite and tantalite to lorries bound for airstrips from which jets shuttled to Kigali.*

(Carroll 2004:10)

15

NORA'S WORK WITH THE WOMEN

NORA'S WORK EXPANDS

After arrival at Bwatsinge, Nora noticed very early, in worship services, that there were children with signs of malnutrition. Her exposure to thousands of Angolan refugees made her very familiar with the symptoms of *kwashiorkor* (advanced malnutrition), evidenced by the extended stomachs of little children, and the loss of pigmentation from their hair, which showed reddish-brown rather than black. She also noticed many children on the street who were half-naked and dirty, and some mothers were not caring well for their children. What could she do about all this?

Nora recalled the nutrition course she had taken at the Centre of Ndjili in Kinshasa. She focussed her efforts on giving instruction to the mothers, and placed much emphasis on making use of foods readily available in the country. She had also observed in Kinshasa that some of the women who had adequate resources were making the wrong choices. Some bought canned goods because they were prestigious, but without attention to food value. Others chose to use milk powder or baby formula rather than breast-feeding their children.

The beginnings of instruction for women were modest. Nora travelled with João to the seminars for leaders that he had scheduled in places like Kirumba, Katwa, and Kanyabayonga. While he was instructing the men, Nora began to gather women for lessons in nutrition. Back at their residence in Bwatsinge, the initial instruction for women would require no special facilities, no special funding, as the Matwawanas subsidized this new project through the supplies from their own kitchen. Sixteen young women began to meet regularly with Nora in her house. Of the sixteen, fourteen were single. Of the two who were married, one had two children.

> *I determined to teach them self-esteem, and how a girl cares for herself.*
> *I taught them how to look after their clothes, to wash and to iron them.*
> *We focussed on how a woman makes herself presentable, how to prepare to go visiting.*
> *There were simple little details that you wouldn't think necessary—things like checking between their toes when washing their feet.*

There was initially some resistance from the parents of these girls. They couldn't see why girls who might be working in the garden or carrying wood or water should be going to the missionary's house. There were even comments that they should not go there to learn bad things. Parents were suspicious that their daughters might be taught to wear pants (Nora explains that due to its altitude above sea level, Bwatsinge was very cold, and that there were times when she found comfort in slacks). But the pastor at the Bwatsinge church was cooperative and allowed Nora to make announcements at the church concerning her work. She would also show samples of items prepared by the young women, and interest in what she was doing began to grow when people started noticing the results.

The Matwawanas were due for a trip out to Nairobi, Kenya, in 1993, and in preparation for that, Nora invited a man who had been teaching literacy in the villages to provide continuity for the work she had begun.

Eric and Merle MacKenzie, based in Nairobi, were CBM's African Representatives, and authorized to make adjustments to levels of financial support. While in Kenya, Nora brought to Merle's attention this work that she had been doing at Bwatsinge, and together they struck a budget of US400 dollars for materials. While in Nairobi, Nora was able to buy cloth, needles, thread, and crochet hooks, which were not available in Kivu.

Growth of the women's work and the need for a Women's Centre

On their return to Bwatsinge after the 1993 visit to Nairobi, Nora discovered that there were no less than a hundred new candidates who wished to sign up for her instruction. She had obviously made a breakthrough. A program of this dimension could no longer be run from her home. They needed facilities.

She was given an abandoned building that had served as a clinic. It took lots of work to clean it up, and even then the roof leaked. The ceiling was also falling. However, the teaching got underway with Nora's students divided into three groups, each having lessons twice weekly. Projects were undertaken geared to the level of the students.

Seeing so many naked children, Nora resolved to teach the women to sew by hand. The cloth she used came from used dresses purchased in the local market and from used curtains bought on sale. She taught them how to mark and cut the cloth and they began by making little things for the kids. Her projects included small tablecloths, how to knit, how to crochet and embroider.

Instruction was enriching the quality of the women's lives in a number of ways. It was obvious that there was great scope for beautification in their drab homes, and it would lift the population above bare simplicity, with impact on all—both children and adults. There was value in the additional cash that became available with the sale of handcrafted items. Providing a deeper and more subtle impact on the society, the self-esteem of the women was lifted, building their confidence and their general productivity, as well. It was easier for people to understand the meaning of Jesus' declaration that he had come so that people might have life and have it more abundantly, when one was able to see some sign of improvement in the quality of life, with dimensions of beauty in the home and in the lives of its occupants. Furthermore, the women found real joy in doing, in learning, in expanding the frontiers of their very confined world. Probably the closest thing to recreation that many wives would have experienced since the time when they were free to play as children, came as they learned these new skills.

Nora's seminars included child care. She also began teaching the rudiments of family planning, and at that point the women began insisting that their husbands be present. Otherwise, family planning would not work.

By 1994, the need for a place from which Nora could conduct her teaching became a serious problem:

We will not ask Canada for money to build a centre. You women will find a way.

Before returning to Canada for a brief four months in 1994, when they took Isabel to get her established in university, Nora collected 180 million zaïres which, at the time, amounted to US 14 dollars. As a result of inflation and devaluation, this amount had been reduced to the value of one bag of cement transported overland from Nairobi. In any case, she told them,

Make bricks and do whatever else you can by yourselves, while I go to Canada.

When Nora returned to Bwatsinge, she found that the bricks had been made and baked.

Then Muriel Bent, as CBM's Development Representative, visited with Matwawanas. She evaluated the program and the progress, and took note of the needs. Muriel wrote an enthusiastic report to CBM's *Sharing Way* Director, Marilyn Smith, saying, "We have no budget, but we must find help for this worthy undertaking." They pledged support of US 15,000 dollars.

By 1995, it was time to begin laying foundations for a new women's centre. They determined that some salaries would need to be paid to specialized helpers. Although that might seem obvious to us, it was actually a radical departure from the past. It was the Bwatsinge people's first instance of paying out cash for a church-related project. All projects had previously been completed by volunteer work and with materials that were either donated or produced by themselves.

Some aspects of the program continued as a volunteer project, such as the carrying of wood, water, brick, and stone. Even the principal and the teachers of the local primary school helped with the manual labour. Their participation was a measure of the esteem in which the project was held in the community.

When cement was mixed for the foundation, women carried the sand. This was carried on their heads 12 kilometres uphill from the river, a round-trip distance of 24 kilometres on foot for each bucket of sand. Some of the girls were up at 2 a.m. in order to be able to make the trip for a load of sand and then be back home in time to go to school. Water for the cement had to be carried up a steep hill and stored in barrels at the work site. This was all done by women and girls. Timbers for the roof were all carried by male students. The distance was 10 kilometres, making it a round trip of 20 kilometres. Men made and burned the bricks, bringing in large tree trunks to fuel the enormous ovens that they had constructed of the raw brick, with tunnels for the firing. This was a process that continued through two days and two nights.

Once the raw bricks were fire-hardened and cooled, each group took its turn carrying them 150 metres or so to the building site. One day it was the primary school students, the following day it was the women carrying brick, the next day the secondary school students, and so forth.

Women carried stones for the foundation, as did students from the High School, together with their principal. Any who have worked in Africa will acknowledge the very high degree of local commitment that would lure a high school principal into participating in such manual labour, as cultural expectations, a holdover from the Belgian colonial era, dictated that those who held positions of prestige, such as a school director, did not participate in manual activity. All this work was voluntary. The new women's centre was obviously high on the local community priority list.

The Mama Nora Centre was a local initiative with volunteer labour

Meanwhile I decided to teach the women how to bake small items which would produce income for them. For this project the only facility available was the wood stove in my own kitchen. The menu read like this:

How to make bread
Peanut butter cookies
Carrot cake
Banana bread
Plum cake
White cake
Sugar cookies

There was a logic behind her cooking menu. It was tailored to materials that were available, and all the items produced were marketable. Where a recipe called for vanilla, she would substitute lemon juice or orange juice.

After the cooking and baking lessons, Nora touched on a number of other topics:
- How to set a table.
- Sitting together for a cup of tea (this was a new concept)
- How to make beds.

Nora would take women shopping with her when she went to purchase materials at Butembo, where she introduced them to the merchants. She took them through what would have been a fearful restaurant experience, had they gone alone. She saw the need to teach women just how to hold a knife and fork when eating at the table. She reminisces when speaking on these topics, "I never dreamed in the early years of my own experience that I would ever be in Canada."

Nora kept busy with a combination of teaching and building. She was her own supervisor of the construction project, although João helped from time to time with the purchase and the transportation of some construction supplies. Securing supplies had become a problem because of the deterioration of the entire administrative system in the Congo. Upkeep of roads suffered and travel became very slow, in addition to being highly uncomfortable. This had its impact on getting supplies, as on so much else.

From the outset, Nora impressed upon the women that they must be prepared to buy their own materials. To help in that preparation, she charged fees. Officers were elected among the women, including a treasurer to handle income. Still, Nora was troubled and puzzled as she faced the issue of program continuity past the time of their projected return to Canada. With this in mind, she approached government representatives responsible for social work and invited them to visit her program at Bwatsinge. Would she be able to get government recognition for the programs she had begun? Would the women who passed through her classes be given access to some sort of employment with the government? The officials agreed to attend. So they hastened to finish the centre and to prepare her students for examinations.

Opening of the new Bwatsinge Women's Centre

May of 1995 was one of those very hectic months. Nora worked around the clock in order to finish her sewing and crocheting classes with the women. Funds granted by CBM had allowed Nora to purchase paint, curtains, and furniture for the new centre.

The Women's Centre consisted of a kitchen, storage, office, two classrooms, a waiting room, and an office desk and chair. There were benches in the classrooms, with cupboards, cutting tables, a sofa and chairs, a lunchroom, and a coffee table.

The highlight of the month was the opening of the new Bwatsinge Women's Centre, and its graduation attended by a government representative.

The government inspector was a lady from Goma. The tests included the baking of a cake to present to the inspector. There had been much fear of the exam, and a few were not prepared to face it. However, all who took the examination passed, and more than fifty government certificates were presented. The centre was inaugurated with honour. They called it the *Centre Sociale Mama Nora*.

Events such as the government inspection, the inauguration of the new centre, and the graduation of sisters, wives, and mothers, could not pass unnoticed. It was a big day and the church bought a cow to be slaughtered for the celebration feast. Women and girls sewed their own uniforms.

The impact of the women's program on the community soon became evident. Because Bwatsinge was changing as a result of it, the men and boys finally came to accept that women and girls must learn. After the inauguration, there were women who came from considerable distances to stay and learn in a two-year program. The projects they undertook were geared to the level of the students.

Following the Matwawanas' home assignment in 1995-96, additional funding from CBM permitted the purchase of sewing machines and a wood stove. Nominal fees were charged for the use of the sewing machine, which had a zigzag feature, and for use of the wood stove to bake bread for sale.

Unfortunately, given the rough years that have intervened, the situation at Bwatsinge has since deteriorated.

16

RECONCILIATION WORK IN RWANDA

INVITATION TO KIGALI, RWANDA

At the end of 1996, João received an invitation to join a Kigali team to conduct four-week healing and reconciliation seminars for ninety pastors and lay leaders in Kigali between February and March of 1997.

The impact of João's work in the refugee camps near Goma was so significant that when those pastors who had lived in the camps and participated in his workshops returned to their homes in Rwanda, the reputation of the seminars spread.

Rev. Faustin Bashaka, General Secretary of the Association of Baptist Churches in Rwanda, had fled to the Congo as one pastor among many in that mass exodus following the genocide. He lived for a time in one of the refugee camps near Goma. There he attended João's seminars and observed the practical and effective work being done, preparing Hutu pastors for the steps needed to reintegrate back into a mixed society.

Pastor Bashaka issued an appeal through Canadian Baptist

Ministries for help to continue that reconciliation and reconstruction process in Rwanda.

RWANDA RECONCILIATION WORK UNDERTAKEN WITH DR. CHARLES FOSTER

The Foster and Matwawana families were both under appointment by Canadian Baptist Ministries:

Charlie and I did some work together both in Kigali (Rwanda) and in Goma (Congo). The thrust of what Charlie was undertaking in reconciliation focussed more on the university level, working with the academic community and in conjunction with L'Université Libre des Pays des Grands Lacs. What Charlie was doing was very necessary, because these university students will be the future leaders and trend-setters. They need a solid understanding of peace and reconciliation. It was a good combination, both of us working there.

The first time we were invited to Kigali, it was scary. At that time, the refugee camps were still in place in Goma. There was no communication then between Kigali and Goma. We were still in the era of Mobutu Sese-Seko as President of Zaïre (Congo). Goma was considered by Kigali to be the enemy camp, and we needed to drive from Goma to Kigali by vehicle.

The question which Charlie and I discussed between us was, "What does Rev. Faustin Bashaka want? We will be killed there!"

But from Bashaka there came only encouragement to proceed. "I have spoken with the government authorities here, and we need you. We want you to do the same things you have been doing in the camps near Goma, because the people here need it, too. They are hurting in the same way that the people in the refugee camps are hurting."

Travel into Rwanda

Officially, the border post was closed. As they arrived at the checkpoint, Charlie Foster stayed in the car as João presented himself to the border official with their two Canadian passports. The official took note of João's birthplace, Mbanza-Kongo, and he recalled from his history studies that this was the seat of the ancient Kingdom of the Kongo. Discussion resulted. Conversation helps, but it does not always remove all the obstacles:

"We are not ready for this yet."
"But the church is ready."
"Canadians, are you? ... Hmmmm. You may go."

They arrived in Kigali on February 4, and found that because of the unstable and perilous situation in Rwanda, the majority of expatriates around them were packing to leave. In a period of less than three weeks, three Spanish aid workers were killed and a sixty-one-year-old Canadian priest was slain as he celebrated mass. These killings were followed by the attack of two mini-buses and five UN human rights observers were killed.

João and Charlie proceeded to the Presbyterian Conference Centre. Its facilities had been bombed. The roof was open to the sky. That is where their meetings took place, before repairs had started. Their first session lasted a week or so.

Their first seminar was attended by eighteen regional pastors, four heads of departments and twelve headmasters of secondary schools. Before the end of their second seminar, other churches and organizations asked them to extend their stay in Rwanda in order to participate in other workshops. João then participated in another one-week workshop which was organized by the Church Council of Rwanda. Speakers dealt with the difficult issue of "The Role of the Rwandan Church Before, During, and After the Genocide."

As an opener to sessions that they conducted together, Charlie encouraged João to tell his own personal story as an Angolan refugee, his journey from hatred to unconditional love. Charlie then followed with biblical texts appropriate to the occasion. They discovered that the pastors were uptight, very tense. Their immediate task was to help people open up, and this was done through eliciting their stories. Pastors and church leaders from about seven denominations participated. They were divided into groups of three. One would tell his story, the second was asked to repeat it, the third to evaluate and point out what was missing:

"You may scream and cry while telling your story. You are allowed to do that. But the others must listen."
From that phase they turned to seek input of a different nature.
"Now let's turn to the positive."
"Let's dream of Rwanda and peace."
"Let's dream of children laughing and playing, of women dancing."

"There were large numbers of people who spent time in the refugee camps who felt they were absolutely innocent," they explained. *"We had to run, just because everyone was running."*

Those were the people who went back to Rwanda out of the camps. Among them were individuals who performed acts of great courage which should be written up, but no newspapers were writing them. These people began coming to the seminars we were giving in Rwanda, seminars designed initially for those who had not fled to Congo, but expanded to include returnees. When we got underway I would ask "Do we have anybody here who lived in a camp? If so please raise your hand." That group might represent up to 50 percent of the attendance.

"So some of you have been through these sessions before?"
"Yes."
"Why did you come back again?"
"Because we wanted to hear it more, and we want to help our brothers."

These were both Hutu and Tutsi people, all mixed together.

Repentance and remorse

Then we would have sharing times, and that's when we would hear of the power of God in forgiveness. There were Tutsis, for example, who would come to a Hutu family and say, "My nephew killed your family. He's wandering in the forest with the rebels. Because of what my nephew did I want to pay compensation, whatever compensation you want."

There was moving evidence of real repentance, real remorse over the inter-ethnic killings, instances of conversations such as these which required deep courage and a long-term commitment to make things right:

"Is there any way I could work in your plantation twice a week to compensate you for your suffering?"
"No, you don't need to do that, we can forgive."
"No, I want to do something tangible. I want to offer myself for all of my life to work two days a week in your plantation."
"That showed a lot of courage. Why don't reporters write about such things?"

An incident witnessed by Nora

On another trip, Nora was attending a women's conference with women present from both Rwanda and Burundi. At the sharing time, one Tutsi woman was crying. Nora listened in on the conversation she had with her neighbour:

"I have a guilty feeling."
"What is this guilty feeling?"
"Because you are Hutu."
"You should not have a guilty feeling, you Tutsi people were the victims."
"You don't have the whole story."

So Nora heard the whole story about how, during the massacre, this Tutsi woman had a close friend who was a Hutu.

> "She called me and my family to her house and she hid us in the attic, because if those young people were to see us they would kill us. We were in her attic about ten days, until the slaughter finished. The lady cooked for us, washed our clothes, she clothed my children."

When the massacre finished, this Hutu lady told the Tutsi family that it was now time to flee, and they did so. However, some of her neighbours working in a garden nearby had observed the Tutsi family as they emerged and fled from that Hutu home which had sheltered them. They betrayed the Hutu lady to the Militia, and the house was surrounded.

> "You were harboring enemies."
> "They are innocent."
> "There is no question of innocence or guilt. Every Tutsi has to die. Why did you hide them?"
> "They are my friends."
> "The lesson we will give you is this. We will not kill you, but you will be in pain for all your life."

The Hutu militia then killed all four children of this Hutu woman because she had demonstrated that she was a moderate. After the conflict finished and the government changed to a Tutsi regime, the Tutsis returned to their villages, including the woman who had been sheltered. The woman concluded the story of her guilt in these terms:

> "Here I am, with all my children, intact. I'm a Tutsi, and I did not suffer in the genocide. I escaped because my friend, who is a Hutu, undertook to protect me. She lost all of her children because of that. Why don't people talk about these things? They say that all Hutus are bad, but this Hutu suffered because of the love she has for me, and that is why I'm suffering."

Some day people will read about this, and realize that where there is love, there are no barriers.

Nora does trauma counselling in Rwanda

RECONCILIATION SESSIONS MAKE A DIFFERENCE

At the end of his reconciliation seminars in Rwanda, it was João's custom to give opportunity to participants who had something they wished to share. One young man who chose to speak was probably nineteen or twenty years old, and he blurted out these statements:

"My family were killed during the genocide."
"I tried to plan ways of getting revenge."
"These seminars have helped."
"Then today, the worship service here was the culmination."
"A big load has been lifted from me."
"As of today I forgive all the criminals and I forgive those who killed my family."

The Occupation of Enemy Houses

There were many Tutsis who had occupied the homes of Hutus, but surrendered them when the owners returned. And cases of those who would *not* surrender them. Here we see the difference between those who have reconciliation in their hearts and those who do not. In fact, there were those who would accuse a returning property owner falsely, wiping out the person as well as their claim to the property:

> *Many encouraging signs of progress in relationships showed up in the villages. There were Hutus and Tutsis who worked together in the co-operatives after the conflict. Not many reporters write about those things because those stories don't seem to sell newspapers. However, if there is one* Interhamwe *attack on a village after months of peace, that will get treated as big news.*

It was important for the Matwawanas to have had time to minister in Rwanda. It was an opportunity to learn of results of their ministries in the refugee camps of Kivu.

Methodology used both in Kivu and in Rwanda

João found that when holding reconciliation sessions with semi-literate people, illustrations are the key. Conference notes might or might not be meaningful or even readable to participants, depending on the state of their literacy and their reading habits. So he focused on the strategic use of illustrations that participants readily grasped and could easily remember.

One particular outline, which João used effectively, concentrated on three components of the human anatomy—"The Head, the Heart, and the Hands."

The head

Consider how much thinking and planning we sometimes go through before we actually do something. Do you think genocide was an accident?

"No, it was not. Our people had been thinking and talking about killing for a long time. As a pastor I didn't believe that it would ever happen," said one Hutu pastor.

"So it was necessary then, that someone should have been cleaning your minds of what you had been talking about?"

"Yes. If we only knew, but now it is too late. I now know people around us were preparing something dangerous without our realizing it. They were saying that if one day we have a way, these enemies will have to be eliminated. They have been killing us and making us suffer over all these years. We called them 'rebels' back then, and they were attacking, killing my people. They invaded too many places in Rwanda. This rebel group has now become the government. They killed so many. They burned hospitals. They burned schools."

The only way those who had been oppressed could envisage a response appropriate to all the suffering that they had absorbed across the decades and generations was to plan ahead for the day when they would be able to eliminate their enemies. When the reality of that sentiment was elicited from them in discussion and dialogue, they could see and readily admit the role that their minds played in leading up to violent action. Our seminars led them through a process that made them conscious of how our mental processes are directly related to any action that we take later on.

Then in due course we would come around to relevant Scriptures.

> Do not conform any longer to the patterns of this world,
> but be transformed by the renewing of your mind.
> Then you will be able to test and approve what God's will is—
> his good, pleasing and perfect will.
> Romans 12:2

The heart

And then we move on to talk about the heart, how the Lord can give one a new heart because of His promise. But you have to give that heart to the Lord first. One makes a direct connection with the gospel, a message with which they are already familiar, but which they have been unable to apply, or have not even tried to apply to the grave ethnic problems that they have been caught up in. People start understanding. They come to the point of thinking, "Oh, so really I need a change?" and that represents a significant step forward.

Then we give more lessons about the heart, like the lessons of the prophets Jeremiah and Ezekiel when they talked about the heart:

> *The heart is deceitful above all things*
> *and beyond cure.*
> *Who can understand it?*
> Jeremiah 17:9

> *"You will seek me and find me*
> *when you seek me with all your heart.*
> *I will be found by you," declares the Lord,*
> *"and will bring you back from captivity."*
> Jeremiah 29: 13-14

> *I will give you a new heart and put a new spirit in you;*
> *I will remove from you your heart of stone and give you a heart of flesh.*
> *And I will put my Spirit in you and move you to follow my decrees*
> *and be careful to keep my laws.*
> *…You will be my people, and I will be your God.*
> *I will save you from all your uncleanness.*
> Ezekiel 36:26-29

Also, we considered the choice of words used by the prophet when he was addressing King David: "The Lord sees the heart," and the importance of the choice coming from the heart. So the people understood in that way, in a simple way.

The hands

The head represents the mind, the heart is the motivation, then we speak of the hands which represent overt action, the concrete actions involved in the doing of evil. In our conferences we remember and speak openly about the machetes, the axes, the hoes they used in the killings—whatever. Then we emphasized the importance of our hands being a gift from God. A gift if properly used, and how these hands can turn into an instrument of the Devil if they are not properly used. They see the difference, and they comment like this:

"Yes, that's true."
"So then even your hands need to be purified."

Then there would be some role playing with two participants, one Tutsi, one Hutu, sitting in chairs facing each other.
"How do you feel when someone says, shake hands with him?"
"I will be frozen."

"So you see that your hands are a real symbol of hostility or of friendship. You see that when your hand is liberated it will bring friendship. It will bring blessing, because you will shake hands, even with the enemy."

Basically in every topic we used some illustrations and some role playing.

Above all else we cannot be hurried. The pace cannot be forced. We people who have a background of experience in western culture, with its rapid pace and with the pride we have in our speed and efficiency, cannot bring these components into a rec-

onciliation process among people who have moved at a different tempo for all of their lives.

The new component introduced by a specifically Christian approach to reconciliation is the component of repentance and forgiveness. This is something which all these other organizations are missing. They introduce principles of mediation, reconciliation, conflict management and skills, they introduce the participants to all these things. What happens is that these people hear it all, yet remain unmoved from their affirmation that they only did what was right and what was expected of them in their culture.

"But I didn't do anything wrong," they would say, "because what I did was simply revenging the suffering of what was done to my uncle and my grandparents. I am revenging what they did to my tribe and that is not wrong. These others were the criminals. They were very bad. What I did was just my duty."

Reconciliation conferences must not be hurried

This is the thing which other organizations don't know. They think that as long as you teach people how to reconcile, and how to solve their difference, it is enough. Well, the heart is not touched.

There was a conference for reconciliation in Nairobi or Kampala, I can't remember which. They took some of our people from Kivu, mostly area chiefs, to go to that big conference. These were people to whom we had ministered already. We didn't think there was any need for them to go, but they went anyway, because everything was paid.

I asked them to give me some kind of evaluation of what happened. These are the comments of one chief who participated in a UN-sponsored set of treaty talks:

"That conference created a lot of confusion in my life. Why? First of all, I didn't understand anything they talked about. Second, they were using methods which ignored the processes which must take place in our communities."

So I said, *"Well, what they had put in writing, you signed it. This peace treaty with the other tribe. How can you say that you didn't understand?"*

"You want to know? I signed because I was under pressure. These people were saying they had to catch the flight at six in the evening. If you don't sign, nobody will pay your ticket back to your village. So I signed under pressure. We had to let these people go, so they would not miss their flight."

"That's the reason you signed?"

"That's the reason I signed. These people almost lost their flight."

"So you didn't understand the conference but you signed just to liberate the others not to lose their flight?"

"Yes."

"Can you remember anything good from the conference even if you didn't understand the reconciliation?"

"The good thing I can remember is that I never slept in a hotel like that. It was the first time in my life. That is something good I can remember. Good food, good drinks, good champagne, and good wine. So those are the good things I could remember. But when it comes to peace and reconciliation, zero." Then he said, *"What you teach, we understand."*

So I said, *"Oh, boy!"* And then, when I saw the budget—oh, the budget! I think it was 1.7 million American dollars spent on that peace and reconciliation attempt with the result of zero.

When the Matwawanas would go to reconciliation conferences, they would travel with an open airline ticket, with no fixed return date. This allowed them the flexibility of staying with people until problems were resolved.

17

BACK TO KENYA

The Matwawanas' work took them in and out of Kenya several times over the years while they were working in Kivu and Rwanda, and eventually the dangers of the situation in Kivu brought them back to teaching in Kenya once more. When João and Nora eventually left Kivu, it was by vehicle across the nearby Rwandan border to Kigali and a flight to Nairobi.

They had become increasingly familiar with Kenya, and by now were comfortable in their working relationship with CBM's partners in that country, the African Christian Church and Schools (ACC&S), and the African Brotherhood Church (ABC).

Teaching at two seminaries

Earlier teaching in Kenya, during 1992, had been at the ABC Divinity School in Mitaboni. When they returned in 1999, unable again to work in an unstable Kivu Province of Congo, it was to teach both there and at the ACC&S Seminary in Thika, an hour north of Nairobi. During the intervening years they had passed through Nairobi many times, but now they were back to make a contribution to two groups of Christians whom they were coming to know well.

Incidentally, they helped lay the academic foundations that helped the students at these seminaries to qualify for participation in a Certificate of Ministry program. This program was developed in conjunction with Carey Theological College in Vancouver, Canada, a logical outworking of CBM's and its staff working in East Africa. The key person in developing this program was Dr. Brian Stelck, who had lived and worked at Mitaboni with his family.

João's courses included Discipleship, Introduction to Chaplaincy, Communication Skills, Conflict Resolution, Christian Ethics, Special Ministry to HIV/AIDS Patients and their Families, Homiletics, and the Gospel of John. Nora taught Home Economics, Christian Family, and the Book of Ruth to seminary students. Both João and Nora were greatly appreciated by the students, who credited them with much innovation. In turn they became part of the family life of students and were invited to special events, which included weddings, birthdays, anniversaries, and family gatherings.

One of the Matwawana letters mentioned the receptivity of the students in both seminaries, and the love which João and Nora had developed for Kenyan Christians in every church. Their activities were not restricted to the classroom. They were out among the churches and the people. They were active in holding retreats and seminars with pastors and their wives. João helped students and pastors to face issues relating to HIV/AIDS. He found both a reticence to touch the topic at all, and a general state of denial, and he helped them to overcome both.

While teaching at the Divinity School of the African Brotherhood Church in Mitaboni, João elected to take his students from Mitaboni to do visitation among AIDS patients in the hospital at Machakos. One of the purposes was to help the students feel comfortable working with AIDS patients. This did not come easily, for there was a lot of denial both in the community and in the churches.

For the chaplaincy training, he rented mini-buses to move the students back and forth for their sessions at the hospital. Every student would pass one hour with an AIDS patient, ministering to them. Hospital staff were appreciative and most enthusiastic. They commented that the hospital atmosphere began to change as a result. The patients felt loved and cared for. Patients included both men and women and covered a range of ages.

Another almost incidental training opportunity emerged in relationship to the ACC&S, when their General Secretary requested that João assume the role of mentor for their young Kikuyu pastor Samuel Ngaruiya, a graduate of the Certificate of Ministry program offered to the pastors of both ACC&S and ABC by Carey Theological College of Vancouver. This involved regular meetings with the student, as well as working with him in the context of the Ongata Rongai church, which Samuel was pastoring while he studied. It was an opportunity for one African-born leader who had benefited extensively through his international contacts to pour something of himself and his vision for Africa into the life and experience of another, much younger, but already in ministry.

The impact of João's ministries has not been the simple result of words or ideas only, for they are enhanced by the charismatic nature of the man, combined with his genuine love, concern, and interest in people. But words and ideas do count.

Thinking about Retirement

As João's formal retirement age approached, the topic of the Matwawanas' return to Canada was raised in conversation with the ABC's revered Bishop Nathan Ngala:

"You say you are going back. But you have just begun."

"I'm going back."

"Shame on you, young people don't retire."

To grasp the significance of that conversation, one needs to know that Bishop Ngala is a big man in every way, not only large of frame, but great in faith, also having a robust vision for his people and his church. Combined with that, he is still both strong and energetic, far more energetic than one would expect to find in a man well along in his nineties. But why should he not expect to have years of active work ahead when his own mother only died in the year 2001. Calculations based on known events placed her age at death as being around 120.

Indeed, people who are young at heart don't retire, and although the Matwawanas' years were advancing toward that North American cut-off age when retirement normally happens, they were constantly aware that Angola, the land of their birth, continued to be a place of suffering and of need. A February message from 1999 reveals the never-failing concern for Angola:

> ... we are settled in Nairobi. João is now teaching at both Thika and Mitaboni Divinity Schools. We also have a busy schedule of seminars for pastors and other church leaders. From time to time we receive news from Kivu. The church leaders are still urging us to remain in Kenya until the situation will improve there.
>
> As you know, we are also saddened by the war in Angola in general. The news of 12,000 Angolan refuges in Bas-Congo, from Mbanza-Kongo area, reminds us of the bad memories of the people's suffering since March 1961. I do hope that the Sharing Way *will reach out to those people as fast as possible.*

PART FIVE

MINISTRIES FOLLOWING RETIREMENT

REAPING THE ADVANTAGES OF AGE AND EXPERIENCE

18

BURUNDI

CANADA: DISTINGUISHED SERVICE AWARD

On the occasion of the Commissioning Service held for its class of 2001, the Acadia Divinity College Alumni Association conferred their Distinguished Service Award on Rev. João Matwawana. Dr. M. Allen Gibson covered the event for the *Halifax Chronicle Herald*:

> *The inclusion of Pastor Matwawana in the list (of distinguished recipients) is a recognition of an individual who has been described as: "one of Africa's best exports to Canada."*

He went on to report on the observations of Rev. Daniel Green, President of the alumni, as he made the presentation:

> *"I would rate him as one of a very choice and small band of African graduates who have done much to bring change to their own lands."*
>
> (Gibson 2001)

João Matwawana

A HEART FOR PEACEMAKING

Early in 2001, João and Nora undertook deputation speaking engagements in Ontario. In discussions with John Keith, João articulated his vision and convictions which had been building in his deeper being:

John, the time has come when we must move peacemaking efforts to a new and different level. It used to be that one could confront and perhaps even solve Africa's conflicts locally. The tensions often related to land, boundaries, property ownership, theft, accidental disfigurement or even death, conflict between families or groups, flocks and grazing rights, or a number of other topics that could be confronted face to face, solutions reached.

These wars Africa is experiencing today are of a different nature. The remote control is in the hands of others, perhaps in Brussels, Paris, London, New York, or Berlin. The root causes, often economic, and often involving rich natural resources, are not always evident. Those who benefit may be invisible and difficult to identify. Solutions must now be of a different nature. At present we do not have access to participation in the kind of peacemaking that is needed.

This was an astute summary, which led to pondering just where beginnings might be made, and how private individuals such as João, or non-governmental organizations (NGOs) like CBM, might be able to make a positive contribution in an arena where only official teams recognized and sponsored by the United Nations held credibility. Some toe-hold had to be sought prayerfully and diligently.

VISIT TO MUHEBA REFUGEE CAMP IN ZAMBIA, APRIL 2001

Since João and Nora have twice been refugees themselves, their concern for refugees has never faded. Whereas they themselves had integrated remarkably into Congolese society, and found acceptance, some of Angola's refugees, especially those in other countries, had been restricted to life in refugee camps for nearly forty years. His visit to Zambia was not in response to any specific request, it simply grew out of this inner concern.

João's first post-retirement sortie to Africa was in favour of refugees. He was aware of the refugee scene in the Congo but hungered to see the condition of refugees in Zambia, Namibia, and elsewhere. He called this undertaking a fact-finding mission. Nora remained at their home at Lower Sackville, a suburb of Halifax.

The visit to Zambia represented another step of faith in the life of our peace and reconciliation consultant, taken without being able to predict either the outcome or the timing, or the nature of the end events.

With John Keith when making plans for peace-building missions in Africa

Travel Documents

In spite of João's intense desire to help Angola when he retired formally, internal conditions did not yet favour his immediate participation in national affairs there, due to the ongoing conflict. Instead, other peacemaking opportunities unfolded, relating specifically to Burundi. This experience equipped him to serve Angola better when the time was ripe. Then, once he began to undertake peace missions to Angola, concerns about documentation were an impediment for two more years. Canadians require a visa to enter Angola. For a prolonged stay, a work permit is needed, involving a complicated process of application procedures. It appears that there is no simple process by which the formalities can be bypassed in favour of someone whose assistance is particularly desirable. João's first few visits to Angola were limited in duration by visa restrictions or difficulty in securing extensions. For that reason, João came to invest considerable time and effort securing the documentation verifying his Angolan birth, the securing of a *bilhete de identidade*, and eventually his Angolan passport, with dual citizenship, permitting him the freedom of entry and exit that would lay those concerns to rest. Later, Nora did the same.

A SIGNIFICANT EVENT AT CAMP IAWAH

In October, a conference was held at Camp IAWAH, north of Kingston, Ontario, co-ordinated by Dr. Charlie and Mrs. Elma Foster, with the help of expatriates resident in and around Kingston linked with Queens University or in the professions. Invitations had gone to diplomats in Ottawa and to immigrants from the Great Lakes region of Africa, living as far away as Montreal. While there were many issues of concern, the agonies of the Hutu-Tutsi conflict of Rwanda were high in everyone's awareness. In fact, a special speaker was invited, Major Brent Beardsley, an officer who served under General Romeo D'Allaire in Rwanda.

The conference was convened under the title, "Conflict Management vs. Humanistic Reconstruction" and was unapologetic in its Christian approach to Africa's needs and concerns. (The name of the camp, IAWAH, is based on an acronym of a scriptural theme, "In All Ways Acknowledge Him.")

The tranquillity of IAWAH's setting, removed from official concerns and demands, created a serene atmosphere in which unusual relationships developed. The two dozen or so participants from Canada, Rwanda, USA, Burundi, and the Congo included politicians, professionals, academics, and representatives of NGOs who had worked in the region. Most of the African participants had lost members of their immediate families within the last eight years. For many participants, given the ethnic makeup of the group, "the enemy" who had taken the lives of loved ones was represented in the room. It was indeed an explosive mix.

> *Hatred is explosive, but God's love and reconciliation and forgiveness are also explosive, and it was this combination which burst in on us at Camp IAWAH, especially on Wednesday, October 31. ... What happened that day to trigger the breakthrough is best classified as "brokenness" on the part of an important participant from Burundi. It brought an inability to communicate in words the depth of grief and suffering that he had experienced.*
>
> *This brokenness was met in turn by tears, apology, and a plea for forgiveness by another of the key players, all this at a level none present would have considered possible. The affirmations of unity and oneness which were then expressed among diverse ethnic and diverse political streams from within Burundi were not orchestrated, indeed they could not have been. They were the work of God. They virtually exploded in our midst, and we rejoiced. Participants referred to the morning as a significant breakthrough in reconciliation between the divided elements of Burundi's community within Canada.*
>
> (InfoMission, January 2002)

The spinoff from this remarkable day led to the formulation of what they called "Operation Osprey," in which João Matwawana became the principal player.

During the discussions that day, Burundi's Ambassador Edonias Niyongabo explained that, when Burundi's President Melchior Ndadaye had been assassinated in October of 1993, he chose to return to Burundi from their embassy in Paris. This was a courageous step he had taken.

"I would do more even now if I had access to a small amount of money."

"That's a surprising statement, Excellency. Most significant events and processes are dependent on initiative, imagination, boldness, skill, or other factors, often combined with large amounts of capital expenditure. It is a rare occasion that small amounts of money can make a difference. What would you do if you had a small amount of money?"

"I would fly two of Burundi's rebel leaders to Ottawa, for I believe I could convince them to join the peace process, which they have been refusing to do for more than two years. I happen to know them personally. I cannot leave my post as ambassador to go to them in Africa. If I were to propose this to my government, the complications and protocol would be long and involved and it would risk not happening."

Soon the basic concepts of Operation Osprey began to take shape. The idea was this: funding would be sought to send João Matwawana to Africa to locate the rebel leaders, speak with them, convince them that he would be their security insurance, accompany them back to Canada, and stay with them until they were again in Africa.

The osprey is Canada's famous fish eagle, which goes fishing, carrying its prey back to the nest. Only then does the action begin to take place. Hence the name Operation Osprey. João Matwawana would go fishing in Africa, but the real action would only begin to happen back in Ottawa, once the rebel leaders arrived there with him.

Testing Options at Foreign Affairs Canada

The next day, João and John were directed to Minister David Kilgour's constituency office in the East Block of Parliament, where both he and Africa Director Arthur Perron and another consultant were waiting. They heard and considered the proposals, and although they had certain doubts, the concept was not rejected entirely. First, they said, civil servants in Foreign Affairs, those relating directly to Central Africa, would need to be convinced. Second, there was a question about the wisdom of trying to bring rebel leaders into Canada.

Six weeks passed before the next significant development. João and John met at Burundi's embassy in Ottawa, to learn from Ambassador Edonias that there were new developments bearing on the Osprey proposal. Four days earlier, the United Nations had issued a press release transferring leadership of the Burundi-related peace mission team from ailing President Mandela to a co-facilitating team consisting of Gabon's President Omar Bongo and South Africa's Deputy President Jacob Zuma. President Mandela had worked for three years without success on this very project, namely, the attempt to bring the *Conseil national pour la défense de la démocratie-Force pour la défense de la démocratie* (CNDD/FDD) *rebel* movement back to the peace table, along with another movement, the *Forces Nationales pour la Libération* (FNL). These two holdout groups had refused to sign the Arusha Peace Accord in Tanzania in August 2000.

Ambassador Edonias' news from Foreign Affairs Canada was not encouraging. First, Canada had capped its contribution to the Burundi peace process and could not be expected to invest more. Second, there was no hope that attempts to bring rebel leaders to Canada would meet with any favour from Immigration Canada. Ambassador Edonias now appealed to João Matwawana and to Canadian Baptist Ministries. Operation Osprey must be adapted or re-designed in some way that would permit João to go to Pretoria, where the ambassador had located the key political advisor to the CNDD/FDD movement, Jean-Marie Ngendahayo. As a personal representative of Ambassador Edonias Niyongabo, João's task would be to convince Jean-Marie and others of his party to return to the discussion table of the United Nations peace process. "Our hope," he said, "lies in you." We shared prayer with him there at the embassy, as we had done before.

The next stop, the same day, was at the Pearson Building of Foreign Affairs Canada. Mr. Perron's assistant was the door opener to our meeting with Louis-Robert Daigle, Director General for Western and Central Africa Division, Francophone Africa, who soon called in Mireille Coderre, the Burundi desk officer.

Ministries Following Retirement

"But we have no financial support for you, so what do you want from us?"

"We seek your moral support, your approval, and the intervention of Canada's High Commissioner in Pretoria to gain access to Deputy-President Zuma."

"You have it."

Accepting Louis-Robert Daigle's conditions, they learned that key players on President Mandela's team had been "Fink" Haysom and Jan Van Eck. They would be continuing on with the new co-facilitators. The beginnings of João's mission must absolutely be made through them, he said. His final word was that any contact with Canada's High Commission in Pretoria could only be made by Minister Kilgour.

When Minister Kilgour heard of our success at the Pearson Building, his guarantee of support was immediate. His signature would go on the introductory letter for João early in the morning.

A call to a special donor confirmed her readiness to provide funding for João's travel to Pretoria, since CBM had no such budget provision.

That evening's reception offered by Kenya's High Commissioner, Green Josiah, provided João with his first opportunity to meet Angola's ambassador to Canada, His Excellency Miguel N'Zau Puna. The Angolan ambassador's greeting was a warm one, and nothing would do but that we visit the Angolan embassy the following morning, a meeting that went well and established the foundation for future contacts. As the story of João's involvement in Burundi's peace process emerged, Ambassador Puna asked, "And when will he be involved with Angola?" To this question the ready response was, "The day after tomorrow, once you have invited him."

João Matwawana to South Africa

As the year 2002 dawned, preparations were well underway for travel to Pretoria, with Minister Kilgour's introductory letter directed to Canada's High Commissioner, Her Excellency Lucie Edwards.

The pace at which developments were unfolding exceeded all expectations. On arrival at Capetown, and even before his first meeting, João checked his e-mail and found a message waiting from Ambassador Edonias Niyongabo in Ottawa, forwarding a message from Jean-Marie that said he was waiting for a call from João, and included his cell phone number.

Before leaving Canada, João had confided his suspicion that it might be days or weeks before he would be able to get down to root issues with Jean-Marie. Not having met him, not knowing his disposition, his attitudes, his orientation, or his level of sophistication, João was prepared to spend appropriate time, African style, establishing some sort of comfortable rapport. Might this "advisor" to a rebel movement be a rough old bush fighter, perhaps wise but maybe unlettered?

It may be days before I get around to speaking directly about peace negotiations. I may have to discuss rainfall, the condition of his chickens or goats, his family matters and whatever other concerns I discover, before it would be the right time to talk about the peace process. I want to do this the African way, and that means not being rushed.

The reality was quite different, and establishing rapport came easily. João found Jean-Marie to be a sophisticated and experienced politician, who had served as Minister of Foreign Affairs in the elected government of assassinated President Ndadaye. No diplomatic footwork was required as a transition to serious discussions. Ambassador Edonias had sent a communication so that all would be in readiness.

The initial phone contact to Jean-Marie was made early on Sunday afternoon, January 27. As soon as João identified himself, the response was "'I have been waiting a week for your call, brother." Plans were made, and he came to pick up João the next morning at ten, when they would go out for a working lunch. The process was under way. João's diary records the following:

Today I will relax and prepare my mind and spirit for the task before me. I am praying that God will grant me wisdom and the leading of the Holy Spirit to convince this man to choose peace instead of war. I will be ready with the Bible I will present to him.

Plans for the day ahead were charted in the diary. João would open with the prayer of St. Francis of Assisi, then a sharing of his own experiences as a refugee from Angola to Congo in 1961, his studies, his return to Angola and his second refugee experience. His decision to forgive the MPLA in 1990 would be described, and the personal peace that came over him as a result. The nine years of working in Kivu would be shared (since Kivu borders on Burundi), especially his awareness of the Hutu-Tutsi tensions from working extensively in projects of reconciliation and counselling with refugees—all this to establish that João knew Burundi and its problems intimately.

Just for example, in Goma under CBK I prepared the two pastors the CBK sent to Bujumbura as Election Monitors for that first democratic presidential election in Burundi, which elected the late President Melchior Ndadaye. Then I was in Goma when the news of his assassination came out. My last visit to Bujumbura was in May 1998, during the International Conference on Democracy, Good Governance, and Development for a Lasting Peace in the Great Lakes Region.

Then, a list of questions about Jean-Marie's own background, studies, family, his hopes for Burundi, what goals he has for our meetings, and this question:

"If he is asked to make a personal sacrifice for the sake of his people and the peace of Burundi, which one will it be?"
Then I will just listen deeply.

They met and went to what João described as a beautiful place, where they talked in privacy for five hours. "He wanted to know me better, but he also wanted me to know him better."

Before leaving Canada, João had asked his supporters to pray that the leaders he was to encounter would be delivered from those evil forces or intentions that keep conflict alive. As that day's conversation unfolded with Jean-Marie, he was deliberating whether to place that request openly before him.

> *I was afraid that his reaction would be negative or one of denial. To my surprise, he started it himself. "What we need is a deliverance. From our grandfathers we inherited this culture of violence and killing, which needs to be delivered from our families by prayer."*

> *I said "Thank you, God!" inside my head, because I believe that God had already prepared Jean-Marie to receive that ministry from me, with support of all the prayer warriors in Canada.*

> *The Bible says there is a time for war and a time for peace. This is a time for peace. The rebellion has already proved to the world the reason for their struggle. Enough blood has been shed.*

The next meeting with Jean-Marie was two days later. In this session, he expressed his wish that João might be given a role as spiritual advisor in the ongoing peace discussions, perhaps even organizing workshops for the belligerents between sessions or even before. João's contribution to the discussion that day included a description of fifteen facets of forgiveness. A new and important consideration introduced by Jean-Marie was that the presence of an additional set of players would be absolutely vital at the next round of peace talks, otherwise they would come to nothing. He was referring to the FNL, *Forces Nationales pour la Libération*, who still refused to lay down their arms.

The FNL had an advisor residing in Holland, Alain Mugabarabona, whose role was parallel to that of Jean-Marie. Alain must meet João face to face, and hear these points that were being considered. They concluded that this might best happen as a stopover on the flight back to Canada. Jean-Marie made contact with Alain by phone, and even facilitated a phone conversation between João and Alain while they were trying to set up a meeting between them in London.

Ministries Following Retirement

The next consideration was how to achieve the goal of introducing a spiritual advisor into subsequent peace talks. The next step was to bring additional diplomats into the picture.

Then a new and surprising development came in the form of an invitation:

> *Jean-Marie asked me if I had time to go with him and his wife to a prayer cell at the residence of the DRC Ambassador. He felt that the Congolese should also hear my message, as the inter-Congolese dialogue of February 25 approached. I accepted the challenge. So by 6:30 they came to pick me up.*

The results of that night's presentation to the group meeting in the Congolese Ambassador's home included a letter sent to CBM, suggesting that João's involvement be spread even wider, to include the Congolese peace process, a suggestion that was carried to Ottawa and discussed there.

The positive responses of the diplomats, Congolese and Burundi officials, and the CNDD/FDD advisor, may constitute the most telling affirmation that an unapologetically Christian approach to peacemaking is still highly appropriate in their countries.

A suggestion to try an Angolan peace initiative

During one of their sessions, Jean-Marie expressed the conviction that João should also make direct contact with Jonas Savimbi, fighting in the forests of Angola, for the same purpose of convincing him that the only reasonable end of the road of violence lay in negotiation.

> *My immediate response to him was that although Jean-Marie had access to the use of a cell phone in South Africa, Jonas Savimbi in Angola's bush did not. Communication with Savimbi is very difficult. However, when I arrived back at the guest house I was unable to rest leaving it that way. So from the guest house I sent an e-mail message to Dr. Ian Gilchrist in Canada, remembering that it was he who had introduced Jonas Savimbi to*

Holden Roberto in Kinshasa, around 1962, suggesting that they work together. Holden proceeded to appoint Jonas Savimbi his Minister of Foreign Affairs in the Revolutionary Government of Angola in Exile, GRAE. Dr. Ian Gilchrist was appointed Medical Director. So, having had that kind of close interaction with Jonas Savimbi, would Ian please try to make contact with him in Angola, informing him that I would like to meet with him personally. Ian's response cited the communications problem and added that he was afraid Savimbi would not accept.

A month or so later, Savimbi was killed in action in the bush.

A Monday phone call from Jean-Marie brought the welcome news that Alain Mugabarabona of FNL was waiting at a certain phone number in Amsterdam, and would he please try a call right then. João's call went through, and was cordially received. By phone, they established their plan to meet in London. Their conversation continued for a half-hour, which allowed a sharing of what had been discussed with Jean-Marie. Just as well that the call was not hurried, for in retrospect it was João's only personal contact with Alain:

Alain listened to all that I had to say. He agreed that there is an urgent need for peace in Burundi. He promised to meet with me as soon as possible, but he couldn't discuss the meeting place with me for security reasons. We concluded that there will now be no need for me to meet with him after all on my way home through London, since we had covered the main points.

Language capacity and familiarity plays an important role. With João, the ability to call on English, French, Portuguese, Kikongo, Kiswahili, and Lingala with ease represented an asset that truly was beyond one's capacity to measure or evaluate. Alain Mugabarabona revealed a surprisingly strong ease in handling English. With Jean-Marie, conversations ebbed and flowed through a combination of languages, and they used whichever was most comfortable to one or the other at the moment:

Sometimes we started in English, then would review a document in French, but when the topic turned to African things we would switch into Swahili. Jean-Marie saw me as a father he can listen to and respect.

Success

João's final day with Jean-Marie was a red-letter day—a day on which Jean-Marie affirmed that nothing would now stop him from participating in the next round of UN-sponsored peace talks. "My team is ready," he said. He even had the list of those who would be representing the CNDD/FDD as they entered the technical phase of defining how to press forward with negotiations. It was the day that confirmed the Matwawana mission to Pretoria as a success, against such odds. In the afternoon, before João's departure to the airport, Jean-Marie arrived with his two daughters to say farewell and to bring a final gift. Appropriately, it was a copy of *No Future Without Forgiveness,* by Archbishop Desmond Tutu. It was a gift, he said, to the man who had given him a Bible. The very choice of author and title was, in itself, an affirmation of all that João had come to do, a signal that his emphasis on forgiveness as an important part of reconciliation was not rejected.

From that point, the process reverted to the United Nations.

João arrived back in Halifax on February 9.

Less than a week after returning to Nova Scotia, he received a message from Jean-Marie by e-mail that carried this request for his continued prayer support:

De notre coté nous nous portons très bien. Je prépare la rencontre du 18 Février sérieusement et dans la prière; jéspère que d'ici le jour de la rencontre vous serez avec moi en conversation avec le Seigneur pour qu'il y ait réellement une avancée significative vers la paix au Burundi. Fraternellement....
[For our part we are well. I'm preparing for the February 18 meeting seriously and prayerfully; I hope that from now until

then you will be with me in conversation with the Lord, that there may really be significant progress toward peace in Burundi. Fraternally....]

CONCERNS ABOUT BURUNDI'S OTHER REBEL FACTION—FNL

Perseverance in the face of setbacks is one of the characteristics of Matwawana the reconciler. Although Operation Osprey's mission to Pretoria had been a success in itself, Burundi still reeled from hostilities. Attacks and killings continued, along with the other unspeakable acts of violence, rape, and cruelty that accompany war in Africa, as elsewhere. Ten days after returning home, João spoke by phone with Jean-Marie in Pretoria. He learned that Jean-Marie's movement, CNDD/FDD, met with the negotiators, but the FNL failed to do so. That troubled João, and brought him back to considering once more the need for face-to-face talks with Alain in Europe. At that point, João was ready to make yet another attempt to meet with Alain.

João made phone contact with a UN Peace team member in Pretoria on March 9, in which he expressed his appreciation. "I am happy for the work you are doing, to persuade individual rebel leaders to join the negotiations. We value your good work. You are part of the peace process." That statement was a counter-balance to the rest of the news, which was that João would not be allowed into Burundi's formal peace process either as an observer or as a spiritual counsellor. These sessions, he said, are closed to all reporters and observers. Even accredited UN observers from two countries were refused entry, due to complications surrounding the issues. João brought him up-to-date on his plans to go to Holland for contacts with Alain Mugabarabona of FNL, and pledged to keep him posted on the results of any meeting with Alain.

On March 11, João flew to Amsterdam, scheduled to stay for one week. His flight was delayed in Montreal, so his phone contact could not be made on time. That alone may have been enough to spook Alain. One way or another, he failed to show up at the rendezvous. The remainder of João's scheduled time in Europe was then re-negotiated with CBM to be used productively in visiting with CBM personnel and with the leadership of Baptists in Belgium. If there was failure, it was not for lack of trying.

Of course I am very disappointed. But also, this warns us not to give up because things didn't come out as planned. Just remember that Nelson Mandela tried for three years, and the Canadian government paid the bill of 2.5 million dollars, and these two parties are still out. ... We should not contact Alain again until we see the results of the next meetings.

Around this time, momentous happenings were taking place in Angola that would soon command João's attention, but Burundi continued and continues to be an item of concern.

BURUNDI: LATER DEVELOPMENTS

To close this part of the story of João's participation in Burundi's quest for peace, we have two bulletins issued by the IRIN news service. The first is dated January 25-31, 2003:

Burundian President Pierre Buyoya and the leader of a wing of the Conseil national pour la defense de la democratie-Force pour la defense de la democratie *(CNDD-FDD), Pierre Nkurunziza, signed a memorandum of understanding on Monday, paving the way for the implementation of a ceasefire accord they reached in Arusha, Tanzania, December 2002.*

The South Africa Broadcasting Corporation reported on Tuesday that the memorandum, signed in the South African administrative capital, Pretoria, was reached after a "marathon meeting," which was supposed to have ended on Sunday. The office of the South African President said the parties agreed to the "urgent establishment" of the Joint Ceasefire Commission; provide information to the facilitator of the Burundi ceasefire talks, South African Deputy President Jacob Zuma, that will facilitate the conclusion of the "Forces Technical Agreement";

and the immediate deployment of the African Union Military Observer Mission. Ethiopia, Mozambique and South Africa have agreed to provide troops for this mission.

The second IRIN bulletin, almost a year later, is dated January 9, 2004:

[Burundi's] hope for peace was greatly boosted on 5 January when the only rebel faction, which had hitherto refused to enter into peace negotiations with the government, announced that it was willing to meet President Domitien Ndayizeye for talks.

The announcement by the Forces nationales de liberation *(FNL) faction, led by Agathon Rwasa, follows December's integration into the government of the main rebel movement, the* Conseil national pour la défense de la Démocratie-Forces pour la Défense de la Démocratie *(CNDD-FDD), led by Pierre Nkurunziza.*

In November, Nkurunziza was named Minister of State for Good Governance, the third most powerful position in the government after Ndayizeye and Vice-President Alphonse-Marie Kadege, who must henceforth consult him on matters concerning state security and government appointments.

On 6 January, Ndayizeye signed a decree appointing 33 members of the Joint Military High Command, 20 from the army and 13 from Nkurunziza's CNDD-FDD, in accordance with a Technical Forces Agreement signed in Pretoria on 2 November, 2003....

Ndayizeye's cabinet shuffle on 23 November 2003, to incorporate Nkurunziza's CNDD-FDD illustrated the country's determination to move toward peace after ten years of civil strife in which at least 300,000 Burundians have died.

Ministries Following Retirement

Besides naming Nkurunziza the Minister for Good Governance, President Ndayizeye appointed three other CNDD-FDD members to ministerial posts. With Nkurunziza's CNDD-FDD now part of the transitional government, ethnic integration and eventually democracy are now within grasp of Burundians, so long as the army does not jeopardize the good gains which the transitional government has made to date.

19

Transition to Angola, Visiting Refugees in Zambia

Let us now turn from considering Operation Osprey and the peace-building efforts relating to Burundi, to focus our attention on how João's ministries relating to Angola unfolded.

Angola had seen no peace since the beginning of its battle for independence in March of 1961. When the Portuguese colonial presence withdrew in 1976, they left behind three movements contending for the mandate to rule Angola, with the prospect of elections on the horizon. UNITA, whose founder was Jonas Savimbi, was strongest in the South. MPLA, whose earliest leader had been Agostinho Neto, was strongest in Central Angola. FNLA, led by Holden Roberto, was strongest in the north. Over the ensuing quarter-century, conflict and violence were constant, and the political landscape had changed. Intervention by the Cuban army secured the ascendancy of MPLA, especially in and around Luanda, and MPLA morphed into the Government of Angola. FNLA had effectively disappeared from the scene as it ceased to be a significant military or political contender. At the turn of the millennium, Angola was locked in the throes of this civil war, in which it was now the Government, under President José Eduardo dos Santos, pitted against UNITA, still led by Jonas Savimbi. Large areas of the countryside, including some major centres, were in effect under Savimbi's military control, and a case could be made for saying that rural areas were actually under a bush-style administration of his making.

A malaise had spread across Angola, and a war-weariness that was still building but had not yet reached its peak. However, there was not yet any organized resistance to ongoing war. In terms of resources, and specifically military resources, the opposing forces more or less balanced each other. The government controlled vast oil reserves, which were coming increasingly under production. UNITA controlled the diamond-producing areas. Both had the buying power to secure military hardware, jet aircraft, heavy armament, and to replace it when required. Both did so repeatedly.

By 2002, Luanda, Huambo, and a few other cities had received 4.5 million refugees classified as "internally displaced persons," or IDPs. An estimated 360,000 refugees were living in Zambia, Namibia, and the Democratic Republic of Congo, and many more were living in Europe and the Americas.

At no stage in his career did Angola cease to be a concern that weighed upon João Matwawana, even in those long years when it was difficult to see how his or any other efforts from outside the country might contribute toward peace.

Rev. Matwawana Becomes Dr. Matwawana

On May 15, 2002, Rev. João Matwawana was awarded an honorary Doctor of Divinity degree by McMaster University, in Hamilton, Ontario. Family members joined João and Nora for the occasion: Samuel and Cathy and Ambrose came from Boston, Edward and Celina from Dartmouth, Julie and Isabel from Toronto, and Raymond from Vancouver.

This well-deserved recognition was by recommendation of the Divinity College, and the degree was awarded by McMaster University's Senate. In recommending conferral of the degree, Dr. Peter

George, President and Vice-Chancellor, reviewed briefly many of the elements of João Matwawana's career. He closed with these words:

Mr. Chancellor, I present to you Rev. João Samuel Matwawana, missionary statesman, refugee worker, pastor and world Christian, so that you may confer upon him the degree, Doctor of Divinity, honoris causa.

The event became significant for relationships with Angola, in that Ambassador Puna flew down from Ottawa to Hamilton and his staff came by car, bringing a magnificent painting that was presented in recognition of the occasion.

Significant developments in Angola

The death of Jonas Savimbi, by anyone's standard, ranks as a momentous event and a critical turning point in Angola's history, leading directly as it did to a cease-fire only eight days later, and then firmed up with the signing of a protocol of agreement between MPLA and UNITA on April 4. No other occurrence since the outset of the war of independence in 1961 competes in importance with that sequence of events in terms of bringing about changes in Angola's political and social landscape. These three events constitute the closing punctuation of a two-part era of conflict, which had opened in March of 1961.

A number of the developments that converged around the ceasefire help to explain why Angola's ceasefire experience of 2002, from its outset, was more permanent than those of other African countries. It differed as well from earlier abortive attempts within Angola. First, this was a purely Angolan phenomenon, not brokered by the UN, by western governments, or by outside forces. Details and arrangements around the time of Savimbi's death and the ceasefire were handled wisely by the government of Angola, contributing to a rapid calming of emotions and the stabilization of UNITA forces. For instance, it was important that MPLA refrained from announcements implying that they had won the war. It was important that steps were taken to integrate UNITA officers into the country's military, without distinction or prejudice. Within days of the March

30, 2002 ceasefire, UNITA's military officers were in public, in uniform, on the streets of Luanda, with transportation and drivers. A joint mixed military commission was established (JMC), charged with oversight of the dissolution of UNITA's military force, through an official process of disarmament and demobilization. By July of 2002, some 84,600 demobilized soldiers of UNITA had been assembled in thirty-four guarding areas, nation-wide, along with 264,000 dependants and non-military officials. The Government of Angola absorbed 5,000 former UNITA soldiers into Angola's armed forces (FAA). Detractors can readily find flaws, lapses and shortfalls, but there was a lot that was done right.

A SPECIAL WORKING PARTNERSHIP IN ANGOLA WITH DEVELOPMENT WORKSHOP

Development Workshop (DW) is an effective NGO actively involved in development projects. It has been a major player on the Angola scene since Allan Cain was invited in 1980 by the Angolan government to develop a self-help housing program. He began with three employees. Today there are 132 in Luanda and 107 in Huambo. Although the number of projects has grown, DW's objectives remain the same, that of human settlements development. Recently DW started focussing on the needs of the poor who have been displaced by the war. This interest corresponded with João's concern for the refugee poor.

Development Workshop's remarkable director came to play a key role in João's Angola work. Allan Cain grew up in St. Catharines, Ontario. He and his wife, Julia, have two children, Mathieu and Rebecca, who spent much of their youth in Luanda, with periodic trips to Canada. In January, 2004, Allan was appointed an officer of the Order of Canada. The citation on that occasion referred to him as a man of courage and conviction, who has dedicated his life to helping the people of Angola. Within Angola, those years of careful and dedicated work have earned Allan a deep respect at all levels of society. The term *cooperante* applies to him for having remained there in Luanda during the long, hard years of the country's internal conflict.

As João Matwawana began to lay serious plans for his first visit to Angola, it became evident that it would be beneficial to make contact with Allan Cain and DW to test the degree to which João, with his experience, his background, his gifts, might be useful to DW in its important work on behalf of Angola, and whether there might be ministries of mutual concern to DW and CBM while pursuing João's vision of fostering peace in Angola.

Through a mutual friend, João and John learned that in the last week of April, 2002, two key people resident in Angola would be in Canada for brief and separate visits. Ben Costello of *Jubilee 200 Angola* would be in Montreal. Allan Cain and family would be paying a visit to Allan's mother in St. Catharines. They agreed on the importance of making contact with both, in preparation for João's first visit to Angola. They agreed that João would travel from Halifax to Montreal to meet with Ben Costello. John would travel from Lakefield to St. Catharines to meet Allan Cain.

It was an excellent meeting with Allan. His quiet competence, his sound judgment on Angola and its needs, his profound understanding of the intricacies of survival and life in Luanda were all obvious assets as João prepared for that first visit. Allan and DW were prepared to facilitate arrival and lodging arrangements and João would make contact with Allan on arrival in Luanda.

To Angola, via Zambia, August 2002

As João and Nora set up their first visit to Angola in decades, travel was arranged to allow João two weeks in Zambia for another look at the Angolan refugee situation in that country, and another visit to the camps. From Zambia he would fly on to South Africa, Nora would join him there, and they would enter Angola together.

This visit to Zambia was planned around two goals. First, João set about to establish a supportive network of contact persons in Zambia's churches who would be his partners in ministering to refugee needs. Then to visit the concentration of Angolans living in Muheba refugee camp. With its population of 50,000 refugees, it was the largest such camp anywhere in the world at that time. Both goals were achieved.

The Matwawana approach was to bring the refugees a message of hope and a ministry of encouragement. He was interested in the needs of all the refugees in the camp, but he had a special interest in identifying pastors and lay leaders. For by giving them additional training and encouragement, they would extend and multiply his vision of ministry, comfort, and encouragement. In two camps, Nangweshi and Maheba, he identified over forty pastors and lay leaders. Speaking directly to them and challenging them to be of support to others gave them a motivation for living. Service to others in need always lifts and strengthens the one who serves.

On returning to Halifax following his Zambia visit, João conveyed his impressions of the visit to his supporters through a local church publication.

> *Not every question makes sense! It is the "simple" things which make so little sense. Sometimes the questions are better left unasked. We asked for a mirror ... a simple thing, to shave. We could not find one.*
>
> *Not quite being accustomed to this life we asked, "Do you people shave?"*
>
> *One old man replied, "What for? We have bigger problems than shaving!"*
>
> *One more question could not hurt. "Do you have breakfast?" A young twenty-year-old man replied, "What is breakfast?"*
>
> *After three failures, we decided not to ask any more questions but to just listen to them tell us about their lives in the camp. After we listened for two hours we discovered that we could, in fact, have a BRUNCH ... that is if we gave them 15,000 Kwachas to purchase food at the market and find a lady to cook it for us.*
>
> Louise Hakizimana

This Rwandan lady fled from the Kivu Refugee Camps at the beginning of the Kabila war. She walked from Kivu to Lake

Victoria and, after crossing by ferry, she continued to walk through Tanzania to the Zambian border with her two children. She has not heard from her husband since 1996.

After this dear lady went to the market...quite some distance away, purchased the food, brought it back and cooked it for us, had a meal. That was the food for that day—NO refrigeration, NO snacks in the cupboards, NO little extras—that was it!

The Oldest Man in the Camp

The oldest refugee had spent 25 years at Muheba refugee camp

Manuel Kavikolo, now eighty years old, entered the Camp twenty-five years ago. He had lost his two sons in the war, and his wife died a few years ago.

When I asked him his life's secret he replied, "Faith in God and a hope of returning to Angola keeps me focussed, living one day at a time." Speaking with this wise man was my most rewarding and inspiring moment of my visit, as we shared with each other our acquaintances and our great desire to return to our mother land.

Education & Government

There was a note of encouragement to be found in the Camp—all of the refugees had access to BASIC primary education—perhaps the equivalent of grade seven. I sensed that the children, the teenagers, and the young adults (19-30 yrs.) are very satisfied probably since they have nothing to compare their experiences with.

The older generation is TIRED...tired of the twenty-six-year-old civil war. There is little wonder that these people are so sad and depressed—they have lost their land and many of their children and grandchildren to the battlefield of Angola.

Religion

There continues to be a spirit of hatred and revenge for their enemies throughout the Camp—only a few have repented of these feelings.

Even those who are faithful remain angry at God, their government, and the rebels due to their situation. How they survive spiritually can be compared to the children of Israel during the Exile (cf. Psalm 137:4). In the middle of their worship there is a small voice crying out, "How can we sing the songs of the Lord while in a foreign land?"

Refugee Pastors

These pastors are in a great need of material assistance (clothes, Bibles, hymn books and bikes).

The Camp is vast—over 35 kilometres from end to end. The refugees are divided into eight zones and visiting members takes many hours of walking from one zone to another. Thus, I am suggesting, for these pastors, that they receive assistance in the form of bicycles.

A Day in the Life

The uniformity of life in the Camp...the housing consisting of grass thatched roofing or recycled tins, contributes to a daily sense of hopelessness.

Women go on a daily basis to get water and food for their families' needs. The children play and the people sell their wares.

Once in a while fights break out among the refugees. Usually these fights occur because of small disagreements in the Camp or because of some news from home.

As evening falls, the refugees retire to their houses. They make life as normal as possible because this is all which keeps them going.

(Matwawana 2002:2-4)

20

First Peace Mission—to Angola
(August 15 to September 30, 2002)

To Luanda

A dream that João and Nora had been nursing for twenty-five years came true on August 15, 2002. He had flown to Johannesburg from Lusaka, Zambia, the previous day. She was flying in from Nova Scotia via London to join him. This new and promising day began for João at 5 a.m. as he met Nora at Johannesburg airport. Together they checked in for the historic flight to take them to Luanda, capital of their homeland, Angola.

> *Our first observation was to note so many passengers of different nationalities waiting for the same flight. That was a sign that peace might be real over there. The flight to Luanda left on time. Nora and I were impatient during those three and a half hours of flying time.*

All sorts of thoughts were running through their heads during that flight. One of Allan Cain's assistants had alerted Matwawanas to Luanda's basics.

"Have your yellow fever vaccinations up to date."
"Don't count on being able to use credit cards."
"Come equipped with American cash, but only the notes with big heads." (Small head bills would be rejected as potentially counterfeited.)

It was 1975 when João was last in Luanda. The circumstances of his departure through the airport on that occasion were unforgettable. In fact, he often repeated them during this first visit back. Now, as they approached Luanda decades later, his mind flashed back to that tense event. Cuban troops had arrived in support of the MPLA faction, and there was gunfire in the streets. Hostilities between the parties were in full swing. João's taxi driver was an older man who gave him special instructions: "Lie down across the back seat. They know me and will let me pass but they don't know you."

On this day, August 15, 2002, their approach to Luanda from Johannesburg was from over the Atlantic.

Nora kept asking if we had not arrived yet. At immigration we saw that there were two lines, one for Angolans, the other for foreigners. Arriving back home it was hard to have to stand in the foreigners' line. But we were travelling on Canadian passports.
"The reason for your visit?"
"Homesick."
That was enough. It was credible, and no other explanation was necessary.

Later, at one of the seminars João was conducting, a lawyer asked him about his nationality. With these many years away from Angola, his Portuguese was obviously not local and current.

We were met in the reception hall at the airport by a group of pastors as well as the driver for Development Workshop....

Ministries Following Retirement

The choice of the Soleme Guest House for our lodging was made by our Canadian Consul. It is centrally located, close to the National Assembly, the President's palace, the Maria Pia Hospital, the Defense Department, and only fifteen minutes' walk from the post office where one can use the Internet. Prices in Luanda have escalated, and we found life expensive according to our budget. The Consul advised us to take it for security reasons. Other areas may be cheaper, but are not as safe. The manager and her workers offered us excellent service, and they didn't mind the daily flow of friends and family to our room.

On this first visit back to Angola, João and Nora were not expecting to accomplish much beyond establishing contact with family, friends, and prior acquaintances. It was planned as a visit of investigation, an opportunity to study the lay of the land and determine if any contribution to the reconstruction of Angola might be possible. The reality was radically different and much more productive than they had dared to hope.

They checked into the guest house at 2:30 p.m. At 3 p.m. Allan Cain of Development Workshop (DW) called, confirming that João should attend a meeting within the hour. Even the fact of just having arrived did not get João off the hook. Allan had been studying their itineraries. Nora would be permitted to rest, as she had been travelling all the way from Canada. Allan noted that João had rested overnight in Johannesburg, and now that he was in Angola there were things to be accomplished. What an affirmation!

That very first day the flow of visitors began, in the person of Nora's nephew, Dr. António Nsumbu Wooding. It became evident that they would need to divide responsibilities. Nora would receive the visitors, while João would plunge immediately into tasks related to his peace mission, which he understood as bringing a message of forgiveness and reconciliation as the solid foundation on which the nation of Angola could be rebuilt.

Productive contacts in Luanda

Allan Cain arranged a preliminary session for strategy planning, meeting with João and one of his associates, Eunice Inácio. They briefed João on a peace conference already in progress there in Luanda, and about to close, sponsored by *Conselho de Igrejas Cristãs em Angola* (CICA), which is Angola's Council of Protestant Churches. The organizers had learned of the Matwawanas arrival, and requested João's presence for the closing of their conference. It offered him the opportunity to meet key pastors and other leaders.

Allan warned João how busy his program would be for the rest of his stay. Seminars were already scheduled in which he would function as a trainer and facilitator. He was expected to teach and to begin explaining his plan as laid out in his "National Fellowship for the Reconciliation of Angola" (reproduced in full in appendix C). João's manifesto was the first document in print on the topic of national reconciliation relating to Angola. Development Workshop also wished to use his prepared lessons in packets of literature they were preparing for distribution. His concepts had already been tested in other countries, specifically in the Congo, Rwanda, Burundi, Kenya, and Zambia. Credibility and field-tested practicality were both important to DW.

For more information on the resolutions and conclusions of the conference, see appendix D.

About 6:30 p.m. Allan and Eunice took me back to the guest house. I didn't expect this many contacts on the first day in Angola. I felt needed. These, my brothers, had been waiting with prayers and anticipation for our return to Angola. This ended the first day's activities. Imagine, all this in our very first day back in Angola! To God be the glory, great things He has done. But we must also thank Allan Cain.

The pace of activity expected of him and the measure of rapid integration into meaningful activity came both as a surprise and as an affirmation. At nine in the morning of his second day, their driver was there to take João to the DW office and a more detailed planning meeting with Eunice. She was to be his contact person, her role being that of co-ordinating DW's peace-building program. They worked together on his calendar and program details for the rest of the visit.

SETTLING INTO WORKING PATTERNS WITH DEVELOPMENT WORKSHOP

Another meeting with Allan Cain firmed up details of how João would be working, and confirmed the training seminars that had been projected. This would be the pattern, João working primarily with Eunice, occasional meetings happening with Allan only when they were needed. Allan confirmed his satisfaction with João's manifesto, "National Fellowship for the Reconciliation of Angola." Eunice introduced João to a Mr. Noé Alberto José, engaged to translate his lessons from English to Portuguese. He was a graduate of the Mindolo Ecumenical Centre, and as part of his studies there he had visited Muheba refugee camp. João took him to Soleme guest house to explain about the lessons and what was expected of him. Through Muheba, he and João had something in common. João's lessons were first taught to Angolan refugee leaders in Ndola Zambia two weeks earlier. Now they were to be used inside Angola itself, closing the circle and preparing the way for the reintegration of those refugees.

Noé Alberto José later became a co-worker with João as they travelled to Malange together and taught the lawyers and journalists together during seminars in Luanda from September 6-12, 2002:

> *We agreed that our first family reunion should be held at the home of Nora's relatives. The site was at the home of Juliana Miezi and her husband Filipe Tanjula and their three boys. Over twenty members of the family made it, with uncles, nephews, brothers, nieces, and in-laws like myself. Nora tried to identify by washing our clothes outside by hand with the help of her older sister, Anna Wooding. Some cousins and nieces arrived early in the morning in order to start cooking the goat which was killed for the occasion, and other kinds of food. At the end there were a few family speeches and even joyful singing. Needless to say, Nora was very happy to see so many of her relatives.*

Nora and her brother reunited after 41 years separation by war

Communications in Luanda were heavily dependent on face-to-face contact. Links with Canada and the outside world were theoretically possible, but not always workable. It was not long before the complications of the Internet age became apparent. Internet cafés were jammed with young people playing computer games online. The number of phone lines available for Internet access was inadequate. Four days passed without being able to send messages. In those four days, João was integrated into the training team of DW's Peace-Building Unit. As he assessed just how and why there was so much for him to undertake immediately on arrival, João's conclusion was that Allan's vision for the peace-building program was both appropriate and timely, but he was short on people who could provide solid content for the program. His arrival on the scene to fill that need was God's doing.

From Militant Rebel to Peace Promoter

This involvement in the training of Development Workshop's peace promoters moved João directly to the heart of what he had come to do in

Angola. There were a number of incidents during this first peace mission to Angola that brought solid affirmation of the importance of his undertaking the assignment, confirming the rightness of his being involved in the rebuilding of Angola. One of these was a conversation with a young man from southern Angola, probably in his mid-twenties, who participated in a DW training session in which João was equipping peace promoters. Felizardo had become one of Allan Cain's peace builders.

Felizardo's story took more than an hour in the telling. He had suffered a lot in a government prison, and had become filled with hatred. He managed to escape prison, and made his way back to his home area where he became a militant in the army of UNITA:

> "How come, with all this hatred, you have become a peace promoter?"
> "Only by the grace of God is this possible. I didn't think I would ever bring myself north again. I once saw it as coming to the enemy camp."

Felizardo's account revealed how pastors continued to function in the bush throughout the war years, ministering to the dispersed population as well as to the military and their families. This was done in hiding, always on the run to avoid attacks and ambushes, as UNITA held out against the government in Luanda. He learned the good news about Jesus and His love, it changed his life:

> "The Lord touched my heart, removed the hatred, and changed my life to the point where I knew that I had to do something constructive. I became a peace promoter."

With his change of heart Felizardo had to live out in a positive way the change that had come over him. He is a man who will make a big impact, in spite of his small stature and the gentle spirit that he now shows. He will become a good leader. He didn't want to miss anything that I was teaching or saying. When the formal seminars finished he still wanted to travel with me, serving, helping, and continuing to learn. He requested that he be able to travel with me to other seminars around Luanda.

That was Felizardo: he helped me during teaching sessions, writing notes on the blackboard. His heart was changed. And when he speaks it comes from the heart. He maintains active links with the church in Southern Angola. He put me in touch with a Pastor Epalanga, from the south, now living in Luanda.

We have to look at the whole picture. Both sides have done wrong in this conflict which has just come to a close. We must forgive, and we must help others to learn to forgive.

This first Angola visit was a relatively short one, the days were full, and a host of known people were eager to make contact. Nora was able to carry much of the social interaction with family as well as with friends and acquaintances from long ago. João's encounters with church and denominational leaders were worked in between meetings and lessons.

Meeting with Non-Governmental Organizations

During an early meeting at the offices of FONGA, the Forum of Angolan Non-Governmental Organizations, ten of the NGOs were represented. They requested first that the Matwawana manifesto be available in a form they could distribute and use. They were all ready to subscribe to it. They also requested that João return to Angola soon to train more people in that program. FONGA leaders also asked João and Nora to visit a certain project in Catete, where IDPs (internally displaced people) have created gardens.

Part of FONGA's programs are what they call *Grupos de trabalho*, work groups, under these headings:

- *Rede de Paz*   Peace network
- *Redução de pobreza*   Poverty reduction
- *Trabalho da saúde.*   Health work

- *Educação*   Education
- *Autoridades tradicionais*   Traditional authority
- *Direitos Humanos e*   Human rights and
  Educação Cívica   civic education.

João and Nora travelled to Catete, a distance of 75 kilometres, to visit the recommended women's centre. This was their first glimpse of life outside the capital. It was important for them to see that the military were no longer on edge with the constant concern about attacks. It was another sign that peace had arrived, or at least was on its way:

When we reached Catete we left the main road and entered the muddy road. Here are the signs of peace we have observed:
- *In every road block we saw only police, no soldiers.*
- *Outside Catete we found an army barracks. The soldiers carried no guns.*
- *Soldiers waved to us!*

On the dirt road we were fearful of land mines but were assured everything was OK. Among the people from FONGA was the President of Women who leads the NGO called TWENDE. She is also the supervisor of the farming co-operatives of the displaced people. The visit was excellent. We saw their beautiful gardens with corn, onions, cabbages, and more. FONGA officials introduced us to the Women's Executive and the population of IDP of Catete. I was asked to address these people about the importance of national reconciliation.

A weekend engagement at a church affiliated to the *Igreja Evangélica de Angola* (IEA), and therefore linked with CBM, also facilitated a meeting with their pastors serving the Luanda area. There was a meeting with a government official, during which João was still careful to guard his "neutrality" stance.

The Seminars in Malange came off without a hitch, and in reporting on them João was euphoric. He went there by plane, the same plane the Provincial Governor was travelling on. When the Governor discovered what João had come to do in Malange, he pronounced this to be a government event, not just something sponsored by one or two agencies. Nothing would do but that it be held in the Provincial Assembly Building, and so it was. The Vice-Governor attended the closing ceremony. Government identification with church-sponsored undertakings distinctly signalled a change in the government's attitude, a melting of the freeze that had gripped state-church relationships.

A subsequent weekend was spent with churches of the *Igreja Evangélica Baptista de Angola*, (IEBA), the denomination in which João was raised. Again he was able to connect with pastors and leaders of the Luanda area. The occasion was their twenty-fifth anniversary of work in Luanda. In spite of years of having been away from Angola, João found old friends and colleagues there.

Survival was difficult in Angola, even for professionals. The salary level for an Angolan medical doctor came to about 100 US dollars per month. Doctors would take on a private practice with some company like SONANGOL, the national oil firm with its international connections, where they would be paid in dollars. However, they would not dare to go full time with such a company because of government attitudes, which were suspicious of anyone not in their network: "So we pretend. We stay with the government, but our heart is not there."

As the days wound down to departure, he met with military officers, political leaders, church leaders, and with Mr. Giovanni Bosco, the United Nations Policy Advisor for Angola.

Most of my lessons on Peace and Reconciliation have now been translated into Portuguese by Mr. Noe of CICA, including my manifesto, "National Fellowship for the Reconciliation of Angola." This and my other lessons are now given by DW to seminar participants as handouts.

Yesterday Nora and I were invited to lunch by an army General. Tonight we are having dinner at the home of Pastor Zassala and his wife Mafuta, whom I taught at IME. Other invited guests include Holden Roberto and his associates.

Tomorrow I preach at the IEBA church on Avenida dos Combatentes. Our schedule is full until we leave Luanda.
Written September 7, 2002

Departure was one week later, September 14.

Throughout this visit, João was diligent in not assuming a partisan political stance. FNLA, by now, had been integrated into Angola's Parliament, represented by five Members of Parliament, referred to in Angola as *deputados*. Holden, the historic President of FNLA, is now the acknowledged leader of the opposition. In that position, he has designated benefits, which include housing, transportation, and security.

He hurried to me one afternoon without an appointment. He wanted a few minutes so I could check on his English in a document that he was preparing for presentation to a diplomat who was passing through Luanda. As a member of the Council of the Republic, Holden Roberto is one of the advisors of President José Eduardo dos Santos.

One of the events of the ensuing week was notable for its participants—a dozen lawyers and journalists who were interested in learning some skills on conflict resolution and reconciliation in this the new era in Angola.

As this ministry tour wound down, there was a session for evaluation with Allan Cain and his Development Workshop staff. An impact had been made, and they attempted to assess the results.

Everybody believes that this time the peace is here to stay.

Just now Nora is calling me to start packing for our travel home, and she is right. We will leave Luanda tomorrow with our hearts full of joy and gratitude for everything the Lord has done.

Dr. João Matwawana's visit of up to six weeks was billed as a fact-finding mission. It certainly was that, but it had become much more. One of the very important questions João had carried with him into

Angola was whether the peace was real, or only a temporary lull in the hostilities that had been prolonged for decades. The assurance of permanent peace was something he had needed to see and evaluate firsthand. He was convinced. It freed him to concentrate on what more could be done in the course of subsequent visits.

Emerging as it was from the throes of a prolonged and devastating war, Angola faced issues of momentous import, with little promise that all of them could be faced or solved in the immediate future.

The issues as João saw them tended to fall into the following categories:

1. Political issues
2. Peace and stability
3. Truth and reconciliation
4. Land Mine Clearance
5. Refugee repatriation
6. Land rights and property issues
7. Violence in society, armaments in society as a carry-over from war
8. Acceptability of approaches to Peace and Reconciliation which are distinctively and unapologetically Christian in content
9. Readiness of churches to come to grips with peace and the need for reconciliation
10. Health programs
11. Education

Of the major issues identified by the Matwawanas during that brief period in Angola, there were a few that João could hope to address directly in some way. The others he could only highlight, and hope to make recommendations either to Foreign Affairs Canada, to Canadian Baptist Ministries, to Development Workshop, or to some other consortium or forum such as the Angola Peace Action Network.

21

SECOND PEACE MISSION—TO GENEVA, DIDCOT (UK), AND ANGOLA
(February 21 to March 30, 2003)

The second tour of post-retirement ministry to Angola by Dr. João Matwawana actually started, not in Angola, but in Geneva, visiting United Nations headquarters. He described this tour to his local supporters in Nova Scotia as a "Ministry of Advocacy". The time in Geneva yielded a series of interviews with officials in favour of Angolan refugees, dealing with issues related to their reintegration into Angolan society.

TO GENEVA

When I left Canada on February 21, I told the churches that my second visit to Angola will have a different goal. That goal is the Ministry of Advocacy....

What is Advocacy?

Advocacy means getting involved in the dialogue that shapes government decisions, speaking out for one's values and con-

cerns. An advocate makes a case for a particular position and then presses that case to those who make the decisions. From Moses addressing Pharaoh and Daniel speaking to Nebuchadnezzar, God's people have acted on the assumption that government leaders are to be held accountable to do what is right and just.

What is the Matwawana case in this instance?

In our report on the Peace and Reconciliation Seminar for Refugees in Zambia, August 5-9, 2002, part of the plan of action was that CBM's Sharing Way *may want to consider being present during the repatriation of over 230,000 Angolan refugees from Zambia and 180,000 from the DRC, to reinforce our concern for the welfare of the refugees as well as to remind them of the peace process they were taught. CBM felt that if representation is possible during the repatriation exercise, preliminary inquiries must start before the operation begins.*

The trip took me first to Geneva Headquarters of the United Nations High Commission for Refugees....

Their response was hearty and appreciative These officials praised CBM's interest in refugee repatriation. They also recommended securing approval of Angola's government for this involvement. One achievement, which exceeded all João's expectations, was that the UNHCR offices sent a letter introducing Dr. Matwawana to all of their representatives in Africa, including Namibia, Zambia, and Congo.

To the U.K.

João spent a two-day interval in the United Kingdom, with a full day at the Didcot headquarters of the Baptist Missionary Society—that historic entity dating from William Carey's commissioning to India in the 1700s. This linkage with BMS firmed up a sense of partnership in the common interests shared with CBM in northern Angola, especially in issues relating to refugee repatriation, reconciliation among estranged churches, and more. He renewed fellowship with missionaries Jim Grenfell, Phyllis Gilbert, and Jean Comber, all of whom had been João's colleagues first in Angola, prior to 1961, and then in Congo until 1975.

On to Angola

New air links from Europe to Angola were being added. The outbound flight to Angola was João's first experience of a direct connection from Heathrow to Luanda. It reduced flying time by seven hours, avoiding the need to double back from Johannesburg. The drawback of this flight is a Luanda arrival at 4:35 a.m., a perilous time for Luanda drivers to be on the streets due to armed vehicle thieves. He was met by Allan Cain's driver and safely installed in the DW transit house. This was soon changed to accommodations at the Mission Aviation Fellowship residences outside Luanda, to avoid having to climb the seventy-five steps in a building where the elevator has not functioned since 1975. These details give a flavour of some of Luanda's inconveniences, which are numerous. Working in Luanda is a far cry from the average retired Canadian's idea of acceptable living and working conditions.

In Luanda, João's ministry of advocacy began with a call to Angola's Minister of Information, Hendrick Val Neto, for the purpose of emphasizing the positive features Angola would gain with the repatriation of refugees. A simple matter like changing the spin on repatriation might do miracles in terms of removing obstacles and prejudices from the path of refugees, for whom repatriation and reintegration would not be easy. The label of *refugee*, whether away from home in the Congo or returning home to Angola, is a description heavily loaded with emotion and prejudice. Refugees have consistently emphasized how they are a despised people, the label *refugee* hanging over them like a curse.

João then contacted the Ministry of Health through Tungavo, a former student at Sona Bata in the Congo.

During his peace missions to Angola, João, the reconciler, was forced to face his personal need to forgive, when he was informed that someone coming to visit with him at the guest house was the very person who had betrayed some of his family members, who consequently ended up in prison. It was an occasion when forgiveness had to be a practical thing and genuine. It was not easy.

The following quote from João's report shows how intricate and how time-consuming it can be to make a single contact, especially with an official at ministerial level, and especially a first-time contact. Even Ambassador Puna's letter of introduction from Canada did not grant João immediate access. However, contact with officials at the *Ministêrio de Assistência e Reinserção Social*, abbreviated as MINARS, was certainly well worth pursuing. The ministry name translates as Ministry of Assistance and Social Reinsertion, therefore highly relevant to advocacy and for dealing with refugees:

> *The first lesson I learned was that I could not start my contacts by phone, because everything starts by personal connections. It took me three days to find somebody who knew someone who works with Minister João Baptista Kussumua at MINARS (Ministêrio de Assistência e Reinserção Social). This is the ministry responsible for the welfare of the internally displaced persons (IDPs), and the repatriation of refugees. The rest of the week was to locate the lady's house. I visited and explained to her why I wanted to see the Minister. She promised to check with the Deputy Minister and the Director of the Minster's office about his schedule the following week. She gave us her cell phone number. Then she requested that I also leave my own cell phone number. I gave Allan Cain's number. I realized that I needed to buy a cell phone before starting such important contacts, thus freeing me to be reached wherever I am. That is what I did.*
>
> *With my cell phone on hand, I was able to keep contacts with Dona Helena. On March 6 she introduced me to the Director of the Minister's office, Mr. Pedro Castello João. He explained to me that they had already received a message from Ambassador Puna about my arrival, that I didn't need to see Dona Maria da Luz, the Deputy Minister, because the letter I*

was carrying from the Angolan Embassy was directed to the Minister himself. "The Minister will be in meeting for the rest of the week. But if you leave your phone number we will call you when the Minister is available, maybe next week." I considered this first contact as very positive.

A SIGNIFICANT MEETING

The meeting with Minister Kussumua was on March 12, 2003.

The office of the Minister called a day before to confirm my appointment. Although I arrived on time at 10 a.m., the red tape took another hour before I entered the Minister's office. He gave me a warm welcome. He asked me a few questions about my experiences working among refugees. After telling him my background, he asked me to write that information for him with a letter explaining the main objectives of our involvement in the repatriation project as monitors.

The Minister added that this work cannot be done until the rainy season ends here in Angola. Most of the roads are impassible in the Provinces of Zaire, Uige, Moxico, and Cuando Cubango, which are scheduled to receive the repatriated refugees. He suggested that I should return to Canada first to wait until the dry season, which starts in early June to the end of August. This contact we believe will shape whatever decision the Minister will take on the issue....

The news of my meeting with the Minister spread faster than I had expected. Many church leaders expressed their satisfaction and addressed my ministry of advocacy. They considered it as being a voice for the voiceless.... Most of these churches and lay leaders have members among those refugees who will be repatriated in June. They appreciated CBM initiatives on behalf of the refugees.

This Ministry, MINARS, is precisely the one relevant, not only to the repatriation of refugees and their reintegration into civilian life in Angola, but also the one relevant to civic education projects which were being addressed by Development Workshop. In the meeting with Minister Kussumua, he and João were alone, and he showed much interest in João's experiences. The intervention of Ambassador Puna, much appreciated, proved to be helpful and effective.

DEVELOPMENT WORKSHOP (DW) AND CIVIC EDUCATION

Allan Cain of DW was disappointed by the slowness of approval from CIDA (Canadian International Development Agency) in funding proposals related to civic education for the reintegration of ex-combatants and returning IDPs, who lived in Luanda's slums in such great numbers. The program could not proceed until CIDA funding was assured, and it was needed immediately.

The Civic Education project was designed to run for a year. João was invited to be part of the peace-building team and his lessons on reconciliation were to have a nation-wide focus. If funding approval were to come through from CIDA, they would work on an extension of João's visa so that an immediate start could be made. João's participation on the team provided a needed link with the north of Angola, where DW had done relatively little. Allan was prepared to help there with the building of schools and clinics and in setting up loans to facilitate small businesses.

When João reported back to him after the meeting with Minister Kussumua, Allan encouraged João to visit Mbanza-Kongo, where he could assess the needs and monitor any movement of refugees returning home voluntarily from the Congo.

From earlier planning sessions with John Keith, a recommendation went to CBM that João's church reconciliation undertaking in Angola be acknowledged as significant, and that some financial provision be made for João's support while doing it, since this class of activity did not fall under projects sponsored by DW. That led to CBM and DW sharing his in-country expenses. João aimed at being a bridge-builder among the leaders, the churches and the denominations.

Ministries Following Retirement

A historic visit to Mbanza-Kongo

The next activity was for João to visit Mbanza-Kongo, his place of birth.

The first thing to consider is the historical significance of the 15 of March. It was this day, forty-two years ago, that the war for independence started in the north of Angola. I was a student at the Bible Institute of Calambata, where John Keith was the Principal. Here are a few contrasts I found: In 1961 British and Canadian Baptist teachers, students, and their families were evacuated by the Portuguese army trucks from Calambata to Mbanza-Kongo (called São Salvador in those days). We were all fearful of war and death. But now in 2003 I arrived here by airplane from the capital of Angola, without fear of war and death. In 1961 the airport was at Bela Vista, 15 kilometres outside the town; this time we landed in the middle of the town.

The second relevance of that historic date forty-two years earlier was the birth of our son, Edward Matwawana, in the Mbanza-Kongo hospital. The war did not spare that hospital, because all that was left was the shell of the operating theatre and Dr. Shields' consulting room.

In 1961, the São Salvador mission station had a printing press and a trade school. Today there are no signs left of all that work. In 1961 São Salvador was the pride of the Baptist work in Angola, being the largest, with a missionary staff of twelve, the two boarding schools, one for boys and another for girls, and many congregations in over 130 towns and villages, with African leadership of high quality.

Most school buildings were destroyed by the war and all the well-trained leaders refuse to leave the capital city of Luanda to lead the church in the provinces. As a result, the less qualified pastors also started to protest the decisions of the General

WARS ARE NEVER ENOUGH

With Samuel and Edward on the day of Edward's dedication

João with Samuel and Edward 40 years later

Assembly, refusing to leave Luanda to their assigned churches in the provinces. Talking with these pastors and their wives, I learned that their fears are real. It is unwise to take their children out of school to go to an area where there are no schools and no medical clinics. Therefore, the rehabilitation of both schools and medical services in the provinces is an urgent need. Pastors are not the only ones refusing to leave Luanda. It was reported that 80 percent of Angolan medical doctors are working in the capital city of Luanda, and the list goes on.

João continued recording his observations about the town itself, a major segment of it, near where the king's palace was located, now desolate. He comments on the surprising and disappointing presence of a whole new generation who grew up waiting for handouts from the government or from non-governmental organizations. This was in dramatic contrast to pre-war Angolans, who were enterprising by nature. He laments their lack of any sense of ownership, and their lack of awareness of the need for people to invest in their town in order to improve it. He observed houses left by the Portuguese which had not been painted for twenty-five years, commenting that there will be a great need for moral and civic education, precisely the activities in which he is involved with DW. The time has come for people to learn their rights and responsibilities as citizens, a daunting task for both government and churches in years to come.

Sunday, March 16, 2003, is another day with nostalgic memories. At the beginning of the civil war in 1975, I was the Senior Pastor of the Baptist Church in Mbanza-Kongo. The whole population fled when they learned of the advance of the Cuban army. I was among the last to leave the town. Being there again brought very sad memories of how it was we became refugees again for the second time. This was the first time I returned in the twenty-seven years since I left in the middle of the war. My tears of joy flowed when I heard familiar hymns and songs, and saw familiar faces. Of course the majority in this congregation are much younger. In order to identify some of them I had to ask first who their parents and grandparents were.

Wars Are Never Enough

There were things which popped into my mind when I stood before my old pulpit. First of all, it reminded me of the day of my baptism, and our wedding ceremony in that same old sanctuary, built in 1900 by British missionary, Thomas Lewis, still standing as a witness, although leaking and in bad shape.

After the service I visited the cemetery of the pioneer missionaries, and visited a few old members of the congregation who are no longer able to walk to the church services. I also visited the old school where Nora and I studied, a red burnt brick house standing in ruin beside the old church.

The Christians are in good heart but the tasks ahead are enormous and beyond their limited resources. They need our prayers and our financial assistance in order to rebuild their churches and their shattered lives. I left Mbanza-Kongo with a lot of hope, because I saw people determined to rebuild their churches and their homes.

João worshipping in a new church in Angola

GETTING DOWN TO WORK ON CIVIC EDUCATION

After this visit to Mbanza-Kongo, consultations with Allan Cain and Eunice Inácio, back in Luanda, focussed on DW's development of program and materials for its civic education project even though CIDA's approval of funding continued to lag. Allan wished to extend João's time in Angola, but could not do it without assurances of funding from Ottawa. For such time as remained available, João and Eunice were to continue to map out their National Civic Education Project.

Dr. Gary Nelson's first visit to Angola fell during João's time in Luanda. As General Secretary of CBM, his contacts would be primarily with *Igreja Evangélica de Angola*, its leaders, people and congregations, including visits to Soyo and Cabinda. João was part of his reception on arrival, together with IEA leaders, and with Karl and Kathy Janzen, also of CBM and on assignment in Angola.

In a resumé of this second productive trip, João was happy to observe that CBM's objectives for the assignment had been met:

When the process of repatriating refugees begins in June, the place of CBM on the monitoring team is now recognized, along with the UNHCR and the government of Angola.

CIDA's approval of funding for Development Workshop's Civic Education Project was granted on July 25, 2003.

22

THIRD PEACE MISSION—TO ZAMBIA AND ANGOLA
(July 29 to October 12, 2003)

The more dramatic highlights of what Dr. João Matwawana called his Peace Mission Number Three to Angola were the teaching sessions he conducted in various refugee reception centres inside Angola. Less visible, but equally valuable, was the considerable amount of time and effort he invested in preparing peace-building materials for use in seminars, to be distributed by Development Workshop, and put in the hands of peace workers as they were trained.

The Civic Education Program, as originally conceived by Allan Cain and DW colleagues, was seen as an instrument to equip ex-combatants for civilian life. Specifically, that meant demobilized troops of UNITA and also those of Angola's armed forces, FAA, whose military careers had ended with the signing of Angola's 2002 *Protocol of Understanding* that ended the long years of warfare. It was becoming obvious now, that program contents were also highly relevant to the communities of refugees being repatriated in 2003.

His two most recent visits back to Angola had convinced João that Angola's population was severely deficient in any sense of collective responsibility, and deficient in personal initiative. Whereas prior to

1961, Angolans, as a people, were not only survivors, they were innovators who turned the most meagre resources into productivity and outshone their neighbours in both creativity and industry. By 2003, Angolans no longer displayed that *élan vital*.

Those findings convinced João that civic education input was vital and that it was a valid companion of personal faith. It was, in fact, urgent to the future of Angola. With that foundation, other efforts aimed at nation-building or development or self-help, whether undertaken by government or by private agencies, would stand a better chance of yielding permanent results. João was ready to pour his energies into the task lined up for him through Development Workshop.

Preparations

João summarized his preparations for Angola Peace Mission Number Three this way:

> *I will bring back my exiled people....*
> *they will rebuild the ruined cities and live in them....*
> *they will make gardens and eat their fruit.*
>
> Amos 9:14

> *... I will heal my people and will let them enjoy*
> *abundant peace and security....*
> *I will cleanse them from all the sin*
> *they have committed against me*
> *and will forgive all their sins of rebellion against me.*
>
> Jeremiah 33:6, 8

The verses above were on my mind when I was saying goodbye to friends and family in Nova Scotia, as I left on July 29, 2003, for Zambia via London and Johannesburg. I was going to Angola just to be God's vessel available to be used by Himself. To be a comforter and an encourager to those exiled who are returning home from Zambia, Namibia, DRC, and other coun-

tries. *They will have many challenges to face. Many will find their lands occupied by others. Returning refugees will clash with neighbouring villages, who will see them as being richer than themselves, because of the settlement kits they have received at the transit centres. This may cause a deep resentment. There will be a need to accelerate community-based programs of reconciliation and civic education, because both local and returning people have little notion of their basic rights and responsibilities as citizens. Someone has called it a* ministry of presence *among suffering people.*

To Lusaka, Zambia

This trip began with a return to the Zambian refugee camps housing Angolans, where João had worked earlier. He arrived in Lusaka, Zambia, on the last day of July, and was met by UNHCR staff and taken to Belvedere Lodge. Their representative had been alerted to his coming by a memo from Geneva, and expressed his personal gratitude to CBM and João for the interest being shown for the well-being of Angolan refugees and specifically for the decision to be part of the repatriation team by way of training and counselling. Before proceeding on to Ndola and his contact with refugees, João met with the Zambian Government's Commissioner for Refugees, Mr. Jacob Mphepo, whose commendation carried a similar tone.

It was a tearful event for many of the refugee leaders with whom João met at Ndola, as they watched the first group of 500 who were Angola bound, in a convoy of trucks provided by the International Organization for Migration. These were from the Muheba Refugee Camp, which João had visited two years earlier. On arrival in Angola they had the promise of food for two months, through the World Food Program. Looking into the details of how this was all happening, João was pleased to see the good organization and a high level of co-operation between UNHCR and the Zambian government. Other provisions on arrival would include blankets, household utensils, seeds, and awareness training related to dangers such as the minefields and AIDS.

Moving on to Luanda, João was hosted by the UNHCR Head of Operations, Mr. Carlos Zaccagnini, helped by Jean-Claude Lude, head of logistics. They booked flights to visit refugee reception centres in Angola's provinces of Moxico and Zaire. The World Food Program has planes that fly to remote areas of Angola. This time in Luanda was a basic orientation to what takes place, how, and in what sequence.

To Kazombo Refugee Reception Centre

A visit to the Kazombo Refugee Reception Centre, located in Angola's Moxico Province, marked a new dimension in João's participation in the refugee repatriation process. Being able to conduct seminars there brought to fruition plans made much earlier. He approached the opportunity with anticipation. UNHCR officers in Luanda had paved the way with fine arrangements for lodging, seminars, and João's presentation to the relevant officials—always very important. He met with the Administrator, the Chief of Police, the army General, and others.

At Kazombo, the results of his visits to Zambian refugee camps beginning in 2001 began to show:

During the tour of that reception centre, I was encouraged to meet some returning refugees who had earlier attended our seminar on Conflict Resolution, Peace & Reconciliation in Zambia. ...One even showed me his binder of lessons he received at the Peace Seminar in Ndola.... It is my hope that as these people return to their home villages they will be able to train many others.

The three main objectives of our peace-building seminars were explained to the Kazombo officials, which are:
(a) to encourage the refugees by bringing them a message of hope in this uncertain time
(b) to empower the leadership and teach them to exercise their duties, in assisting the local officials in conflict resolution
(c) to provide care in the form of counselling and teaching through workshops.

The beneficiaries were the refugees, camp leaders, women, youth, and volunteers. The first seminar was attended by seventeen people. They were challenged to train others after they settle in their home areas. In turn they will be the torch bearers of the Peace and Reconciliation message to their fellow countrymen.

João made virtually no mention of the loss of his luggage, on August 9, between Lusaka and Johannesburg, en route to Angola, which he said "caused some inconvenience." The best face was put on this misfortune, as he added "...the good thing about it was that I felt very much at home in refugee camps, being dirty and not wearing fancy clothes."

The loss of his luggage was an inconvenience which he did not allow to become an impediment. There were many other inconveniences. One recurring problem, mission after mission, related to problems in communication. One of the requests for prayer sent to his friends in Canada, was that he would have the necessary patience (again and again) when electrical power is cut in the middle of a partially composed e-mail message!

Pursuit of Reconciliation among Churches and Denominations

Once back in Luanda again, contacts resumed with church leaders, pursuing reconciliation, mutual understanding, and a spirit of fellowship and cooperation. Rifts had developed between churches in exile and those which remained in Angola during the long years of war. There was constructive work to be done as well among those who had remained in Angola, coming to grips with long-standing issues large and small which had simply never been resolved. A series of contacts were undertaken with the following:

- UMC, the United Methodist Church
- IECA, the Evangelical Church of Central Angola. This is the traditional partner of the United Church of Canada.
- IEBA, the Evangelical Baptist Church of Angola, the traditional partner of the UK's Baptist Missionary Society

- IEA, the Evangelical Church of Angola, the traditional partner with CBM
- CICA, the Council of Christian Churches in Angola

The Visit to Kiowa Refugee Reception Centre at Mbanza-Kongo

In September, João made another foray into his area of origin. Discussions with the UNHCR Field Director at Mbanza-Kongo took on special significance as he learned of difficulties in bringing returning refugees to their home communities because of damaged roads. These were roads João had walked repeatedly. So could he possibly stay on for a while and help with logistics, providing insights to local issues? Unfortunately that would not be possible, a heavy agenda, limited time, and visa restrictions being among the complications. But he was certainly working on very familiar ground.

As he joined the convoy of trucks taking refugees from Congo back across the border into Angola, there were incidents that brought back nostalgic memories of his childhood, and he observed that some of the simple technology (or lack of it) still prevails more than sixty years later.

The lamps João used when in school around 1952-54 were simply a sardine can or a milk can with paraffin or palm oil for fuel. The wick was a piece of cloth from an old pair of trousers. These lamps smoked profusely, gave limited light, and were obnoxiously smelly, but they were what was available and they gave the light that permitted the students to study for their exams and eventually their diplomas. Those who fell asleep were in danger, for they could easily burn the house down if the lamp were accidentally bumped from whatever perch held it in a position to provide that minimal lighting needed. On at least one occasion, while studying for an exam, João was awakened from sleep by the smell of his own hair burning. During this 2004 visit to Angolan refugees at their camp in western Congo, and accompanying them on their journey of repatriation to the reception Centre at Kiowa, near Mbanza-Kongo, João was astounded to find those primitive lamps still in use, but burning diesel fuel.

Ministries Following Retirement

Experiences at the Angola/Congo frontier

Crossing the Congo border into Angola with the refugee convoy, they made it safely through half of the border formalities, exiting Congo in time, but arrived too late to be processed that day for official entry at Luvo on the Angolan side. The convoy of perhaps five trucks prepared to hunker down in the open to await the opening of Angola's border post the following morning. As part of this migration, with observer status, João was able to absorb and reflect on the realities of prevailing conditions in rural Angola today, affected by many years of warfare. He found the situation to be a shambles:

> I asked immigration if they have some place where a person can spend the night.
> "No, but try with the security people."
> Security had nothing.
> "Try the administrator."
> The administrator's wife said that although they might have a room, she was alone and was not allowed to host anyone, especially men. This was understandable.
> "But I was introduced to your husband during my last visit to Mbanza-Kongo."
> "Maybe so, but I can't let you in. Try the military commander."
>
> The commander spoke no Kikongo, only Portuguese, which indicated that he was from a different part of Angola. I identified myself and my mission of visiting refugees.
> "Because there was so much delay I am late. Can I just sleep anywhere inside in a corner somewhere, maybe even in your office?"
> "I have confidential documents in my office, I can't put you there. Even we ourselves are suffering. We have no place. You may have to sleep outside like others."
> His assistant was there nearby and he heard me muttering to myself, "Ofuku mfwidi kwa mbu."
> The commander asked his assistant what the old man said.
> "He said, 'Tonight I will die from mosquitoes.'"

The commander then authorized his assistant, whose name was Eduardo, to question João in Kikongo:

"*Tell me a little of your story.*"
So I filled him in.
"*We should do something to help you, but we have no resources.*"

João made the most of the fact that the assistant's name was Eduardo, like that of his son. Eduardo informed his commander that one of their tents was empty, a soldier being on assignment to Mbanza-Kongo.

"*His tent is empty. We will put you there.*"
Approval was granted.
"*Is the tent clean?*" (It was the commander who asked.)
"*The tent is never clean, but it has a bamboo bed.*"
I found a mosquito net as well, riddled with holes. And darkness.

"*I want to buy candles.*"
"*Candles are not allowed here, you might burn down the tent. If it were a market day you could buy a lantern. We have diesel oil.*"

The wife of a soldier heard some of this conversation and said that maybe the old man could borrow a lamp from her, since she had two. She filled one with diesel fuel and lighted it:

I was astounded at my memory flashback. I had used one precisely like this from 1951 to 1954, fifty years earlier. It was just a small condensed milk can with a hole in the top, with a simple cloth as a wick. Of course the smell was of diesel oil rather than kerosene or palm oil. Among three or four truckloads, I was the only one to sleep inside, because I had persisted (afraid of malaria). I was honoured to receive such treatment, with hundreds outside. I had shelter and an oil lamp.

Ministries Following Retirement

The immigration department's opening hour for border crossing the next day was governed more by prevailing conditions than by any established official working hours. Of course there were no showers available. All the male officials headed for the Luvo River around seven. They returned from the river with towels wrapped around them, and then it was the women's turn. The women washed dishes in the river, washed their clothes, had their own bath, then came back to make breakfast for the men who might then open the border not long after eight, if all went well.

The convoy with its refugees made it through:

The following days my time was divided as follows:

In the mornings I conducted the Seminars on Peace and Reconciliation attended by twenty-eight people. That workshop included representatives from different churches and leaders of the refugee camp and of the local communities.

Afternoons were spent at the Refugee Reception Centre, where I assisted during the arrival of convoys from DRC. I found the centre well organized. There was tremendous sensitivity given to specific needs of refugees returning home after many years in exile. I highly commend the excellent work they are doing. Also I observed another excellent working relationship among the HCR staff and other NGOs. I felt welcomed by both the refugees and the HCR staff and my presence and recommendations were much appreciated and accepted.

Contacts with Angolan authorities on this visit included the Ministry of Social Affairs in Luanda, where their blessing was given to João's ongoing training programs among refugees. The Governor of Zaire Province was absent, but João met with the Deputy Governor, the representative of the Minister of Social Affairs, the Provincial Director of Public Works, the Director of Industry Commerce and Tourism, and the representative of the Director of Culture, who also attended the seminar in Mbanza-Kongo.

The report on his third Peace Mission to Angola wraps up with his own resumé of highlights:

- *It was a joy to realize that the head of the Southern Africa Desk of UNHCR in Geneva kept his word. This was proven by the warm welcome and good co-operation I received from their staff in both Zambia and Angola.*
- *To recognize some refugees I met in Zambia. One of them exhibited his last year's binder of lessons he received in Zambia. This alone made my trip to Angola worthwhile.*
- *To see the enthusiasm in the face of these refugees when they were leaving the transit centres by trucks to their last destination singing and jumping. I agree with Kenneth King when he wrote, "One of the enduring mysteries and marvels of Africa is the ability of its people to pick themselves up from the most appalling disasters."*
- *The joy of finding my lost suitcase with everything in it. A sign of improvement in the Angolan customs services.*
- *When I received an invitation from Allan Cain (Canadian Consulate) to work with Development Workshop to be their Peace Advisor for a national project funded by CIDA.... Their task is called Civic Education, and their goal is to provide mini libraries and train people who will teach Angolans how to live as citizens of a free society.*

23

FOURTH PEACE MISSION—TO ANGOLA
(December 6, 2003 to February 28, 2004)

ANGOLA'S PEACE AND THE FAITH FACTOR

During this fourth Peace Mission, João noticed that in worship services, the nation's present state of peace was publicly acknowledged as an answer to prayer. The Angolan people had prayed faithfully for years that their war would end and that peace would be established. There was never a lack of personal or collective prayer for peace. However, the collapse of the Lusaka Accord created a new level of spiritual crisis that drove Angolan churches to their knees collectively.

Never in the history of Angola did the churches pray so audibly. They even rented a stadium and prayed publicly in a way which impressed the power of prayer on those outside the church, to the point where non-believers feared. The President even came to one of those public prayer sessions. Things began to change.

My first observation is to see the spiritual side of the peace in Angola. It is God's peace. The people believe this is not the politicians' peace, but God's peace. The Generals were directed by God to make this peace accord because God heard the cry of the people. Furthermore there has been a mental shift on the part of government officials to acknowledge the appropriateness of the church's share in peace and reconciliation.

After conducting his seminar at Malange, João was introduced to the District Governor, and received the Governor's affirmation:

"We are very grateful you came to do this because the church is credible to do it. We politicians talk of these things in speeches but it is really your task."

It is now possible to look back and contrast this attitude with the earlier hostility toward the church that has since disappeared.

"If we staked out property to build a church in a prominent place the local population would usually pull up our markers at night. It was considered too dangerous to live near a church, because of the government's hostility to churches. Eventually we came to establish our churches virtually in the bush, only in bad places where people didn't want to build houses. The government called itself a lay government but this was the reality of the situation."

Today there is a certain amount of respect that the government has for churches as a whole, and a recognition of what the churches accomplished in the gaining of peace. When Angola's Council of Churches holds conferences, the government sends representatives.

Kimbanguism is a Protestant religious denomination, active in Angola and in the Congo. When it underwent a rift, Angola's President Dos Santos wrote them, registering his concern: "If you start breaking into pieces, this gives a bad example to the nation." João sees this as a sign that the President now looks on the church as a potential unifying force in the process of nation-building.

Ministries Following Retirement

Back to Development Workshop's Civic Education Project

Getting into the substance of the work of Peace Mission Number Four, João was plunged into the details of making Development Workshop's *Civic Education Program* a success.

"Civic Education," he says, "is simply teaching people how to live. Under the communist system that responsibility was not theirs, individually, rather it belonged to the government." He speaks of a middle generation of people who had no civic education and who grew up during the war without any concept of either responsibility or ownership. Under the communist upbringing, property belongs to all of us. What you have is mine. Any appeal for accountability and transparency in management and reporting, whether in government, business, or industry, is dependent upon Civic Education's processes of de-programming or re-programming communist patterns of thinking.

For example, João was travelling north of Luanda, along the coast. He and his colleague had brought their own food from Luanda, and took it into a restaurant. The waitress told them that it was a very good idea to bring their own food, since the restaurant had none to offer. What was her job then? To sell drinks. The waitress approached João and requested that she be able to taste his fish. Everything belongs to everyone!

His colleague commented to João in this context that in the communist environment, the person who lives with nine poor people becomes the tenth. Against such a background, João describes civic education as re-programming the thinking of people to include their responsibilities as well as their rights.

Giving a further practical example, João cited how he had bought milk and juice to put in the shared refrigerator at the Luanda guest house. When it consistently disappeared, he used the opportunity to share lessons in personal ownership and responsibility, including the importance of asking the owner's permission prior to "borrowing" or helping oneself.

From a DW document, "Questions About the Revision of the Civic Education Project," the following translation states one of their missions:

DW as an organization of the International Social Society, is not responsible for carrying out the activities of civic education directly in the communities. Its mission is to work with other organizations of civil society with the purpose of equipping them to act.

Results which the project hopes to achieve are listed as these:
- *A structure of coordination and a network of participating organizations in each of the twelve provinces which the project touches.*
- *Guaranteed access to materials for consultation in civic education in each of those twelve provinces.*
- *Advocacy for the Program of Civic Education promoted.*

Beyond all formal declarations of programs and structures, João had found his "fit" in working with Allan Cain and Development Workshop, even though it originally seemed to him that civic education might be outside his focus on peace and reconciliation. As he looked at Angola, its situation and its needs, he perceived that civic education was, in fact, vital, with so many issues to be addressed.

Peace depends upon a change in the attitude of people. They had assumed that with peace all would be rosy. Reality was just the contrary. Peace came, money disappeared, hunger, frustration, and violence emerged. "What is peace all about?" Through DW and its civic education program, João found his channel through which to address those issues.

The parallel thread of activity that always preoccupied João was his goal of making progress in reconciliation among various denominations of churches which were not in step with each other. One of his goals in this was to aim for a reconciliation conference to be held in 2004. Progress toward this goal could only be achieved by working both sides of the street, so to speak. During this Peace Mission Number Four, he made progress in his contacts with some movements, and he continued in constant interaction with the parent bodies IEBA and IEA, from whom they had separated. He found that he already had an unexpected advantage when he contacted Rev. João Kiala Kiasiswa of the IBLA cluster of churches. This younger man informed João that he had been the youngest student in the primary school João had founded at Mongo Zulu. João, while serving as chaplain at Kimpese, had also been influential in his admission to the Bible School at Vanga. "So the meetings were very family-like, as father with son."

To Cabinda

A visit of three days to Cabinda was the object of much prayer. The heart of João's mission to IEA church leadership was to approach them concerning a reconciliation conference. He found them open, endorsing his proposal, and planned a similar meeting with IEBA leadership in Luanda. When it came down to discussions about participating in an eventual church reconciliation conference, the Matwawana logic was presented in this way: Peace and Reconciliation is like waiting at the train station: you may have the right ticket, but unless you get on board, you will be left behind.

In his church reconciliation attempts João acknowledged the importance of the churches as a role model:

We have to attempt great things for God in order to expect great things for Angola. There is no point of pressing the government to show some changes and acceptance of the idea of reconciliation if the churches are in the same sin.

Canadian government delegation to Angola

The arrival in Angola of a delegation from Foreign Affairs Canada was a special event for DW, and also for João. Allan Cain's position as Canada's honorary Consul placed him in a special category. It was he who introduced the Canadian delegates to each department of the government.

Meetings with the Government of Angola occupied the first days, then João met with them on January 19. FAC's Minister Graham had appointed Mr. David Strangway as his Special Ministerial Envoy to Angola, and Strangway was the team leader on this delegation, with

David Angell as Area Director and Denan Kuni as Desk Officer being key players. Ambassador John Schram, who also covered Angola from his primary posting in Harare, Zimbabwe, was a key participant. He commented to João that it was good to meet him in person after having heard of him in Canadian Baptist churches. The Strangway appointment had been an astute one, since David's father, Dr. Walter Strangway, was an outstanding surgeon who served his career in Angola under the United Church of Canada. This was a serious delegation and one which both Denan Kuni and David Angell has worked hard to put together. It began to give substance to a Canada-Angola joint working group, a step in the direction of more formal diplomatic relations between the two countries. Angola has an embassy in Ottawa but Canada's representation in Luanda is only through our Honorary Consul, and of course through Ambassador Schram, based in Harare.

Oxfam Canada approached Development Workshop to discuss working together. At the request of the director and other staff, João read through their documents and shared his commentaries and recommendations as requested.

In a separate development, DW's team of three met with Angola's Vice-Minister of Education, Mr. Mpinda Simão, who showed much interest in working with them. He invited them to participate in a team of government education experts beginning the following day. In retrospect this contact with Mr. Simão was a significant one in the opening up of a partnership with the Ministry of Education.

Changes for the better in Angola

On this mission, as on others, the appearance of outstanding people in certain offices serves as an encouragement as Angola moves along its path toward democracy and accountable government. One such person is General Pedro Sebastião, the Governor of Zaire Province, with his headquarters at Mbanza-Kongo. Born at Kinzau, in the region of Nzeto, he has served as Minister of Defense, as well as having been a diplomat in Europe.

To give a glimpse of how security in the countryside has been improving with the passage of time, João reflects on the difference between travel concerns in 2002 and those in 2004:

During our 2002 Mission, DW faced a big decision relating to our desire to visit Catete, 60 kilometres from Luanda. Most were afraid that was too far to go.
"Why go to Catete?"
"To see the displaced persons there, and their gardens that we have been hearing about."
This was just four months after the peace agreement had been signed, and Catete seemed too far. Planning went on for a week. Catete was President Agostinho Neto's place of birth. UNITA had destroyed it by bombardment. Furthermore, it would be necessary to leave the road to get to the people's gardens. Two years has made an enormous difference. We travelled 500 kms by road to Mbanza-Kongo and nobody questioned the security. Every 5 kilometres or so other vehicles would be sighted. There is now international food traffic. A great improvement.

While security on the road speaks to the issue of the national situation, in Luanda one notes a more perilous banditry. In Luanda there may be more than a million small firearms, for the population has never been disarmed. There is a general sense that it is right to own arms, since they were distributed by the government in 1992.

At the end of this fourth trip, the privilege of working with Allan Cain and Development Workshop was especially appreciated. "Everybody wants to work through Allan Cain. DW is the most mature of Angola's NGOs. Everyone consults Allan, he is a very busy man." There were occasions when he asked João to meet delegations on his behalf. João was happy to do so.

On Monday, March 1, João was safely home again after a ministry in Angola of three months less eight days.

Church and community support for Nora

Dr. João Matwawana's absences from home have been both frequent and prolonged. Both he and Nora comment on the solid support from both church and community which have made it possible for Nora to survive at their home in Lower Sackville, Nova Scotia, while he has been away.

João and Nora are active members of Grace Baptist Church in Lower Sackville. It has provided them with a broad spectrum of friends and supporters, among whom some are very close and have functioned like family when João is absent. They have helped Nora in meeting appointments, caring for grandchildren, getting her to emergency out-patient treatment, sometimes even giving financial assistance. They remember birthdays and special occasions, and call to know how things are going.

The Matwawanas' immediate neighbours have also gone out of their way to show themselves helpful in very practical ways, whether assisting with snow removal, starting a stalled vehicle, or dealing with the aftermath of storms (not unknown in the Halifax area!), mowing the lawn, and generally being good neighbours.

Of course that kind of friendship and helpfulness from neighbours and from church family does not end with João's return from overseas travels. Assistance of the kind one might only expect in an African village can go beyond being just helpful. In one instance it even extended to the entire re-wiring of their home, which had not been wired originally according to code. Friendship flows back and forth, help is always just that close when needed.

Sons Edward and Ambrose are both in the greater Halifax area, both a comfort and a practical help. Nora shares one incident:

> *When one of the hurricanes was building I had a bad migraine and took medication which makes me sleepy. I went to bed and heard nothing at all. At eight the next morning I got a call from Edward.*
> *"Any damage to your house, Mom?"*
> *"Damage from what?" I was unaware even of the hurricane.*
> *"Go and check."*

I found leaves everywhere, and heard the banging of people repairing their roofs. Only then when I got up and around did I discover that we had no power in the house. Our barbecue on the back porch had a propane tank, so I went there to boil water for coffee. I was drinking it on the street as I examined what the neighbours were doing. I found no damage to our own house at all!

"How did you get hot water for your coffee?" the neighbours asked. So then I invited them to come and boil water on our barbecue, make lunch, or whatever. Neighbours are invaluable. Disasters are a time when people help each other. Our church and our neighbours have been a great help to me.

Matwawana family gathering at their home in Nova Scotia

Events in Ottawa between two peace missions to Angola

Development Workshop's able Ottawa representative, John Van Mossel, convened a March meeting in Ottawa that brought together the

NGOs related to the Angola Peace Action Network, APAN, for contact with Foreign Affairs Canada (FAC), and specifically with the FAC delegation members who had visited Angola in February 2004. Reports were heard from those who had visited Angola recently, so in addition to David Strangway and Ambassador Schram there were reports from Gary Kenney (United Church of Canada), Dorothee Ngolo (Kimberley Process), and João Matwawana (CBM). Contributions from David Angell and Denan Kuni of FAC were also welcomed.

This was the latest in a series of several such meetings with Foreign Affairs Canada, the range of interest and topics being very wide, but with special attention to these items:

- Canadian government assistance to Angola, especially through CIDA
- Angola's progress toward holding free elections, and the timing of elections
- The ongoing peace process, stability and order in Angola
- Land mine control/clearance
- The hope that Angola's wealth of riches may benefit her population
- Transparency and accountability of Angolan government reporting on its resources
- Canadian diplomatic representation in Luanda
- An independent media
- Cessation of conflict in Cabinda
- Programs to help small industries
- Continued human rights monitoring and intervention
- The ethics of big business
- Publish what you pay
- Conflict diamonds

The occasion of this Ottawa consultation permitted participation in Canada's National Prayer Breakfast and associated events.

24

FIFTH PEACE MISSION—TO ANGOLA AND CONGO*
(May 5 to August 8, 2004)

The fifth Peace Mission to Angola got underway with João and Nora's arrival in Luanda airport at 4 a.m. on Saturday, May 8. They were met by Mr. Agostinho of Development Workshop, but they experienced an hour of anxiety, standing by their luggage, as they learned that their guest house reservation had been cancelled. "Welcome to the Angola system," said their driver.

That Sunday afternoon they visited relatives in the Luanda hospital, and on Monday they rested, as they were still fighting jet lag.

STRUCK BY A CAR

On the Tuesday, his first full day back at work in Angola, João suffered a mishap. He refers to it as being snatched from the power of death, Psalm 49:15:

> *Little did I foresee that it could also have been my last day of work and of this life altogether. At around 10 a.m. I was knocked down by a car as I was crossing the street from the*

Canadian Consulate office. I never saw the car coming, because it entered the main street from a small back road and started speeding. Fortunately I was able to get up by myself, assuring the driver that I was alive, but I needed urgent medical attention. At the clinic Dr. Xavier informed me that I suffered no broken bones, and that the bruises on my knees, elbows, feet, and right arm would be healed in two or three weeks, so I was treated and released.

Since my first mission in the summer of 2002, I witnessed many car accidents and many deaths as a result of this never-ending traffic jam in Luanda, but when my turn came I was not prepared. It was so fast, there was no time to think. When I returned to my room several hours later to tell Nora what happened, she was in panic for a week. During my recovery days I read Psalm 91 several times, stopping for a few minutes on verse 11: "For He orders His angels to protect you wherever you go."

Looking back, God has reminded me that this has been a reality in my life, not only in Angola but also in other countries like the DRC, Rwanda, Burundi, Kenya, Zambia, and South Africa, where we carried out a similar ministry. I give thanks to my Lord for His protection and for you, my dear friends and prayer warriors, wherever you are.

In the next couple of weeks two significant events happened, in addition to the inter-church discussions with his potential reconciliation conference always in mind. The first of these events was that they located an appropriate apartment where Nora was able to equip her own kitchen, not a small consideration when away from home for protracted periods. The second was that João finally received his *Bilhete de Identidade* (birth certificate), a landmark event. No matter that there was a misspelling of his name. That was corrected. And of course work continued with DW on its civic education program, which was still the core of Peace Mission Number Five.

Ministries Following Retirement

Visit of pastors from Canada

Visitors from Canada soon joined the Matwawanas. Four Canadian Baptist pastors came to assist them in the IEA, the Angola Evangelical church:

- To assist in the ministry of reconciliation
- To encourage IEA church leadership
- To teach during pastoral retreats in Cabinda and Nzeto, May 24-30, 2004

With only a few hours' rest, they were informed by Rev. Simia and his staff that they were off to preach in churches in Luanda. Departure for the countryside was set for the following morning. There was to be no delay in putting them to work! John Churchill, George Alves, and Sheila Smith flew to Cabinda, while David Watt travelled with João and Nora to Nzeto, six hours' travel by road.

It was a generous act when Mr. Israel João Costa, member of an IEA church in Luanda, put his truck and his driver, Mr. Pedro, at our disposal for the whole week. We were able to travel with less problems, because the driver fixed the truck on the spot every time it was out of order. [To qualify as an excellent driver one must also be an excellent mechanic.] He even invented some car parts in our presence. We think that new missionaries who plan to work outside the cities in Angola should be equipped with a book such as Where There Is No Canadian Tire Store. *We reached Nzeto in late afternoon and found all the participants waiting for us—pastors and their spouses from four areas of the IEA: Luanda, Bengo, Nzeto and Soyo....*

Participants asked questions after each session, and then were given questions for discussion in small groups. Each group reported back their findings on the topics of:
- *Leadership development*
- *Spiritual formation*

- *Biblical peacemaking*
- *The role of the Church in Angola's reconciliation*

Some afternoons Nora had separate sessions with the pastors' wives, in order to discuss in detail some of the morning lessons like, "The Ten Pillars of Marriage" or, "Marriage and the Pastor and His Family". Nora was able to share with them from her personal experiences and the lessons learned as a result of her travels and work among women of other cultures. She was a valuable member of the team.

The highlight was the big closing Sunday service attended by over 2,000 people, including local authorities and representatives of other denominations.

Parallel ministries had been happening in Cabinda with the other Canadian visitors. When they were all reunited in Luanda, they held an evaluation session with IEA leaders, and also visited the offices of NGOs. João observed:

We were glad to note that in the midst of suffering, the church is having such a distinguished part in the rebuilding and reconciliation of both the church and the nation. During the long war the Lord has taught them much.

The impact of this Canadian team was reinforced a week later with the arrival of Terry Smith from Canadian Baptist Ministries, on his first visit to Angola. His purposes included the firming up of the partnership between CBM and the IEA. Terry's totally bilingual abilities with English and French contributed notably to his facility in communication. Many Angolans speak French in addition to Portuguese and one or more other languages.

João gave a real shout of victory on June 14 when he finally received his Angolan passport, the culmination of a long struggle. The event was so important that he even noted the time of day when it was in his hand—nine-thirty in the morning!

Ministries Following Retirement

Before Nora's departure, she started the documentation process to get her own *Bilhete de Identidade*, as João had done. She also made her own pilgrimage to Mbanza-Kongo, her town of birth. That also allowed her to visit her parents' graves there for the first time. She returned to Canada on July 4, with João remaining behind for additional work among refugees.

Accounts of João's participation in collateral activities must not obscure his ongoing involvement in organizational aspects and work for DW's program of Civic Education. He held or equipped workshops and seminars to train Peace Promoters, prepared material and trained Peace Promoters, collected content for handouts or to be part of the micro-libraries going to the twelve provinces of Angola's eighteen that were most seriously affected by war—the provinces DW was pledged to assist. Much of the material was for use by other NGOs, who would become the delivery agents. The task of DW was not to make face-to-face contacts with all of the target audience. Rather, DW was the master strategist, the generator of concepts and ideas in civic education, the trainer of trainers and promoters, the equipper of other agencies for the mammoth task of touching recipients in villages across much of Angola. Between March and August of 2004, DW held a national training workshop for thirty-six Peace Promoters, and gave training seminars of one month in all of the designated twelve provinces.

The civic education materials produced by João and his colleagues are too extensive and detailed to cover in depth. Their value, however, can be gathered from one representative sample, the list of topics included in the micro-library kits that they sent to the designated twelve provinces affected by war. The first unit is a weighty document, actually a book. The rest of the documents are booklets:

1. Training for transformation
2. The rights of a child
3. The power of participation
4. Knowing one's rights
5. Conflict resolution manual
6. Moral and civic education
7. The Lusaka Protocol
8. What is democracy?

9. Human rights
10. The role of the activist
11. Legal framework for resettlement and return of the populations directly affected by the conflict
12. The constitutional law of the II Republic of Angola
13. Study methods
14. Communication and personal integration
15. Tolerance
16. The joy of being a citizen of the universe
17. The joy of growing up in a family
18. The joy of not being alone
19. *Ei! Malta calados porque?* (Hey! Everybody clammed up, but why?)
20. Justice and peace
21. Principles to orient internally displaced people
22. Social projects
23. It's time for change
24. The joy of being a person of dignity
25. Education for living in a peaceful culture
26. The citizen and politics
27. The art of living, in four parts
28. Workshops for growth
29. The ethic of tolerance
30. A tour through vocabulary

Some of the problems João and his colleagues in DW's Peace-Building Team faced as they set out to design the civic education program are as follows:
- How can you teach someone justice who knows only injustice?
- How can you teach someone to respect human life who saw his relatives killed?
- How can you teach someone to respect state property, or someone else's property, who never owned anything in his life?

That, João says, is why reconciliation and civic education must go together. People need to know their rights and responsibilities. As they learn these, they need to be able to fit them into an entirely new pattern of looking at all of life with respect and dignity—their own lives as well as the lives of others.

REFUGEES ARE NOT FORGOTTEN

To the end of this fifth peace mission to Angola, João sustained the same concern for the well-being of refugees that he brought to his very first visit to refugee camps in Zambia. That interest has never wavered. Who better to be a spokesperson for refugees?

> The plight of the refugee. *Many people have asked me, João, what has refugees to do with reconciliation ministry? My answer is always this: Reconciliation has many facets, one of them is advocacy. Refugees are marginalized, and sometimes put down and abused. They can't defend themselves, because sometimes they don't know their rights or nobody will listen to them. The main goal of this ministry of advocacy is to give a voice to the voiceless and restore their dignity as citizens of the country with the same rights and privileges as those who stayed home by accident during the war....*

Among those refugees in the Congo who did not live in camps and who found opportunities to advance their education and experience, many had become multi-lingual, and many had already found ways of integrating back into Angolan life.

Services to refugees that João has provided and continues to provide are these:

- Tracking the progress of repatriation, being aware of how many have returned, how many Angolans still remain in exile
- Bringing encouragement and hope through visits
- Training refugee leaders in counselling, conflict management, and mediation
- Warning them of difficulties and perils, from AIDS to land mines, which they will face as they return home
- Spiritual healing, including reconciliation and forgiveness

- Monitoring
- Advocacy
- Identification of needs as voiced by refugees themselves (often an integral part of advocacy)

Consistent with his never-failing support for refugees and his preoccupation with their concerns, it is not surprising that the final days of João's Peace Mission Number Five were spent in a visit to the Kilueka refugee camp in Congo and then at the reception centre at Mbanza-Kongo. This allowed him to monitor the progress of repatriation, and to evaluate the work of assisting refugees that was being provided by UNHCR. It would also allow him to interact in person with refugees both before their repatriation and as they arrived at their destination. He gives UNHCR a high rating for their compassion, efficiency, and effectiveness, even though logistical problems had reduced the actual number of refugees repatriated to well below the goals they had set for themselves. The second phase of repatriation began July 5, with convoys of trucks carrying refugees from Kilueka camp to Mbanza-Kongo every two weeks.

Conversation with refugee leaders, parents, and elders alerted them to dangers, problems, and disappointments they were about to encounter in post-war Angola, which had changed so much from the Angola they knew previously. He encouraged the leaders and elders to be peacemakers and mediators when they arrived at their areas of destination. The report on this trip, prepared in Portuguese for Allan Cain and others of DW, called attention to the valuable contribution returning refugees were bringing to the communities where they take up residence:

In refugee camps many were able to conserve valuable customs and traditions, due to the low impact of the outside world there within the camps. In there the family still begins the education of children from infancy, through childhood and adolescence to maturity. Even until now, in refugee camps they believe that the child reflects the life model seen in the parents. Whereas in the new post-war Angola, morals fail due to the absence of norms in family conduct.

To Congo and back to Mbanza-Kongo

João made some important links again at Mbanza-Kongo on that mid-July visit, beneficial to refugees as well as to Allan Cain and DW. They included contacts with the Provincial Vice-Governor and the Provincial Director for MINARS, the ministry directly involved with the reintegration of refugees. These encounters paved the way for future seminars sponsored by DW. A third contact was with the Department of Education at the Provincial level.

João's travel to Kinshasa by air and return overland to Mbanza-Kongo were both undertaken on his newly acquired Angolan passport, an effective and affirming test of the ability to come and go through Angola's immigration posts without requiring further attention to visas. This was a great load lifted. Exiting from Luanda, protocol looked after his documentation, saving an hour of standing in line. Arriving at the Kinshasa airport, Nora's brother, Captain Alvaro, who is an attaché at the Embassy there, had his documents processed while they conversed in the VIP lounge.

In late July, the Executive of the Council of Christian Churches in Angola concluded their forty-eighth meeting by issuing a final communique that João considers significant, because he feels it reflects the real sentiments of the Angolan population. Certainly a broad spectrum of churches was represented in its drafting, and he was a participant in that session. The document, datelined Luanda, July 23, 2004, addresses the national scene and directs a list of expectations and requests to the government:

> 1. Cessation of hostilities in the Province of Cabinda, and resolution of conflict there through permanent dialogue
>
> 2. Disarming of the civil population, using methods of exchange for arms turned in
>
> 3. Creation of minimal conditions for those demobilized as a result of the various peace accords and dislocated populations
>
> (CICA 2004)

Several events came together in late July which served to cap this fifth peace mission. Development Workshop signed a Partnership Protocol on July 23, 2004, with the National Institute for Investigation and Development of Education, INIDE, the most important technical body of the Angolan Ministry of Education. This was DW's seal of approval for their work. At that point, DW was involved in a partnership with the Ministry of Education, and the content of its civic education program began to be implemented across the nation through the Republic's educational network. It was the culmination of many months' work by the peace-building team. Then at the CICA Executive meeting, referred to above, João was able to meet and converse with Dr. Francisco Lisboa Santos, General Director of the National Institute for Religious Subject, within the Ministry of Education and culture. There was an additional affirmation that the government was accepting the churches' role in nation-building as the government made reference to restoring the ethical and moral values lost due to the war.

João arrived back in Halifax on Sunday, August 8, 2004, one month after Nora's return.

João and Nora Matwawana

25

SIXTH PEACE MISSION—TO ANGOLA AND CONGO
(January 27 to February 13, 2005)

This sixth undertaking following re-establishment of peace in Angola was brief, intense, focussed: a tour by road of the coastal areas north of Luanda, included Bengo and Zaire provinces, touching Ambriz, Kinzau, Nzeto, Tomboko, Soyo, and a number of smaller villages. This itinerary, undertaken with Brian Malcolm of CBM's *Sharing Way* division, permitted João to reach rural areas where the peacebuilders would be unlikely to penetrate.

THE PROGRAM

In one intense week, João and Brian spoke more than twenty times, with the turnout, on occasion, numbering over 500. At each community visited, they met with the local government Administrator and with community leaders. Their goals included the defining of specific projects to be undertaken with assistance from *The Sharing Way*. They were attentive to progress being made in the resettlement in these areas of refugees and internally displaced persons, with an eye to both resettlement and rebuilding, assisting the countryside to return to some degree of normal living. In daily messages, the emphasis upon repentance, forgiveness, and reconciliation, which had become so much a part of João's life over the last three years, came to the fore with regularity.

Back in Luanda, after the visit to the towns north of the capital, João was able to visit with personnel in Angola's Ministry of Foreign Affairs. It was his plan to make personal contact again with Georges Chicote, but he was out of town. The welcome accorded João was a warm one, renewing acquaintances established at Ottawa when the official delegation visited Canada in October 2004.

Findings

During this brief visit João Matwawana and Brian Malcolm identified five needs which they defined as basic and immediate. *The Sharing Way* is committed to respond as soon as possible to these:

- Food security:
  Many of the internally displaced persons—IDPs—have not had access to land for cultivation. Those who cease cultivation no longer have seeds. Those returning from exile may gain access to land but lack tools and agricultural basics. All need support to get started in agriculture and the raising of poultry and small animals. They need tools and heavy equipment for increased production, both for their own consumption and to market.

- Rehabilitation:
  Some infrastructure needs reconstruction. Most of the structures used during the pre-war era of activity need to be rehabilitated—whether residences, schools, health centres, or church sanctuaries.

- Primary Health Care:
  The Ministry of Health is appealing to Churches, Missions, and other NGOs for assistance in this area. Lack of primary health care is a basic cause of infant mortality up to age five. All areas of the IEA are faced with this problem, which is a universal

calamity. The IEA is also eager to undertake programs in nutrition and maternity health education.

- Basic Sanitation:
  Community training programs concerning basic sanitary matters such as waste disposal, water treatment, latrine construction, the establishment of wells with manual pumps.

- Income-generating projects:
  To teach a new generation about the value and use of local resources, transforming that knowledge into useful items of value which could produce income.

Angola and the future: Hopes and expectations

Hopes for Angola and its future as expressed by Dr. João Matwawana align closely with the thrusts of the programs he undertook with Development Workshop. Programs in Civic Education were designed to create the conditions which would facilitate the rebuilding of Angola as a participatory democracy. That vision is entirely in line with the promises made as Angola was launched on its course toward a multi-party democracy. The transition to democracy is still a work in progress, still incomplete. We wish it well. The role of the Central Committee continues to be a vital part of how Angola is governed.

The legitimate aspirations of Angolans, individually and collectively, are that they may pursue their lives with dignity and in security, benefiting fairly and appropriately from the rich natural resources that allow Angola to be qualified as one of the wealthy and privileged nations of the world. The government has taken constructive steps toward integrity and transparency in accounting for those resources in the period from 2002 to 2004. The pursuit of those goals, from within, not just under pressure from the international community, is vital. Its progress needs to be accelerated, and it must be absolutely relentless.

One of the areas where real progress needs to be made is in establishing fair and just processes for appointments, procurement and hiring, and special study privileges. Secret arrangements still bring advantage to the children of key people. The establishment of a process for candidatures would be a significant step toward justice in the society. There continue to be insiders and outsiders.

Angola's ethnic and linguistic diversity was seen by the former colonial power as an obstacle to be overcome, and sometimes as a tool of governance to be used in the "divide and conquer" mentality which its administrative officers exploited so effectively. Independent Angola need not subscribe to that mentality nor stoop to that methodology, for the nation is richer acknowledging its diversity and coming to terms with its plurality in a spirit of peace and reconciliation. At this critical moment, Angola holds the potential to become a model to be copied by other African countries needing to find their way past ethnic conflicts that are insurmountable by comparison. Justice and fairness, both in sharing of the responsibilities of government and sharing in the resources of the nation, are within reach, free and fair elections in 2006 being the very obvious stepping stone in that direction. More than forty years of internal conflict have been devastating at all levels of Angolan society. If the population has learned adequately from the sufferings of those tumultuous years, they will be alert to any candidates for office who seek to build their platforms for the upcoming election on hatred, suspicion, or rivalry. If the politicians have learned adequately, they will seek to serve their people, and will be returned by the voters to office in subsequent elections.

Angola's linguistic heritage includes 400 years of the Portuguese language for shared communication, and a much deeper history of linguistic diversity, which has been the principal line of communication for traditional cultural and family values. There are signs that these mother tongues may be about to receive recognition as legitimate teaching languages, including their introduction into the classroom. The soul of an African people resides in the stories and legends that are passed from one generation to another through these avenues. Already Angola's national television networks allow elders to appear and tell stories in Kikongo, Kimbundu, Umbundu, and Chokwe.

Conclusion

Looking back and looking ahead

We who have followed João Matwawana's life through its diverse stages are able to see unique and remarkable patterns with threads of consistency throughout. We glimpsed his childhood, youth, education, and marriage in pre-war Angola, and followed him and his family through two refugee experiences. We saw him through programs of training, to ministry as hospital chaplain and respected community leader in Congo, to community pastor and prison chaplain in Canada. In Kivu he was first an educator, then an encourager, speaking with a prophetic voice to refugees. Finally he emerged as a reconciler both in Kivu and in Rwanda.

João's transition to statesman happened around the Burundi peace process, working from both Canada and South Africa. Other countries such as Kenya and Zambia benefited along the way, and in return, the cultures and experiences of each country added to the reserves of wisdom and experience from which he has been able to draw. These rich and varied phases of life, so densely stacked in one person's experience, have all shared in the shaping of the character and outlook of one who sees himself primarily as a servant of God, and of Jesus, Lord of his life. At the appropriate time, he emerged well equipped to participate in the rebuilding of Angola, his country of birth, once the pieces came together to create the political context in which that could begin to happen. The task of rebuilding Angola is far from finished, but Dr. João Matwawana has had a part in it.

At the end of six peace forays into Angola, one aspect of Africa's proverbial divisiveness still troubles João as he seeks to overcome those barriers which someone, in every community, seems eager to erect. He has painstakingly maintained a political neutrality, seeking to serve Angola in its entirety, yet he has consistently found that both the government and political parties doubt the integrity of his neutrality. The opposition parties see him with what they consider to be immediate access to government offices in Luanda, after many years away. "How can this be? He must have been in their pocket all along." He may approach opposition politicians individually, but they are cautious and they do not extend invitations to him:

> *They are unaware of my ministry, especially my ministry of advocacy. They are unaware of the process I have been through in re-establishing links with Angola through its embassy in Ottawa. By resisting invitations to be part of either government or opposition, I now reap the disadvantages of not integrating into one party or another. But I like the situation in one way, for the doubting is almost equal on both sides.*

The government, in turn, appears to still be suspicious that because of his region of origin, his mother tongue and his ethnicity, he must be, at heart, an FNLA person. He may approach government offices, and be received, but they do not extend invitations to him.

Looking back over six peace missions to Angola, which unfolded in less than a three-year time span, we are allowed to glimpse the various struggles which accompany the emergence of a new nation. Angola already differs from its colonial roots, and it will be radically different from the country that was ravaged by war until so recently. We see this through the eyes of one who was the right person in the right place at the right time with the right history, the right skills and experience, and who came in contact with the right organization, Development Workshop, under the sponsorship of the right agency, Canadian Baptist Ministries. João would say that God brought these elements together, and we agree with his conclusion.

As João first began to bring his experience and convictions together for inclusion in DW's packets used for training peace workers and to strengthen civil society, there were those who insisted it was too early to include the reconciliation theme, but he included it. Some said it was too risky to address issues like human rights, democracy, and citizenship directly, for he would be perceived as meddling in politics under a government that would not allow such, yet he included them. There may be those who would insist that he was too religious in his approach, but he did not bend to any of those pressures, holding, instead, to his own sense of rightness, which proved to be entirely correct. At the end of his fifth tour, João commented that, in fact, the Angolan government is more ready to work with churches at this juncture than is the government of Canada. A specific example of this came from Dr. Lisboa in the Ministry of Education and Culture, whose plea was, "Help us bring back moral and civic education...."

The Great Lakes region of Central Africa continues to be dogged by armed struggle, with both individuals and governments, African and non-African, willing to keep the political pots boiling at the expense of myriad lives lost, oceans of blood spilled, untold suffering by the population, and agony beyond measure. There are those who profit from turmoil. One recent report suggests that a thousand lives *per day* are being taken in the Congo alone (Crisis Group 2005: Africa Report # 91). Individuals such as Dr. João Matwawana, who work in the private sector, are not readily admitted to the inner circle of players in what is termed the "peace process". And even if he were invited, the conditions necessary to success might not yet be at hand. This, however, is certain: Wars are never enough to bring permanent closure to situations of such profound tragedy. Would he be willing and open to work along with the peace processes in these countries?

Remember that much of my life has been invested in that part of Africa. Four of our six children were born in the Congo. We lived and worked for sixteen years in the Bas Congo, then for nine years in Kivu Province. Much of my heart is in that part of Africa still, for there were the additional undertakings involving both Rwanda and Burundi. In some ways I find myself less hampered by ethno-tribal suspicions when working at some distance from the country of my birth which I so love.

For Dr. João Matwawana, there is no established roadmap for the journey ahead, just as he had no firm plan at the turn of the millennium. In the place of a fixed plan, he has a willingness and an openness to undertake new challenges on the same basis as he faced them in the past, with resources that include wisdom, tact, insight, compassion, experience, the approach of an African elder, a convinced political neutrality, a vast resource of patience, and a profound faith which, although it is traditional, is by no measure sectarian. Beside him, behind him, supporting him, we find resourceful Nora. This has been their story, and it is not yet finished.

THE END

Appendix A: Key to Abbreviations

AACC	All Africa Council of Churches
ACEBAC	*Associação dos Cristãs Evangélicos Baptistas de Angola no Congo*
AFDL	*Alliance des Forces Démocratiques de Libération* (Great Lakes)
AEA	*Aliança Évangélica de Angola*
APAN	Angola Peace Action Network, a consortium of NGOs
BMS	Baptist Missionary Society: early influence on Matwawanas, based in Didcot, U.K.
CAREP	*Centre Africain de Recherches et d'Éducation pour la Paix et la Démocratie* (Goma, Kivu, Congo)
CBK	*Communauté Baptiste au Kivu*: later renamed *Communauté Baptiste au Centre de l'Afrique*
CBCA	*Communauté Baptiste au Centre de l'Afrique*: formerly

CBK	
CBM	Canadian Baptist Ministries: sponsor of João and Nora Matwawana in Africa
CEC	Council of European Churches
CEZ	*Communauté Évangélique au Zaïre*
CICA	*Conselho de Igrejas Cristãs em Angola*: Council of Christian Churches in Angola
CMA	Christian and Missionary Alliance
CNDD/FDD	*Conseil national pour la défense de la démocratie–Force pour la défense de la démocratie*: Political movement, Burundi, convinced by Matwawana to return to peace talks
DFAIT	Department of Foreign Affairs and International Trade (Canada): later FAC
DRC (RDC)	Democratic Republic of Congo (*République Democratique du Congo*): generally referred to as Congo
DW	Development Workshop: Allan Cain, Director
ECZ	*Église du Christ au Zaïre*: equivalent of a Protestant Council of Churches.
EBF	European Baptist Federation
ECUA	*Église Chrétienne Unie de l'Angola*: Angolan Protestant churches in exile in Congo
EPI	*École de Pasteurs et d'Instituteurs*: located at Kimpese, Congo
FAA	*Forças Armadas de Angola*: Angolan Armed Forces
FAC	Foreign Affairs Canada
FLEC	*Frente Pela Libertação do Enclave de Cabind*

Appendix A: Key to Abbreviations

FNL	Forces of National Liberation (Burundi)
FNLA	*Frente Nacional Pela Libertação de Angola*
FONGA	Forum of Non-Governmental Agencies
GOA	Government of Angola
IBLA	*Igreja Baptista Livre de Angola*
IDPs	Internally Displaced Persons
IEA	*Igreja Evangélica de Angola*: partner of CBM.
IEBA	*Igreja Evangélica Baptista em Angola*: partner of BMS
IME	*Institut Médical Évangélique*: at Kimpese, Congo
INIDE	*Instituto Nacional de Investigação e Developemento da Educação*: The most important technical body within Angola's Ministry of Education
IRIN	A United Nations humanitarian information unit copyrighted by the UN office for co-ordination of humanitarian affairs
JMC	Joint Military Commission: mixed FAA/UNITA
KETI	Earlier acronym for what became EPI, see above
KJV	King James Version of the Bible
MAF	Mission Aviation Fellowship
MAP	Medical Assistance Program
MINARS	*Ministério de Assistência e Reinserção Social* (Angola)
MPLA	*Movimento Popular pela Libertação de Angola*
NIV	New International Version of the Bible
NGO	Non-governmental Organization
PEC	*Projeto de Educação Cívica*: Civic Education Project
PIDE	*Polícia Internacional e Defesa do Estado*: Portugal's

	dreaded secret police
PNUD	*Programme des Nations Unies pour le Développement.*
RPF	Rwanda Patriotic Front: primarily Tutsi
RVA	Rift Valley Academy: School for missionaries' children
UEBA	*União Evangélica de Baptistas em Angola*
UN	United Nations Organization
UNHCR	United Nations High Commission for Refugees
UNICEF	United Nations International Children's Emergency Fund
UNITA	*União Nacional pela Independência Total de Angola*
VEM	*Vereinte Evangelische Mission*: of Wuppertal, Germany
WCC	World Council of Churches

APPENDIX B: CHRONOLOGY OF THE MATWAWANA FAMILY

1930s & 1940s
1935	Feb. 20: João Matwawana born at Mbanza-Kongo (São Salvador), Angola
1939	July 27: Nora Artur born at Mbanza-Kongo (São Salvador), Angola
1949	João enters BMS boarding school at Mbanza-Kongo

1950s
1954	João finishes *quarta classe*
1954–58	João's teaching assignments begin, at Mbanza-Congo
1955–57	João opens a rural school at Buela
1956	Nora finishes *quarta classe*
1957–58	João opens a new school in Mongo Zulu; Nora teaches school in Mbanza-Congo
1958	Sept. 20: João and Nora married by Clifford John Parsons at Mbanza-Kongo
1958–59	Teaching assignment for João and Nora at Lomba, opening new school

1959	July 5: Son Samuel is born at Mbanza-Kongo
1959	September: Enrollment at Calambata Bible Institute

1960s

1961	Mar. 14: First open hostilities near Calambata, in afternoon
1961	Mar. 15: Son Edward is born the night of March 15, at Mbanza-Kongo
1961	Mar. 15: Commonly accepted date for beginning of hostilities in Angola
1961	Apr. 24: Matwawanas flee from Mbanza-Kongo as refugees to the Congo
1961	Apr.–September: João serves as a helper in relief services for Angolan Refugees in the Congo
1961	Sept. '61–Aug. '62: Studies at Kinkonzi, Congo
1962–66	Sept. '62–June '66, João takes theological studies at EPI Kimpese
	Nora studies English and home economics
1963	Apr. 16: Birth of son Ambrose
1965	Nov. 11: Birth of daughter Julie
1966–67	July '66–July '67: João studies in Birmingham, UK
1966–67	Nora teaches student wives at Mbanza Ngungu Bible School
1967	João participates in 10 day Billy Graham School of Evangelism, London
1967–75	João serves as the first African Chaplain at IME Kimpese, Congo
1968	Nora studies nutrition at Ndjili Health Centre in Kinshasa, works at IME
1968–70	João now Secretary-Treasurer, Provincial Evangelism, Église du Christ au Zaïre
1969	Nora: President of women at IME Kimpese, teaches literacy to young women
1969	João elected Provincial Secretary-Treasurer, ECZ Committee for Evangelism
1969–73	João teaches religion at Secondary School, EPI Kimpese, and IME nursing school

Appendix B: Chronology of the Matwawana Family

1970s

1970	June 7: Ordination of João to Christian Ministry at Kimpese, Congo
1970–74	João: President, Angolan Refugees Scholarship Fund
1971	João elected to National Committee on Evangelism, ECZ
1974	Nora: Treasurer of women's work at IME Kimpese
1970	Sept. 29: Birth of son Raymond
1971–1975	João serves as Deputy Hospital Superintendent, IME Kimpese
1972–75	João elected General Secretary of Église Chrétienne Unie de l'Angola
1972	João organizes first Hospital Chaplains' Conference in the Congo
1974	João and Nora to 3 months' ministry in India, CBM assignment
1975	Jan. 15: Alvor Accord signed with Portugal—MPLA, FNLA and UNITA share equally in transitional government
1975	July: Family to Mbanza-Kongo, Angola, as senior pastor, "permanent"
1975	Nov.: João goes to Sweden, Holland, and England, representing ECUA
1976	Jan.: Nora returns to Kimpese, Congo with the smallest children, for Isabel's delivery, (Feb. 12)
1976	Late Feb.: João, Samuel, Edward, and seven relatives return as refugees
1976–77	From Feb.: João serves one year as Coordinator of Refugee Services
1976	Dec.: To Nairobi for PACLA (Pan African Leadership Conference)
1977	Feb. 8: João arrives in Canada for studies at Acadia Divinity College
1977	Sept. 9–10: Nora, with Ambrose, Julie, Raymond, and Isabel, comes to Canada
1978	João to Calgary Missionfest (CBM) as facilitator, senses missionary call to Kivu

1979	Oct.: João's ordination credentials recognized by Atlantic Baptist Convention CBM appoints the Matwawanas for service in Kivu, Congo
1979–80	Cross-Canada speaking tour under CBM sponsorship

1980s

1980	May: João graduates, Master of Divinity, from Acadia
1980	May 22: Hearing, Immigration Canada, at Acadia campus in Wolfville
1980	Sept. 4: Matwawanas granted refugee status in Canada Fly to Nairobi for study of Kiswahili, refused entry, deported by return flight
1981–84	João becomes Pastor of Lockport and Ragged Island churches, Nova Scotia
1981	Oct. 21: João registered in Nova Scotia to solemnize marriages, #5307
1984–91	João serves as Chaplain at Halifax Correctional Centre
1985	Canadian citizenship granted: João, Nora, Julie, Ambrose, Raymond and Isabel
1986	João to Kivu for CBM on his first one-month visit of investigation
1987	Re-appointed by CBM for service in Kivu, but continues in prison chaplaincy
1988	Kivu departure postponed for family considerations, after just selling house
1989	June 22: First MPLA/UNITA cease-fire, signed at Gbadolite, August collapse

1990s

1990	Jan.: João launches National Fellowship for the Reconciliation of Angola
1990	Mar. 21: Namibia becomes independent of the Republic of South Africa, a condition for Cuban troop departure from Angola
1990	Dec. 6: UNITA agrees to cease-fire if MPLA introduces multi-party rule

Appendix B: Chronology of the Matwawana Family

1990	Dec. 10: MPLA Congress endorses multi-party rule
1991	Mar. 17: Savimbi declares at Congress "War is finished...now to the ballot box."
1991	Apr. 24: Dos Santos to Congress: "Cease fire in May.... Elections in 1992."
1991	Apr. 28: MPLA Congress abandons Marxism/Leninism
1991	Apr.: CBM renews Matwawana appointment to Kivu, with CBK
1991	May 1: "Spirit of Estoril" agreement, MPLA /UNITA ends 16 years of civil war
1991	May 31: Peace Agreement (unsuccessful) at Bicesse, Portugal, MPLA/ UNITA
1991	June 30: João officially terminates service with Halifax Correctional Services
1991	Aug.: João, Nora to Swahili studies, Nairobi. Isabel to Rift Valley Academy
1991	Dec.: João is invited to teach at Mitaboni Divinity School
1992	Jan.–May: ABC Divinity School, Mitaboni Kenya (looting, unrest in Kivu)
1992	May 30: Arrival at Bwatsinge for service throughout Kivu province of Congo
1992	Dec.: Political turmoil around Bwatsinge, Toyota vehicle to Brazilians
1993	Mar.: João goes to Masisi, deals with inter-ethnic fighting, gives seminar
1993	May: João goes to Beni, contracts malaria
1993	Nov.: "Foreigners must register."
1993	Other events of '93: Arthroplastic surgery on Nora's hand; João condemns corruption & looting in a sermon, soldiers take exception
1994	Apr. 7: Assassination of Rwanda's President ignites frenzy of murder. More than 800,000 Tutsi killed.

1994	May: João and Nora to Bas-Uele Province leading 20 days of conferences
1994	July–Sept.: In Canada for short furlough, medical care, Isabel to university
1994	Nov. 20: Lusaka Accord signed, called "flawed" in absence of Savimbi himself
1994	Also in '94: João has cerebral malaria; Medical team to Kivu from Edmonton
1994	Mass exodus from Rwanda to Kivu, Congo; João begins reconciliation ministries in refugee camps Katale, Kahindo, and Kibumba
1995	Jan. 25–29: Foster & Matwawana to Kigali for first Reconciliation Seminar
1995	Mar.: João participates in Medical & Chaplaincy Conference, Nairobi
1995	Apr.: Billy Graham evangelistic outreach in refugee camps
1995	João begins trade schools for Rwandan refugees
1995	May 6: Dos Santos and Savimbi meet in person. Savimbi: "You won..."
1995	May: Mama Nora Women's Centre opened; João goes to South Africa chaplaincy conference, starts preparation for program in Goma
1995	June: The Matwawanas return to Canada
1996	Aug.: The Matwawanas return to Kivu, relocate to Goma
1996	Fall: Hostilities break out: the Kabila rebellion
1996	Oct.: Evacuation of all foreigners except the Matwawanas
1996	Dec.: *Great Lakes Regional Conference on Peace, Reconciliation and Community Reconstruction*, at Nairobi; invitation from Rwanda, Rev. Bashaka of AEBR, to continue reconciliation ministries

Appendix B: Chronology of the Matwawana Family

1997	Jan.–Mar.: João goes to Kigali, Rwanda, for ministry
1997	Mar.: Kigali international conference, Council of Churches of Rwanda Matwawana and José Chipenda are among the speakers
1997	Nora to workshop with 30 women of Rwanda & Burundi: *A Woman: The leavening in the reconciliation process....*
1997	May 25: Bomb thrown into Virunga Baptist hospital
1997	July: To Nairobi for one-month retreat
1997	Aug.: First visit following the war, to Bwatsinge, then Katwa
1997	Aug 28: Armed soldier shoots 4 people dead across the street from João's office
1997	Sept.: Three-day consultation on theological education, Goma
1997	Oct.: Participation in Francophone Baptist Consultation at Liège, Belgium
1997	Nov.: To North Kivu, Nora alone 10 days, working with women
1997	Dec.: First seminar at Kalunga area of Kivu; youth conference
1998	Jan.: Following youth retreat, João has typhoid fever, to Virunga hospital
1998	Feb.: Nora works with women teaching knitting, crocheting
1998	Apr.–June: João teaches ethics to about 50 student nurses at Goma
1998	Apr. 8–10: Youth conference on Peace and Reconciliation, Sake, Congo
1998	May: João to (1) Rwanda for seminar on healing, repentance, forgiveness and reconciliation, (2) attends *Conference on Democracy, Good Governance, and Development for a lasting peace in the Great Lakes region of Africa*, Bujumbura
1998	ACC&S Kenya, João serves as facilitator at seminars,

	Methods of Conflict Resolution in Churches and Families, around 300 attending
1998	June: The Matwawanas return to Canada. João attends July Baptist Gathering, Calgary. Another rebellion begins in Eastern Congo, aimed at toppling president Kabila. Home assignment in Canada extended to year end
1998	João and Nora visit with retired BMS missionaries in UK, attend CBM follow-up Francophone Partnership consultation, in Strasbourg, France
1999	Jan.: The Matwawanas are assigned to Kenya to work with CBM's partner churches ABC and ACC&S, as Kivu is politically unstable. João teaches at seminaries in both Thika and Mitaboni.
1999	Feb.–Aug.: Kenya, João gives regional seminars in 7 areas of ACC&S as follow-up to conference on reconciliation. Nora accompanies, teaches women
1999	Aug.: Return to Canada for official retirement following deputation

2000s

2000	Aug. 31: Official retirement from CBM
2000	Nov. 17: Retirement banquet celebration for the Matwawanas in Nova Scotia
2001	Feb.: João & Nora based at the Keith residence for Ontario deputation
	João first articulates vision for a different level of involvement in the peacemaking process in Africa
2001	Mar.: João recipient, Acadia Divinity College Distinguished Service Award
2001	Apr. 4–26: Visits Angolan refugee camps in Zambia
2001	Aug.: CBM awards João and Nora service pins & plaque for service to Congo, Kenya, Rwanda, 1991–2000

Appendix B: Chronology of the Matwawana Family

2001	Oct.: Matwawana and Keith attend conference at Camp IAWAH, coordinated by Fosters: "Great Lakes." Meetings with Burundi's Ambassador Niyongabo lead to formulation of *Operation Osprey* plans
2001	Nov. 1: João and John discuss *Osprey* proposal with Minister Kilgour
2001	Dec. 7: UN Press Release terminates special peacemaking role for Burundi of Nelson Mandela. New process has 2 mediator-negotiators: President Bongo of Gabon and Deputy President Zuma of South Africa
2001	Dec. 9–13 João and John Keith visit Ottawa re *Operation Osprey* João invited to the Angolan Embassy in Ottawa, at Ambassador Puna's request Minister Kilgour issues letter to High Commissioner Lucie Edwards in Pretoria, introducing João & *Operation Osprey*
2001	Dec.: CBM designates João Matwawana as Peace and Reconciliation Consultant
2002	Jan. 22–Feb. 8: João goes to Pretoria in support of Burundi Peace Process and a modified *Operation Osprey*.
2002	Feb 18–22 First phase of a new round of UN peace talks, Burundi, a direct result of *Operation Osprey*
2002	Feb. 19: In Halifax, makes contact with Robert Fowler, Special Representative of Prime Minister Chrétien to G8 meeting
2002	Feb. 22: Jonas Savimbi killed in Angola
2002	Feb. 27–Mar. 2: Liconga & Pindi of Angolan Embassy, Ottawa, visit João in Halifax
2002	Mar. 11–19: João goes to Amsterdam for contact with FNL advisor, Alain Mugabarabona, who fails to show
2002	Mar. 30: Cease-fire agreement announced between Government of Angola and UNITA
2002	Apr. 4: Official Protocol of Agreement following Angola's cease-fire signed at Luena, Moxico Province, Angola

2002	Apr. 15: McMaster University confers doctorate on Rev. João Matwawana, Angola's Ambassador Puna attends
2002	July 31–Aug. 15: Visit to Angolan refugee camps in Zambia
2002	Aug. 15–Sep. 30: Matwawana First Angola Peace-building Mission, following visit to refugees in Zambia
2002	Dec. 2: Burundi cease-fire Accord reached in Arusha, signed Jan. 28, 2003
2003	Jan. 3: Memorandum of understanding signed in Pretoria between Burundi's President Buyoya and the CNDD/FDD, represented by its political and diplomatic advisor, Jean-Marie Ngendahayo
2003	Jan. 9–20: Path to UNHCR Geneva established via European church contacts
2003	Feb. 21–Mar 30: Matwawana Second Angola Peace-building Mission Received in Luanda by his Excellency João Baptista Kussumwa, Minister of *Assistência e Reinserção Social da República de Angola* (MINARS) discusses repatriation of refugees (Mar. 12)
2003	May: Burundi's new Ambassador, Her Excellency Epiphanie Kabushamene Ntamwana, presents credentials as replacement for Ambassador Edonias
2003	July 29–Oct. 12: Matwawana Third Angola Peace-building Mission, after refugee camps, Zambia
2003	Dec. 6–Feb. 28, 2004: Matwawana Fourth Angola Peace-building Mission
2004	Canadian government delegation visits Angola: David Strangway, Schramm, Angell, Kuni (Jan. 18–25). Visits Cabinda, contacts IEA leaders and churches, also former colleague André Conga da Costa (Feb.17–20)
2004	May 6–Aug. 8: Matwawana Fifth Angolan Peace-building Mission UNHCR (Congo) initiates 2nd phase repatriation program for Angolan refugees João visits refugee

APPENDIX B: CHRONOLOGY OF THE MATWAWANA FAMILY

camps in Congo (July 7–12) Civic Education Project of DW signs protocol agreement with INIDE, Angola's Ministry of Education At CICA Executive meeting, meets with Dr. Francisco Lisboa Santos, General Director, *Instituto Nacional Para os Assuntos Religiosos do Ministério da Educação e Cultura* (July 17)

2005   Jan. 27–Feb. 13: Sixth Angola Peace-building Mission with Brian Malcolm of CBM: tour by road of the coastal areas of Zaïre province, defining projects to be undertaken by *The Sharing Way*

Appendix C: National Fellowship for the Reconciliation of Angola

Motto: Peace, Love, Unity

PREAMBLE: The national Fellowship for the reconciliation of Angola is open to all Angolans who desire peace and justice. Membership is available regardless of race, colour, religion, language, or party affiliation. By joining the NFRA, a person commits himself or herself to work for peace and the reconciliation of Angola.

RATIONALE: Peace in Angola will not sink in the hearts of people easily after 30 years of war. The war caused terrible ruin in the land and deep scars in the hearts of people. Peace must start in the heart of the person who pursues it. Peace will not come out of the accords and cease-fire documents that the government signs, though these will help. Many will need help and encouragement in order to catch the vision and understand the benefits of national peace. We have a vision for peace and rebuilding but this vision needs to be shared widely.

Program of the NFRA

OUR AIM: To create an independent, non-partisan force for peace among all peoples of Angola, a grass-roots movement of youth, churches, communities, regions, cities, and businesses.

Our Message of Peace

- Say NO to guns and war; Say YES to PEACE, LOVE, AND UNITY.
- All Angolans must learn to be peacemakers. It is the blessed thing to do for your country.
- Love is the key. All Angolans must learn to love and forgive. It is the best gift that you can give to your people.
- Forgiveness will proceed one heart at a time.
- Unity is essential. In unity there is power. It is better to work in co-operation with people than against them.
- Coming together is beginning, keeping together is progress, working together is success.
- Justice, fairness toward every individual and ethnic group is vital for peace.

Our Methods

- Talking together. We use our African approach and wisdom for solving conflicts.
- Praying together. We encourage all Angolans to pray for peace.
- Targeting our youth. Our first concern is for our youth. We have created in Angola a generation who know nothing but war because some were born in exile, some in the bush camps of the freedom fighters and others were born in cities besieged by armies.
- Working together. We seek to replace the economy of war with an economy of peace. Jobs encourage peace.
- Restitution. We seek, through Supporters of Angola, to put some small financial aid into villages and families shattered by war. Our

Appendix C: National Fellowship for the Reconciliation of Angola

input will help those who have lost so much to receive a token toward repayment of their loss and to assist them to begin rebuilding for themselves.
- Communicating. Our message will be carried throughout Angola and throughout our network of Supporters of Angola.

Our Goals

- Support base: Establish a support base with initial funds to launch the program.
- Meeting in Luanda: Meet with Angolan leaders in government, churches, and businesses, including elders and women, and discuss the pursuit of peace.
- National tour of Angola: We will travel through all the major centres of Angola encouraging peace through meetings, media, and education.
- Home office: Establish a home office in Luanda with representatives in every province. The office will seek to encourage a wide participation in the Peace and Reconciliation movement.
- National Congress for Reconciliation: All the ethnic communities of Angola will participate. The aim of the Congress is to encourage love, forgiveness, and unity across ethnic divisions in Angola and to celebrate the recovery of peace.

Conclusion

We believe that reconciliation is vital for the reconstruction of Angola. Reconciliation is the only hope left to us. Now is the time to rebuild the country together in peace, love, and unity.

For further information write or call: Rev. João Matwawana
Telephone: 1-902-865-8850
Email: jmatwawana@hotmail.com

BIBLIOGRAPHY

Africa Files	2003	"South African Deputy President affirms role of faith groups in quest for peace," *Africa Infoserve* E-mail and web clipping service, Toronto, Canada.
Andersen, Frank	1968	*Annual Report 1967-68*, Institut Médical Évangélique, Kimpese, Congo.
Balandier, Georges	1965	*La Vie Quotidienne au Royaume de Kongo du XVIe au XVIIIe siècle*, Paris, France.
Carroll, Rory	2004	"Rwanda masses troops on Congo border," *The Guardian Weekly*, December 3-9, 2004.
CICA	2004	*Final Communique*. 48th meeting of the Executive Council of CICA, July 23, 2004. Council of Christian Churches in Angola, Luanda, Angola.

Crisis Group	2005	*Africa Report #1* Source website: http://www/crisisgroup.org/home/index.cfm?id=3342&f=1.
d'Hertfelt, Marcel	1965	"The Rwanda of Rwanda," *Peoples of Africa*, edited by James L. Gibbs. Holt, Rinehart and Winston, New York.
Fegley, Randall Arlin	2005	"Mobutu Sese Seko," *Microsoft® Encarta® Online Encyclopedia* 2005 http://encarta.msn.com © 1997-2005. Viewed April, 2005.
Foster, Charles	1995	"Come Over and Help Us," *Tidings*, April 1995.
Gibson, M. Allen	2001	"Matwawana honoured for distinguished service," *Halifax Chronicle-Herald*, April 7, 2001.
Grenfell, James		*The History of the Baptist Church in Angola and the influence on the life and culture of the Kongo and Zombo people, 1879-1940.* Unpublished manuscript.
Immigration Canada	1980	"In the matter of an examination under oath relating to an application for the protection of the United Nations convention and protocol on refugees. On behalf of João Samuel Matwawana, Nora Isabelle Matwawana, Ambrois...Raymond...Julienne...Isabel. Held at Canada Employment Center, Acadia University Wolfville May 22, 1980 before N.C. Beaton, Senior Immigration Officer."
Keith, John F.	1971	*Stability and Change in Bantandu-Kongo Systems of Kinship and Authority.* Thesis submitted in fulfilment of requirements for the Ph.D., Boston University Graduate School.

		University Microfilms, Ann Arbor, Michigan.
	1998	*The First Few Wars Are The Worst: His Grace Has No Measure.* Canadian Baptist Ministries, Mississauga, Canada.
Lightstone, Michael	2001	"Bank card's return 'miracle' to minister," *The Halifax Herald*, Friday, September 28, 2001.
Mandiangu, Mbongi Kiletu		*Annual Report, 1971-72.* Institut Médical Évangélique, Kimpese. Congo.
		Annual Report, 1972-73. Institut Médical Évangélique, Kimpese, Congo.
Maquet, J.J.	1960	"The Problem of Tutsi Domination," *Cultures and Societies of Africa*, edited by Simon and Phoebe Ottenberg. Random House, New York.
Matwawana, João	1980	*Team Ministry in Cross-Cultural Setting, with particular reference to Angola and Zaïre.* Thesis submitted in fulfilment of the requirements for the M. Div., Acadia Divinity College, Nova Scotia.
	1986	"Talking of being a modern-day Jonah," *Missionary Herald*. Baptist Missionary Society, Didcot, U.K.
	1987	"Halifax Correctional Institute Chaplaincy Ministry," *The Atlantic Baptist*.
	2001	*A Vision for Central & Southern Africa*, unpublished manuscript.
	2002	"The freedom of a refugee prison," *The Baptist*, Vol. 5, No.7. Seabreeze Ministries, Hammonds Plains, Nova Scotia.
Ross, Miriam	1971	"João Matwawana, a Man of

		Understanding and Love," *Link & Visitor*, May, 1971.
Stuart, Charles H	1969	*The Lower Congo and the American Baptist Mission to 1910*. Thesis submitted in fulfilment of requirements for the Ph.D., Boston University Graduate School. University Microfilms, Ann Arbor, Michigan.
Van Wing, J.	1959	*Études Bakongo*. Leopoldville (Kinshasa), Congo.
Wilson, David	1967	*Annual Report, 1966-67*. Institut Médical Évangélique, Kimpese, Congo.